Transport

Transport

Strategy and Policy

STEPHEN J. SHAW

First published 1993

Blackwell Publishers
108 Cowley Road
Oxford OX4 1JF
UK

238 Main Street,
Cambridge, Massachusetts 02142
USA

British Library Cataloguing in Publication Data
A CIP catalogue record for this book is available from
the British Library.

Library of Congress Cataloging-in-Publication Data
Shaw, Stephen J., 1955–
       Transport : strategy and policy / Stephen J. Shaw.
          p.   cm.
       Includes index.
       ISBN 0–631–18639–5 (pbk. : alk. paper)
       1. Transportation.   2. Transportation and state.
    3. Transportation — Great Britain.   4. Transportation and state —
    Great Britain.   I. Title.
    HE147.5.S52   1993
    388'.068 – dc20
                                                                92–44817
                                                                CIP

Typeset in 11 on 13pt Palatino
by Graphicraft Typesetters Ltd., Hong Kong
Printed in Great Britain by Page Brothers, Norwich, Ltd.
This book is printed on acid-free paper

Contents

List of Plates

List of Figures

List of Tables

Acknowledgements

The author acknowledges with thanks the kind assistance he received from the following organizations in preparing the text: Air Transport Users Committee; Brighton Borough Transport; The Bristol Port Company; British Airways; British Rail; Bus and Coach Council; Busways Travel Services; Chamber of Shipping; Chartered Institute of Transport; Devon County Council; Greater Manchester Metro; Greater Manchester PTE; Institute of Logistics; London Coaches; London Regional Passengers Committee; Manchester Airport; NFC; Olympic Airways; P & O Containers; Port of Felixstowe; Road Haulage Association; Sainsbury's; Sealink Stena Line; Stansted Airport; TNT; Toronto Transit Commission; Virgin Atlantic Airways; Yorkshire Rider.

He would also like to thank the following individuals: John Cartledge; Stuart Cole; Tim Davis; Tony Davis; Ian Farris; Norman Funk; Helen Grahame; Sandra Gross; Barry Humphreys; Sarah Kendall; Susan Kerr; John Parr; Thomas Savva; Lisa Tully; David Whiteside.

1

Introduction

Since the early 1980s, transport in the UK has experienced radical change. Road, rail, sea and air carriers, once run as public services, have become commercially-led businesses. The shift towards a market economy has been far-reaching:

(a) Most of the former State-owned transport undertakings are now in private hands.
(b) Competition has been stimulated, not only between operators of the same mode, but also between different modes of transport.
(c) Operating subsidies have generally been reduced, and in some cases eliminated.

Some other countries are taking steps in the same direction – encouraging greater competition and commercial orientation. Where like-minded governments negotiate liberal agreements, international services are given similar treatment. Within the European Community, 'liberalization' and 'harmonization' of transport between the 12 Member States are essential principles of a Single Market with free movement of people and goods.

Enthusiasts for a free market for transport emphasize the intended benefits. Competition means choice. It provides a powerful incentive to control costs, lower prices and improve service quality. Operators respond more effectively and rapidly to changing patterns of demand. It encourages innovation and creative thinking. In general, it is argued, governments should serve neither as providers nor as regulators of the supply of transport. Rather, they should create the right conditions for entrepreneurial talent to flourish.

There is, however, growing concern that the markets for some transport services may be very different from the economic ideal of 'perfect competition' – a fair contest between a multitude of suppliers for the custom of well-informed buyers. In some modes of transport, big operators may use anti-competitive, predatory tactics against smaller fry. Some fear that competition may be self-extinguishing, leading to cartels, oligopolies and even monopoly after a period of time. Robust controls may therefore be necessary to arrest this process.

It can also be argued that transport is fundamentally different from other commodities which are bought and sold in the market place. Both passengers and freight shippers tend to use transport as a system of interdependent services. The customers often require through transits, and expect good co-ordination between different routes and modes within a network. They also expect the advertised services and prices charged to have reasonable stability and continuity. Can the free play of market forces satisfy these user requirements?

The reader is encouraged to assess the free market philosophy against the alternative of State intervention in transport. Consideration should also be given to the prospects for building a 'partnership' between commercial enterprise and the public sector, where each plays a complementary role. The implications of these different approaches should be thoroughly examined with regard to:

(a) the mission and objectives of the transport operator;
(b) the role of government and its agencies at local, national and international level;
(c) the influence and function of user bodies and trade associations.

Furthermore, transport should be considered in its broader context. The movement of people and goods affects many aspects of public life, and has ramifications for national and international politics. The wider issues include:

(a) national defence;
(b) public safety;
(c) personal mobility and access;
(d) economic development and employment;
(e) land use change and urban planning.

Last, but not least, there is the question of whether current strategies and policies for transport can be sustained. As we approach the year 2000, there are issues which cause anxiety for the future. Various forms of environmental pollution not only affect the quality of life, but may also endanger the health of people, plants and animals. Our transport systems consume non-renewable energy resources, and all modes suffer from problems of congestion. What long-term solutions are possible and practical?

Part I

Structure

2

Owners and Entrepreneurs

The form of ownership may have an important bearing on whether a business can obtain the necessary funds to establish itself, to renew assets and to expand. Ownership determines accountability. It may also affect the motivation and performance of managers and other employees. This chapter examines the significance of ownership in the transport industry.

Private Ownership

Many small firms are **sole traders** – owned and run by one person. In modes of transport where market entry is relatively easy, such as coaching and road haulage in the UK, an owner-boss can acquire the necessary assets and take full responsibility for the enterprise. Quite commonly, that person will drive the vehicle(s) and carry out many other functions personally, or with assistance from their family. Specialist services such as vehicle maintenance, accounting and legal advice can be bought in as required.

Some sole traders expand and take on staff such as drivers and mechanics, and thus become employers. Some choose to subcontract work which they cannot carry out themselves. Some pool their resources and go into a formal **partnership** with others. For many such people, the satisfaction of owning or part-owning a firm, as opposed to being an employee of someone else's, is an important motivation. If successful, the hard work that they put into building up the operation will bring financial reward and assets which can be passed on to their children who may wish to continue the family business.

It is a sad fact, however, that many such firms are not successful. Particular difficulties are experienced during periods of economic recession when the demand for passenger and freight transport falls, and the volume of trade for carriers goes into decline. In free or deregulated markets there are no controls over the prices charged to the customer, nor over the number of operators allowed to trade. A general downturn in business may force down prices as rival operators offer discounts and undercut one another's rates in order to bring in orders from customers. This situation does not necessarily deter new operators from setting up, hoping to make a living. Fixed costs tend to be high. Wages, road tax, insurance, depreciation, rent for premises, repayment on loans for vehicles and so on still have to be paid. The income, reduced through lack of trade and lower rates, may no longer be enough to cover outgoings. Some firms will cease to trade. Thus, a general shake out will occur until demand and supply come back into balance, trade eventually picks up again, and prices stabilize.

A serious disadvantage of the sole trader or partnership arrangement from the owner's point of view is that should the venture fail, and its assets prove insufficient to pay creditors, their personal property can be seized to make up the shortfall. So, liquidation may mean that their house, furniture and other possessions are forfeited. Another disadvantage is that the amount of money which can be obtained from loans to finance growth may be somewhat limited. High interest, collateral and other onerous conditions may be imposed if the bank or other lender perceives the risk to be high.

An alternative method of ownership is the formation of a **limited company**. The people who hold shares or **equity** in such a company take the risk that the value of their holding may go down. Should the business fail, they may lose their entire stake, but no more. This arrangement has enabled some transport enterprises to acquire substantial capital to invest in vehicles, infrastructure, land, buildings and other assets. Expansion can be funded by further equity and/or by loans.

Indeed, as Alan Kelsey has pointed out,[1] transport played an important role in the history of the equities market. By the sixteenth century, the cost of trading expeditions by sea was often well beyond the resources of an individual merchant. The expense was therefore divided among a group of investors, each of whom had a **share** of the ship or company. Furthermore, these shares could be sold on to others during the period of the voyage, which generally took several years.

As technology developed, new forms of transport, requiring even greater capital outlay, were also financed by issuing shares. These included docks and harbours, canals, railways, steamships, tramways, and omnibus companies. The risk to those who bought such shares was often as high as with earlier issues for trading expeditions. Yet, if the venture proved profitable, the shareholders could gain through the paying out of dividends and through any appreciation of share value when they chose to sell them on. To supporters of the free market it is therefore appropriate that recent transport projects, such as the Channel Tunnel, should be financed, at least in part, through share flotation.

Kelsey comments that whereas in 1885 there were over 450 transport companies quoted on the London stock exchange, in 1985 there were less than 30. The spread of public ownership earlier this century reduced the transport sector's presence to little more than 1 per cent of total market capitalization. Nevertheless, in the mid to late 1980s, privatization of large State undertakings meant that British Airways, BAA (formerly British Airports Authority) and others joined existing **quoted** companies such as P & O and Transport Development Group. Thus transport may be returning to its former status on the London stock exchange.[2]

In addition to quoted companies, there are many other public limited companies whose shares are not traded on the stock market. Nevertheless, their shares can be bought and sold by the public. There are also many private limited companies in the transport sector. In some cases, their shares are owned by the members of one family. and passed on through inheritance. Indeed, a substantial amount of the equity may be owned by one person. In 1984, entrepreneur Richard Branson established his own airline Virgin Atlantic Airways on this basis.

In some cases, privatization has allowed transport managers to acquire equity. Many of the former National Bus Company subsidiaries were sold to their managing directors and other senior managers as private limited companies. In the case of the former State haulage undertaking, now NFC plc, the ownership was more broadly based within the company. In the UK's largest employee buy-out, some two-thirds of the workforce became shareholders, including lorry drivers, clerks and typists. Sir Peter Thompson, who was appointed Chairman of the company in 1982, described this as 'the added dimension of people sharing in as well as creating the wealth'.[3]

Transport operations, small and large, have thus been established and developed by private enterprise. It should not be assumed, however, that short-term profit maximization has necessarily prevailed as the main driving force. Indeed, one could argue that better returns on investment can often be earned elsewhere. Historically, transport entrepreneurs have demonstrated a remarkable commitment to ventures and projects which take several years to bear fruit. Yet, without profits, a commercial operation cannot survive for very long. Where transport cannot be provided by the private sector, and where it is deemed necessary for the 'public good', the State may intervene in various ways – one of which is through public ownership.

Public Ownership

Public policy may favour State ownership of a particular transport operation, or several different operations which can be combined to form a wider network. The reasons may be concerned with economic and social goals, civic or national prestige or defence strategy – a wide range of issues discussed in part IV below. Existing undertakings may pass into the ownership of local or central government, and entirely new projects may be financed from public funds. A variety of forms of public ownership are possible.

Some transport undertakings are owned by local authorities. Throughout the world, there are public transport systems which are run as **municipals**. Amsterdam Municipal Transport (GVB), for example, dates from 1900, when the city's local authority acquired the Amsterdam Omnibus Company from its former owners, and began electrifying its 15 tram routes. Since then, an expanding network of tram, bus, ferry and metro services has been run as a public service. New transport infrastructure has been planned to accommodate growth and redevelopment of the urban area.

In the UK, municipal public transport was also firmly established by the early part of this century. Many town and city councils took great pride in the high standards of service which were achieved. For example, on the South coast, Brighton Corporation Tramways started operating in 1901. Its cheap and reliable services were well used by people living and working in the area, as well as by visitors to the seaside resort. Although the electric trams were

BRIGHTON CORPORATION TRAMWAYS.

TOURIST CARS

LEAVE THE

SEA FRONT ←

At the AQUARIUM TERMINUS,

EVERY WEEK DAY AT

11 a.m. & 2.45 p.m.

FOR A

9 MILES TOUR

ALL ROUND BRIGHTON,

WITHOUT CHANGE OF CAR.

Special Conductors travel on the top and describe all the objects and places of interest passed.

FARE 1/- Children 6d.

Full particulars can be obtained from the Timekeeper at the Aquarium Terminus.

TRAMWAY OFFICES,
LEWES ROAD, JULY 11th, 1910.

WILLIAM MARSH,
ENGINEER AND MANAGER.

Plate 2.1   Brighton Borough Transport, now at 'arm's length' from local government, courtesy of Brighton Borough Transport

abandoned in 1939, trolley buses and motorbuses replaced them and the operation continued to provide a network of local routes, as did scores of other municipals in this country.

The 1968 Transport Act created Passenger Transport Authorities (PTAs) in the metropolitan areas. Following local government re-organization in the early 1970s, these became policy-making bodies with powers to plan and control public transport within their territories – the six large conurbations in England, and Strathclyde in Scotland. Implementation of their policies would be carried out by the professional officers of the Passenger Transport Executives (PTEs). Under this arrangement, smaller municipal bus under-takings were often combined to form subregional networks, and in some cases augmented by other bus services operated under contract. Furthermore, local rail services such as the British Rail networks in West Yorkshire, South Yorkshire and Merseyside could be subsidized, enabling lines to be upgraded and fares kept down. Through central planning and co-ordination, some were also able to put a strong emphasis on integrating the various services and modes of transport.

The 1985 Transport Act has, however, transformed the municipals and PTE operations into 'arm's length' Public Transport Companies (PTCs). Before this legislation, such public transport undertakings were directly accountable to local government, which was free to support them through subsidy. Under the new arrangement PTCs are limited companies, as described above. The shares of each company are held by the local authority or PTA, with provision for sale, subject to approval by the Secretary of State for Transport. It was recognized by central government that any continuation of financial support would give PTCs an unfair advantage in the deregulated market for bus companies created under the same Act. Whether in public or private ownership they must therefore be financially self-supporting. Their revenue must at least cover costs, and they are generally expected to return a healthy profit. A few municipals have proved commercially unsuccessful, and have been declared bankrupt – an unthinkable event before the Act.

The following case study describes how a local government owned bus undertaking became an arm's length company, and was subsequently taken into the private sector through an innovative scheme with a high degree of involvement by the employees.

Case study: Busways Travel Services' employee share ownership plan

Busways Travel Services Ltd, a medium-sized bus and coach operator in the North-East of England, underwent a dramatic change of ownership structure during the 1980s. Formerly a group of municipals, with a long and proud tradition of service to people living in the locality, Busways is now owned by its managers and entire workforce under an arrangement known as an Employee Share Ownership Plan (ESOP). Relatively new and still unusual in the UK, ESOP companies in the United States have demonstrated an impressive record of performance, which is largely attributed to a greater level of employee motivation than is found in many conventional companies. The case of Busways suggests that the form of ownership may have a significant bearing on the corporate culture and ethos of service industries such as those in the transport sector.

With the creation of Tyneside PTA[4] which later became Tyne and Wear PTA,[5] the municipal bus undertakings of Newcastle, South Shields and Sunderland were merged. The Authority had a strong and consistent commitment to the concept of an integrated public transport network for the subregion, guided by social, economic and environmental policies for public benefit. When, in 1980, the Tyne and Wear Metro started to operate, many bus routes were recast as feeder services into the new Light Rapid Transit system. The public transport network of the metro, buses and ferries was centrally planned and co-ordinated.

The 1985 Transport Act, however, brought far-reaching changes. The bus operation became a limited company whose equity would be owned initially by the PTA, with provision for sale, as described above. Under the same Act, the PTA was no longer allowed to make good the bus undertaking's deficit through subsidy. Thus, public transport would be operated at arm's length from local government and would be fully accountable for its own costs and revenue. Implementation of the Act also brought about deregulation of local bus services.[6] Thus, the new bus company had to compete with others, some of which were from the former nationalized sector and some of which were independents. Unlike some other bus undertakings in metropolitan areas, Tyne and Wear's had never dominated the subregion, their market share being roughly one third of the total, with a fleet of less than 600 vehicles.

The corporate name 'Busways Travel Services Limited' was chosen for the company. Recognizing the importance of local identities and traditions, its principal divisions were named Newcastle Busways, City Busways, South Shields Busways and Sunderland Busways. These operating units were registered as subsidiary companies. Other divisions included the Blue Bus Services, Economic and Favourite Services, to which its former competitor Tyne and Wear Omnibus Company was added in 1989, when Busways bought this rival operation. Non-operating units include Busways Marketing, which has built up a reputation for designing high-quality promotional material such as service information leaflets and posters as well as for marketing consultancy in the UK and abroad.[7]

As Peter Nash, Commercial Director of Busways, has explained, this structure gave the new company the opportunity to push responsibility down the line to 'field commanders' who now had a mission in life. The head office establishment was substantially reduced in size and its function changed – no longer controlling day-to-day operations, but directing policy and dictating events, monitoring performance, advising and assisting when required: 'In summary, the organisation was beginning to tick as a business enterprise should. Decision making, bereft of any political dimension, became much easier. When you ask yourself the question "How will this decision directly benefit the business?" it's amazing how easy it is to come to the right conclusion.'[8]

Under the previous arrangements, direction had come from the policies of the local politicians who served on the PTA. Decision making within the bus company was highly centralized as the senior management team took responsibility for interpreting the wishes of PTA and for translating them into operational plans and programmes. In those days the 'field commanders' were not given much freedom. Under the new regime, however, attention focused upon the clear remit to survive and prosper in a competitive commercial environment. Thus, the culture of management was transformed into one which encouraged the spirit of entrepreneurship, whilst still retaining the public service ethic.

This was taken one stage further when, in 1988, consideration was given to full privatization. Unlike many of the ex-nationalized sector bus companies, which were wholly purchased by their senior managers, Busways, its parent PTA, and its trade unions were keen to encourage wider participation by its employees. After assessing the merits of various options, the proposal for an ESOP received the support of all parties concerned. Having received formal permission from the Secretary of State, the PTA sold the company for just over £14 million. Following the example of Yorkshire Rider Ltd, formerly West Yorkshire PTA's bus undertaking, Busways became the UK's fifteenth ESOP company in May 1989.

The equity of Busways is 51 per cent owned by its ten senior managers, led by Chairman and Managing Director Eric Hutchinson. The other 49 per cent is owned by the 1,800 or so employees. The money to fund the ESOP holding was raised through loans secured on the company's assets. Employees who leave are required to sell their shares back to the trust, and are paid in cash for them. Any future proposal to sell the company to an outside interest would require the consent of 75 per cent of the shareholders. This makes such a sale unlikely.[9] Thus, the arrangement ensures that the bus operation remains in local hands.

The PTA benefited from the money received from the sale, some of which it used to finance an extension of the Metro to Newcastle

Airport. Since the senior management team now own just over half of the company, they have a vested interest in its commercial success. Likewise, the employees can identify with the performance of the company. Although they do not risk their own money, they can be rewarded through the profit-sharing scheme. As well as three executive directors, there are also two non-executive directors nominated by the employees, who make up the Board of the company. As Peter Nash has commented, the people who work for Busways 'know that they are working for themselves since profits can't leak from the business to absentee shareholders. Employees all receive our Annual Report and Accounts. Now, for the first time ever, our management accounts are accepted as statements of fact. Together we discuss the fortunes of the business and its prospects for the future.'[10]

Municipal operations have sometimes extended to other modes of transport. For example, until its sale to the private sector in 1991, the Port of Bristol Authority was owned by the City Council of Bristol. The Port Director was accountable to the Docks Committee made up of 12 local councillors.[11] Thus, the Avonmouth, Portishead and Royal Portbury Docks were operated as a municipal. Financial support for the port was considered to be a worthwhile investment to encourage economic development and employment growth in the area.

Some airports have also been operated as municipals for similar reasons. Manchester Airport, established in 1938, accommodates over 90 airlines who fly to over 160 destinations worldwide. In the early 1990s work continues on development and upgrading of facilities, including phase I of a new international terminal to raise capacity to 18 million passengers per annum. As the airport's Chairman has commented, all this will 'reinforce Manchester Airport's position as the major hub airport outside London, and as the major growth point for jobs and prosperity in the North-West'. Like the PTCs described above, the 16 largest municipal airports were established as limited companies with the local authorities retaining 100 per cent of the shares, under the 1986 Airport Act.[12] The government have subsequently announced their intention to proceed with full privatization.

Transport can also be owned by central government. There are several types of nationalized industry. The ownership structure, and amount of discretion allowed to the managers, have important implicatons for the development and growth of such undertakings. The most direct form of government control is a **State department** where the Minister of Transport personally supervises the operation which, in effect, is run as a branch of the Civil Service. The Italian Railways, Ente Ferrovie dello Stato (FS) for example, were run as a State department until 1985.

In the UK and some other countries, however, a different formula was adopted. The arrangement, known as a **public corporation** is based on the principle that the managers of a nationalized industry should have reasonable freedom to take operating decisions. The Chairman and Board of the nationalized industry are usually appointed by the Secretary of State for Transport who is, in turn, accountable to Parliament. In broad terms, the Minister will give direction on matters of policy, subject to constraints imposed by other government departments, notably the Treasury and the Environment.

When the assets of the four regionally-based railway companies were acquired from their former owners in 1948, British Railways was established as a public corporation on this basis. Under the 1962 Transport Act, the Board has a legal obligation to operate rail services in Great Britain with due regard to economy, efficiency and safety. Beyond this, the Secretary of State has the power, under the 1974 Railways Act, to set the Board specific objectives. These create a medium-term framework of aims, within which it is the Board's day-to-day responsibility to manage the railway.[13]

In theory, then, the Secretary of State should not be involved in detailed management decisions. In practice, however, it may be hard to draw a clear line between policy and implementation. Furthermore, there may be conflicts between what is 'good for the operator' and what is 'good for the country'. For example, a State airline may be denied the freedom to acquire foreign-built aircraft that its senior managers consider appropriate for the task, and value for money. Instead, they may be required to procure them from a national aerospace industry in order to protect employment at home and to improve the balance of payments. Similarly, a nationalized bus or coach undertaking may be required to renew its fleet with vehicles built by another State industry.

The very strength of public ownership from an interventionist government's point of view may therefore be a weakness for its Board and managers. Lord King, Chairman of British Airways during the transition from public to private ownership, has commented:

No nationalised industry Board can be quite certain of the role it is supposed to play in the life of the nation. In four decades of peacetime existence, British Airways and its predecessors have been expected to maintain Commonwealth air links, support the UK aircraft industry, further British foreign policy, earn hard currency, create employment . . . you can write your own list. Sometimes the Foreign Office won, sometimes the Treasury, and sometimes the British aircraft industry.[14]

The availability of finance may present a further problem for many State-owned transport undertakings. Railways, airlines, airports and seaports, in particular, require large-scale capital for renewal of assets and expansion. Where the operator is wholly dependent upon government for grants and loans to fund investment, proposals often have to compete for Treasury finance with many other items of public expenditure outside the transport sector – for example defence, health and education. In the UK, tight restrictions have been placed upon public sector borrowing, and some applications from public corporations to go ahead with projects have taken a very long time to approve. Furthermore, the pay increases of public sector employees have often been kept to an 'exemplary' low level. This has done little to improve the morale of those working in the industry, and has sometimes created difficulties with recruiting suitable people from outside.

Conclusions

Privatization and increased competition has brought about a resurgence of the risk-taking, business-led approach to transport operation in the UK. Diverse forms of ownership structure have emerged as transport undertakings, formerly owned by local or central government, have been taken into the private sector. Those undertakings which remain in public ownership are also expected to become commercially-led and to compete with the private sector, yet in practice many constraints and obstacles are placed in their path.

Notes

1   Kelsey, A. (1986) 'Transport Finance and Investment', Chartered Institute of Transport Occasional Paper.

2 Ibid.
3 Freight Transport Association (1986) *National Freight Consortium* – supplement, June, p. 3.
4 Under the 1968 Transport Act.
5 Under the 1972 Local Government Act.
6 An explanation and discussion of bus deregulation under the 1985 Transport Act is given in chapter 9 below.
7 Morris, S. (1989) 'Around the PTCs, 2: Busways Travel Services' in *Buses*, February, pp. 58–62.
8 Nash, P. (1991) 'The Effect of Deregulation on the Large Urban Operator', a paper given to the Summer Conference of the Organization of Teachers of Transport Studies.
9 Abbot, J. (1990) 'Management Set New Priorities after City Bus Firm Buy-Out' in *Urban Transport International*, May/June, p. 29.
10 Nash, P. (1991) op. cit.
11 Port of Bristol (1990) *Handbook 1989/90*: Port of Bristol Authority.
12 The role and status of local authority airports is discussed in P. Swan (1988) 'Fighting the Big' in *Transport*, November.
13 British Rail Public Affairs Department (1992) 'Rail Facts and Figures' p. 4.
14 Lord King (1987) 'The World's Favourite Take-Off' interview in *The Observer*, 25 October, p. 78.

3

Managers and Professionals

Entrepreneurs may provide the energy and drive to initiate a business venture. Local or central government may provide the framework of public policy for a State undertaking. Yet, both private and public sector employers need to appoint transport managers and professionals to run the operation. This chapter examines the special features which distinguish transport from other industries. It assesses the implications of these characteristics for the organizational structure and for the strategy and style of management.

Special Characteristics

The verb 'to manage' has various meanings in the English language – not all of them are complimentary to those who do the managing! Thus, the Oxford Reference Dictionary's definitions include:

- to organize or regulate; to be the manager of (a business etc)
- to succeed in achieving, to contrive; to succeed with limited resources or means, to be able to cope (with)
- to secure the co-operation of (a person) by tact, flattery etc . . .[1]

Essentially it is, however, about achieving desired results by planning, organizing, leading and controlling the actions of others. This necessarily involves **delegation**. Managers must accept responsibility for those below them in the hierarchy who perform these actions under their guidance and instruction. The people who are thus managed should be sufficiently motivated to identify with the aims and objectives of the organization as a whole. Transport undertakings, by their very nature, require good **communications** and **co-ordination** of effort in order to put these principles into practice.

Many transport undertakings are labour-intensive. Wages and salaries commonly represent 50–70 per cent of total running costs for road freight, road passenger and railway operators in the UK. Many of their staff receive low pay relative to other industries. Yet, in order to meet the customers' needs, they must accept shift work and unsocial hours as conditions of service. Transport is often round the clock.

Larger transport operations require people with diverse skills and specialist knowledge. Railways, for example, need managers and professionals for train operation, maintenance, permanent way, signalling and telecommunications, civil engineering and many other functions. In all transport, the services provided for the customers must be co-ordinated in space and time. Each specialist function is interdependent and one weak link will generally result in failure of the entire system.

Managers and staff involved in these disparate activities, then, are spread out geographically over the service network. In the case of airlines, shipping and international haulage they may be separated by distances of thousands of miles. Furthermore, the output of transport cannot be stored, but must be provided as and when the customers require it. All this creates particular problems of supervision and control.

Transport is highly visible to the public's gaze. Problems cannot be hidden from general scrutiny. A discourteous driver, a dirty vehicle or a breakdown will be noticed. More important still, customers entrust their own bodies and/or possessions to the carrier, who must ensure that their arrival is safe, as well as on time. Awareness of the potential dangers and hazards, and vigilance to prevent accidents, is required of all employees.

These special characteristics have an important bearing on how transport is organized. The different modes of transport have their particular requirements, yet some common principles may be identified. A **structure** is necessary to determine lines of authority and to channel the flow of relevant information to ensure that the transport product is delivered effectively and efficiently with consistent quality, day after day.

Organizational Structure

In small transport firms, such as the sole trader haulage and coach hire operators described in chapter 2, there is usually a simple 'master/servant' relationship between the owner-boss and any people he/she may employ. The style of management is often **personal** since the proprietor will usually be closely involved in the day-to-day running of the business, and with the recruitment and selection of staff.

In larger organizations such as national railway systems, international airlines and shipping lines, decisions taken by the Chairman and Chief Executive must rely upon a great deal of specialist expertise provided by managers and professionals further down the hierarchy. Such undertakings require firm and decisive leadership, but may need to adopt a **corporate** structure for decision making. A good deal of consultation may be required to ensure that the full implications of any proposal, such as acquiring new rolling stock, aircraft or vessels, are fully explored at each stage as the proposal is progressed through to implementation. Thus, the process of resolving issues is depersonalized in a search for rational decision-making.

The levels of decision making in a large organization may involve several tiers in a hierarchy:

(a) **Senior managers** make up the small group of people who head the organization, and who have responsibility for the strategic, long-term goals.
(b) **Middle managers** are responsible for working out the medium and short-term tactics to convert these goals into a workable programme of action.
(c) **Supervisory managers** represent the lowest tier and have no other managers below them, but perform the very important role of overseeing the staff who carry out the work.

In larger transport operations of this kind, the organization is often complex but, as in other industries, it is possible to distinguish 'line' from 'staff' management. **Line management** refers to the chain of command, or line of authority for the core business or main activity, for example delivering parcels by road or transporting passengers and vehicles by ferry. In the case of London Underground, reorganization in 1988 defined the core business as the 'Passenger Services Directorate', responsible for operating the trains and stations, the delivery of all services to the customers to meet quality, safety, security and financial performance targets. Here, the line of authority runs from the Director, through the General Managers of the various routes (e.g. Piccadilly Line) down to the drivers, guards and station staff. Line management is supported by **staff management** which provides the necessary services and advice for the core business. In the case of London Underground, staff support includes the finance, development, engineering, marketing and personnel functions. These staff managers have no direct authority over the train crew or station staff in the Passenger Services Directorate.

In transport, a distinction can also be made between functional and divisional management. Where a transport operation has a fairly small geographical spread, its activities may be directed from one operating base such as a haulage depot or bus garage. Such a business may be organized with a **functional structure**. For example, the small bus company in Figure 3.1 has a service network, small enough to be run from one garage. Its six functional managers each head a department: a chief engineer (maintaining, repairing and cleaning the vehicles); a company secretary (legal and administration); as well as managers responsible for personnel, marketing, finance and the core business operations (running the buses to an advertised schedule). In most organizations of this type, these specialists report to a general manager with overall responsibility for co-ordinating these various functions.

Where the operation has a wider geographical spread, however, responsibility may be delegated on an area basis; for example, north, south, east, west. Each area will have a **divisional manager** responsible for the services within that territory. The divisional managers will then report to a general manager (or equivalent) with overall responsibility to co-ordinate the various area-based units and any central functions at the headquarters.

For example the bus company in Figure 3.2 is large enough to have:

(a) headquarters functions consisting of fleet engineering, company secretary, and managers for operations, personnel, marketing and finance;
(b) divisional managers responsible for garage engineering and local operations with clerical support at each of the company's three local depots.

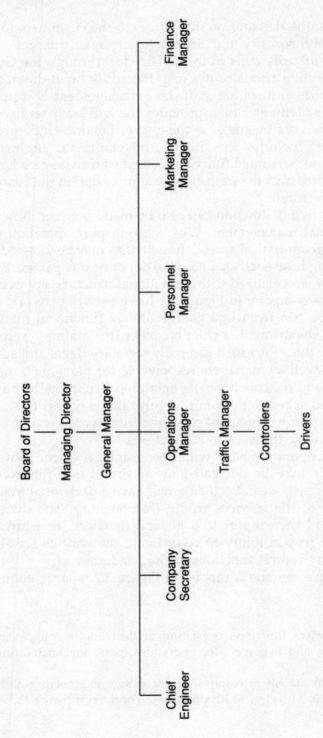

Figure 3.1 Example of small bus company with functional management structure

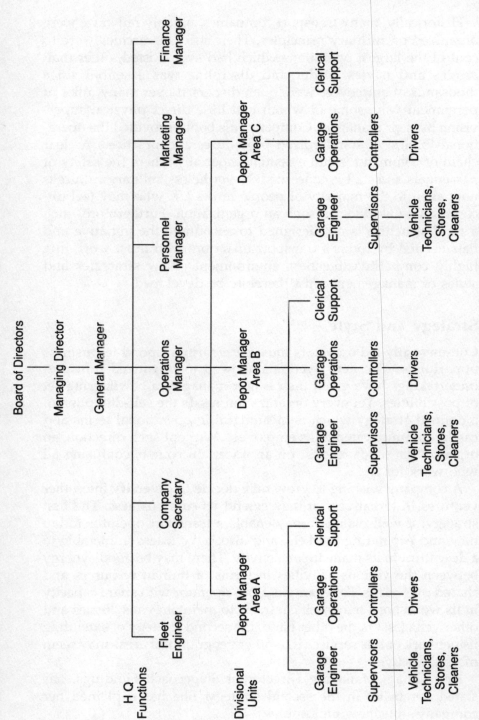

Figure 3.2 Example of a large bus company with divisional management structure

Historically, many transport companies, notably railways, were organized on **military** principles. Their strict hierarchies were to control the largest operations which had ever existed, other than armies and navies. Order and discipline was essential since thousands of employees were often dispersed over many miles of permanent way, some of whom had little direct physical supervision by their managers. Company rule books provided the operational 'bibles' of standardized procedures and practices. A clear chain of command is still essential, especially where the safety of passengers and staff is concerned. Nevertheless, military culture is now alien to the majority of people in the UK who may feel uncomfortable working in such an organization. Furthermore, such a rigid structure is not designed to encourage the initiative and flair needed by today's transport operators who must work in a highly competitive business environment.[2] New strategies and styles of management must therefore be developed.

Strategy and Style

Commercially-led operators must necessarily respond to business opportunity. The new freedoms allowed to privatized transport undertakings have given their senior managers a bewildering set of possibilities. Yet every organization needs the self-discipline of a defined **strategy** which is meaningful in operational terms and can be communicated to its employees. Without such direction, an organization tends to drift on an uncertain course, confusing all who work for it.

A company wishing to grow may decide to **diversify** into other ventures. Alternatively, it may **extend** its core business. The first strategy, if well planned, may enable a transport operator to tap new and expanding markets, and also leave it less vulnerable to a downturn in its mainstream activity. There may be good synergy between the various activities in terms of human resources and shared overheads. For example, a bus operator with spare capacity in its workshops may seek contracts to maintain vans, lorries and other vehicles. On the other hand, the second strategy of extending its network of bus services into other geographical areas may seem more attractive.

Ann Gloag, Managing Director of Stagecoach Holdings, has stated her belief in the second strategy. She has explained her company's business philosophy:

From the very beginning we had to address and decide exactly what kind of business we wanted to be in – in very specific terms – otherwise we and our management would not have a clear view where to apply resource and effort. Should Stagecoach be a conglomerate group? Did we want to be property speculators and developers? Heavy vehicle engineers? Express coach operators? Retailers? Or bus operators? All . . . some . . . or one of them? Should we be a leader or a follower? We looked at what other bus companies were doing to diversify into travel agents, advertising agents, computer suppliers, petrol stations, tobacconists. What a wonderful army of projects to dissipate effort and consume resources![3]

In recent years a number of leading transport organizations have sought to define exactly what sort of business they are in, or should be in. This may be refined into a **corporate mission statement** – a unique aim which sets the organization apart from all others. Such a statement should set direction. Hopson and Scally have discussed the approach taken by Jan Carlzon, when he became Chairman of Scandinavian Airlines (SAS), 'he found that the airline was trying to be in every kind of airline business – charter flights, special trips, holidays, business travel, cargo. After an analysis of where the income was generated, Carlzon redefined the core business of SAS as that of being a business person's airline. From then on all activity would be centred on making SAS the best business airline in Europe.'[4]

The following case study illustrates how British Rail, a very large and complex transport undertaking, has refocused its strategy and style of management to suit a changing commercial environment. To support the reorientation of its activities, a new organizational structure has been developed for the 1990s.

Case study: British Rail, organizing for quality

In his valedictory paper to the Chartered Institute of Transport in 1990, the retiring Chairman of British Rail, Sir Robert Reid, commented that the organization of the railway changed little between 1947 and 1982. He emphasized two dominant features which survived throughout these years: 'First was the primacy of the regional general managers. These were the railway barons exercising great power. The second was the railway's traditionally strong functional hierarchies. The engineers in particular were powerful people whose word tended to be law.' He concluded that, during this period, perhaps the only person who could take a grip of both costs and revenue simultaneously was the Chairman.[5] In 1974 the government gave British Rail the somewhat uninspiring mission 'to operate its railway passenger business so as to provide a public service which is comparable generally with that provided by the Board at present', in return for receiving a Public Service Obligation grant each year.

Meanwhile, the competitive environment for transport in the UK had changed a great deal. The percentage of households in Great Britain with one or more cars had risen from just 14 per cent in 1951 to 61 per cent in 1982.[6] Construction of the national motorways network during the 1960s and 1970s had reduced journey times for inter-urban travel by private car, lorry, and coach. Deregulation of road haulage in 1968, and of scheduled express coaches in 1980, further strengthened road competition in the railway's traditional markets. By the early 1980s improved domestic air services were beginning to erode the railway's premium business traffic on Anglo-Scottish routes.

Reorganization in 1982 established five **Sectors** to focus management effort upon the markets which the railway served. These were as follows:

(a) InterCity – long distance, inter-urban passenger services.
(b) London and the South-East (later Network SouthEast) – commuter services into the capital.
(c) Other Provincial Services (later Regional Railways) – urban, rural and cross-country passenger services outside the South-East.
(d) Railfreight (later split into Trainload Freight and Railfreight Distribution).
(e) Parcels – including Red Star express delivery services.

Each was headed by a Sector Director who was accountable for financial performance, marketing and customer service. The Sectors were responsible for product design and setting the specification for new investment, such as electrification of the East Coast Main Line from London King's Cross to Edinburgh, in the case of InterCity.

The 1982 organizational structure was, however, a complex three-way matrix. The six Regions remained with responsibility for production, working to the specifications and costs established by the Sectors. Thus, the majority of people employed by British Rail worked for Anglia, Eastern, London Midland, Scottish, Southern, and Western Regions. Furthermore, the Board of British Rail retained headquarters Functions including central engineering, finance and personnel services. The contractual arrangement between Sectors and Regions improved cost and service quality performance, but the arrangement was not wholly satisfactory. As Chief Executive John Welsby has pointed out, with significant decisions being taken by the Sectors it became more difficult to create satisfying jobs and career structures within the Regions and central Functions.[7]

In the early 1990s the restructuring was taken one stage further under the project 'Organizing for Quality' (OfQ). This completed the process of devolving responsibility and accountability to organizational units which focus on the markets served, rather than arbitrary geographical regions – as far as possible within the constraints imposed by the Board's statutory duties.[8] The main aims of OfQ are to:

(a)   simplify the matrix management structure, by bringing marketing, financing and production management together;
(b)   decentralize, within the business framework, by bringing power, responsibility and accountability closer to the customer;
(c)   address recommendation of the Hidden Report (following the Clapham accident) that 'British Rail shall ensure that the organizational framework exists to prevent the commercial considerations of a business-led railway from compromising safety'.[9]

The completion of OfQ in 1992–3 meant that the Regions disappeared, and a small strategic corporate or Group Headquarters took responsibility for ensuring that the new system works to provide the best possible service to customers as a whole. It also remains responsible for securing finance, for ensuring satisfactory business performance and for setting policies and standards for the running of the railway. A National Safety Audit is also placed at Headquarters to ensure high safety standards throughout the system. A Central Services unit supervises functions which are kept together in order to retain their integrity and economies of scale, for example Information Systems and Technology, Architecture and Design Group, Personnel Services, and the international consultancy Transmark. Increasingly, where possible, their services will be subject to competitive tendering, and some will have scope to trade externally.[10]

The central principle, of reducing the distance between the railway and its customers, is achieved through a simplified structure with the creation of **Business Units**. These have 'ownership' of the assets – locomotives, rolling stock, track, signalling, stations, depots and so on. Hence, they are responsible for most of the production aspects of the railway, formerly carried out by the Regions and headquarters Functions. Legally employed by British Rail, the majority of managers and other employees therefore work for the Business Units. This refocusing of responsibility is supported by a long-term initiative entitled 'Quality through People' to foster team-building, delegation of responsibility and control, and the freeing of decision making to encourage initiatives and effective contribution from all levels.[11]

Six of the Business Units have been developed from the Sectors – InterCity, Network SouthEast, Regional Railways, Trainload Freight, Railfreight Distribution and Parcels. A further two – European Passenger Services and BR Telecommunications – have been established to exploit new business opportunities arising from the opening of the Channel Tunnel and from the freer telecommunications market respectively.[12] Most of the Business Units have their own headquarters and then delegate responsibility to Profit Centres. These represent the most important level of the organization since they are closest to the market-place. Directors of Profit Centres are accountable for their costs and revenue and, as far as possible, have ownership and control of their assets and resources.

Under OfQ InterCity, for example, manages a business which had a turnover of over £850 million, and an operating surplus (before interest) of nearly £50 million in 1990/1.[13] It operates a high-speed passenger network linking centres as far apart as Inverness, Penzance, Fishguard and Hull. It aims to attract both business and leisure customers (currently a 30:70 split). It is unique amongst European railways in that it operates without subsidy. It has defined its mission statement: 'To be the best, most civilized way to travel at speed from centre to centre.' Responsibility is delegated from InterCity headquarters to five Profit Centres based on line of route – effectively a form of divisional management. These are as follows:

(a)   East Coast Main Line.
(b)   West Coast Main Line.
(c)   Great Western Main Line.

(d) Midland Main Line.
(e) Anglia and Gatwick.

The government's programme for privatization, set out in a White Paper published July 1992,[14] will necessitate further reorganization. In the first phase, train operation will be separated from the track, signalling and other infrastructure, through the creation of 'Railtrack' – an agency which will charge the businesses and other rail operators a market price for their use of the permanent way. Franchising of passenger train services will allow access for private operators. The freight businesses will be sold outright. Some passenger stations will also be sold off. An independent rail regulator will ensure 'fair play'.[15] These proposals will present challenging problems for railway personnel. Nevertheless, a decade of progress towards a business-led railway under public ownership has done much to prepare British Rail's managers and professionals for the new commercial environment.

Objectives and their Usefulness

A transport organization, such as British Rail and its Business Units, will adopt a structure, strategy and style of management appropriate to its function as a carrier of people or goods. Whether commercial or non-commercial, the unique aim of such an organization may be formally expressed as a mission statement. This may give it strength of purpose and overall direction. Yet the mission must somehow be made concrete through the actions of the people who work for the organization. Aims must therefore be translated into **workable objectives**.

Objectives set out precisely what is to be achieved and by whom. Individual managers may be given objectives in the expectation that they will use personal initiative, and the resources at their disposal, to produce the desired results. In transport, as in many other industries, such results can only be achieved through team effort. Sometimes this involves the work of one self-sufficient team, sometimes the co-ordinated effort of several interdependent teams, each with its particular specialism or area of responsibility. Objectives should serve not only to clarify what is required of an individual or team, but also to motivate them. Objectives must therefore be far more than vague aims or lists of good intentions.

To be useful as instruments for managing an organization, objectives should be:

(a) **targets**, i.e. commitments to achieve a particular result within a specified timescale;
(b) **quantified**, i.e. wherever possible, expressed in figures so that performance can be measured on a numerical scale;
(c) **understandable**, i.e. explained clearly and unambiguously in plain English, so that all involved can comprehend what is required of them;
(d) **credible**, i.e. providing a reasonable challenge, yet sensible and realistic in view of the resources available and the external business environment;
(e) **selective**, i.e. homing in upon current priorities in the organization's strategy.

There may also be a hierarchy of objectives, creating a distinction between strategic and operational targets. **Strategic** objectives are those which address the more fundamental and long-term commitments of the organization. Responsibility for carrying through and achieving these will rest with senior management. For example, the Chairman, Chief Executive and Directors of a commercial long-haul airline may have a set of strategic objectives which set the priorities for a five-year programme of expansion. Some of these might be:

• to increase market share on North Atlantic scheduled services from 6 per cent to 12 per cent;
• to increase staff productivity on cargo handling operations by 20 per cent;
• to achieve a three-fold increase in turnover on passenger charters.

Operational objectives are concerned with the detailed realities of implementing the strategic ones. They have shorter timescales, and are commonly translated into monthly or annual targets. Responsibility for taking appropriate action and achieving objectives will tend to rest with middle and supervisory management. Some operational objectives will be concerned with costs and productivity, some with sales and revenue, some with quality of service. For example, a nationwide distribution company delivering beer from a major brewery to public houses, private clubs and supermarkets, must satisfy their client's service specifications set out in the contract, yet the carrier must also establish its own targets to be implemented by the managers and staff at its various depots. For such an operation, quality of service objectives might include:

- deliveries completed on schedule, or within 20 minutes of the specified time, to be at least 90 per cent of the total;
- orders fully satisfied from stock held at the depot to be at least 93 per cent of the total;
- orders satisfied within a lead time of two days to be at least 95 per cent of the total.

In this way an operational objective is established as a standard or norm. Actual performance can then be measured against such a benchmark. In road passenger transport, for example, standards such as cost per passenger-mile, or ratio of cost to revenue, can be used to make comparisons between different bus garages owned by the same company. Comparisons over time can also be made. For one garage, performance in a particular month can be compared with the same month in previous years. If output measures show improvement, the standards can be raised from year to year in order to encourage better results.

Performance measures should be quick and relatively easy to calculate, so that current information can be reported to those who are responsible for achieving the operational objectives, as well as those who are responsible for strategic matters such as investment in vehicle fleets and operational bases. It is also an advantage to establish a system of **exception reporting** in order to reduce the volume of data to that which is most relevant to immediate problems and issues which managers face. Thus for example, revenue performance which is, say, 10 per cent or more above or below the target should be highlighted. A systematic appraisal of accurate, up-to-date, and relevant data will provide the basis for management decisions, including corrective action when performance falls below target.

Conclusion

Transport is an instantly perishable product which must be made available where and when the customers require it. These distinguishing features have influenced the organizational structure of transport undertakings. Nevertheless, different transport operators have developed their own strategies and styles of management, appropriate to the particular tasks their organization has to carry out. A corporate mission statement may serve to establish clearly the fundamental goals which distinguish one undertaking from another. This, in turn, may provide the basis to formulate strategic and operational objectives, which set out in precise terms the desired output which is to be achieved by managers and other employees, individually or, more often, through team effort.

Notes

1   *Oxford Reference Dictionary* (1986), p. 508: Oxford University Press.
2   Shaw, S.J. (1991) 'Seeking Equality' in *Transport*, March/April, p. 64.
3   Gloag, A. (1989) 'Stagecoach: Exploiting Opportunities' in *Bus and Coach Management*, November, p. 10.
4   Hopson, B. and Scally, M. (1989) *12 Steps to Success Through Service*, p. 14: Lifeskills Publishing Group.
5   Sir Robert Reid (1990) 'On Track for the 1990s' in *Transport*, January/February, p. 15.
6   Department of Transport (1989) 'Transport Statistics Great Britain 1978–1988', Tables 2.11 and 7.2.
7   Welsby, J. (1991a) 'Regions Give Way to Businesses' in *Railway Gazette International*, April, p. 217.
8   Ibid. p. 217.
9   Welsby, J. (1991b) 'Organised for Quality' in *Transport*, September/October, pp. 138–9.
10 Welsby, J. (1991a) op. cit. p. 219.
11 Welsby, J. (1991b) op. cit. p. 138.
12 Ibid. pp. 138–9.
13 British Rail Public Affairs Department (1992) *Rail Facts and Figures*, p. 16.
14 HMSO (1992) 'New Opportunities for the Railways: the Privatization of British Rail', Cmnd 2012.
15 See discussion of the Labour Party's response in chapter 13.

4

Understanding the Market

Many people wrongly assume that marketing is concerned only with selling and advertising activities. These functions are certainly elements of the whole, but they do not convey its full scope. The concept of marketing is better understood as a philosophy of business which puts the customer at the centre of things. This chapter discusses the relevance of marketing to the transport operator.

Moving Markets

Marketing should begin with a thorough appraisal of the needs and wants of the customers. In passenger transport, this includes a proper understanding of **why, where, when** and **how** they wish to travel. It includes an understanding of the level of service and degree of comfort they expect, and are prepared to pay for. In freight, the same basic principles apply. Some freight transport operations such as postal services and household removals are for consumer markets – that is, they serve the requirements of individuals and households. Many others are for shippers who have customers of their own. Thus, the carrier must provide services of the right quality and at the right price, which enable the shippers to keep **their** customers satisfied, delivering their goods safely and reliably on time.

Market Intelligence is the process of gathering and analysing all information relevant to the success of the business. This involves a continuous scanning and review of both demand and supply. Firstly, as Professor John Hibbs has pointed out, a wealth of valuable information may be available within the operator's own organization, if it can be monitored systematically.[1] For example, electronic ticketing systems used by local bus operators and computerized reservation and ticketing systems used by airlines and inter-city railways yield data which can be analysed in order to identify patterns and trends, responses to fare increases or discounts and so on. On the supply side, useful information may be obtained by scrutinizing digests and market reports published by government departments, commercial consultants and other organizations. Furthermore, the 'hard' data on both demand and supply can be complemented by 'soft' information gleaned from a variety of sources, for example from articles in journals and newspapers, from user bodies and trade associations,[2] and personal observations of competitors' services.

Market research may be needed to fill in the gaps of information not obtained through the ongoing process of intelligence-gathering. For example, an airline may have an accurate picture of the number of people carried on each flight, and of the revenue generated, but it will not know the reasons why the passengers travelled. Were they on their employers' business? On holiday? Visiting friends and relatives? On urgent personal business? The carrier will not know the proportion of people in different age groups, or socio-economic groups. Nor, unless passengers take the trouble to offer praise or to complain, will the carrier know whether the customers were satisfied or dissatisfied with the service provided, nor how they felt it compared with that of rival airlines. Thus, surveys may be required to investigate specific problems or issues.

Transport markets are seldom static – sometimes they change in a rapid and obvious fashion, such as when a run-down urban centre is redeveloped. Sometimes the change is slower and more subtle, for instance when a rural or coastal area becomes attractive for retirement homes, and the average age of the population gradually increases. A transport operator must therefore use market intelligence and research to interpret and reinterpret the market, and respond by offering services which are in tune with what the customers require. Thus, existing services must be adapted and developed, for example by adjusting routes and timetables. Appropriate new services must be offered through a process of innovation and experiment.

Marketing has been defined as 'the management process responsible for identifying, anticipating, and satisfying, customer requirements profitably.'[3] This concept rests on the principle that customers are free to exercise **choice** between rival suppliers who are keen to obtain their business. If one transport operator fails to satisfy their needs and wants, they know that they can take their trade elsewhere. Thus **competition**, or even the threat of it, should provide the vital spur which encourages road, rail, sea and air carriers to adopt the marketing approach.

Market Orientation

Marketing theory identifies three philosophies of business. An organization may be:

(a)   production-oriented;
(b)   sales-oriented;
(c)   marketing-oriented.

Indeed, an organization may evolve, passing through the first two stages before reaching the third.[4] **Production-orientation** is where management attention is focused on existing products, and pays little attention to the changing needs and wants of the market-place. In transport such organizations may concentrate their efforts on the output – running trains, producing bus passenger-miles and so on. This tends to occur when the customers have little or no effective choice. **Sales-orientation** is where attention shifts towards sales effort. It is assumed that demand can be created by hard sell techniques such as using a highly motivated sales force, or by heavy advertising spending. This tends to occur if there is a glut of a product or service – where supply exceeds demand. **Marketing-orientation** is where the organization first investigates what the customers require, how much they are willing or able to pay, and whether or not these needs and wants are being met by the products or services currently available to them.

In the context of local bus services, newly deregulated under the 1985 Transport Act, Yorkshire Rider Ltd's Chairman and Managing Director Bill Cottham explained the significance of market-orientation in his company's commercial success:

It is important to realise that a marketing-led approach is not in-dulging in expensive and flamboyant advertising and public relations, although creative promotions are obviously an important

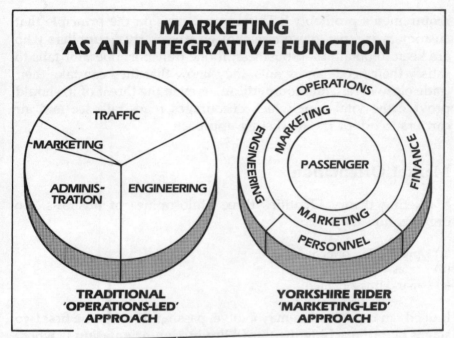

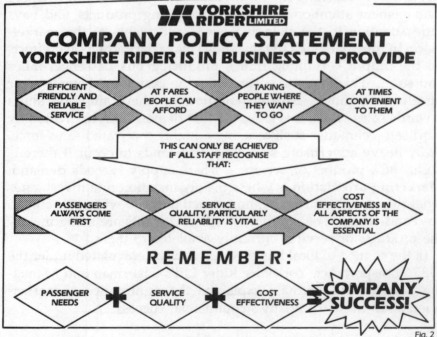

Fig. 2

Plate 4.1   Yorkshire Rider's approach to market-orientation, courtesy
Yorkshire Rider Ltd

element . . . marketing is not merely a separate activity only loosely connected with other key activities, rather it must be recognised as an integrative function, one which permeates and even preconditions all other management activities.[5]

With regard to scheduled airlines whose routes have been opened up to greater competition, Derek Dear emphasizes the need to embrace the marketing concept. He criticizes the complacency of a previous generation of airline executives who had spent 'large sums on advertising to tell travellers "We take more care of you". Research showed the customers took a different view.' He describes how British Airways developed a fresh approach, which involved investment in training before moving into promotion. Customers' reactions were constantly monitored to ensure that the marketing team understood how people perceived the airline and its services. He summarizes the market-led approach of his airline as 'making what you can sell, not selling what you can make'.[6]

As shown in chapter 2, entrepreneurs respond to actual or latent demand for transport. There is often a strong element of risk, and some fail, but some build up successful businesses based on innovative ideas which they put into practice. In the early 1970s, for example, a young American businessman named Fred Smith set up Federal Express (Fedex), to offer a reliable, next day parcel delivery service using dedicated all-freighter aircraft and road vehicles. Customers soon developed sufficient confidence in Fedex to use it on a day-to-day basis. In less than 20 years it expanded into a worldwide operation, offering a wide range of products. With the globalization of many businesses, the market for express parcel services continues to grow. Nevertheless, despite the enormous capital investment required for market entry, the business has become highly competitive. In the 1990s, Fedex must compete, not only with international postal services, but also with other private sector global carriers including TNT, UPS and DHL. Furthermore, all carriers now face a degree of competition from electronic mailing systems which offer an alternative to physically sending certain types of document. The competitive environment has encouraged an emphasis on quality and customer service. In order to keep existing customers happy, and to win new customers, express parcel operators must live up to their promises of guaranteed, on-schedule delivery to the highest standards.

Competition from other operators, other modes, and even other

Plate 4.2   Sealink Stena Line Ferries, courtesy of Sealink Stena Line

service industries may, therefore, encourage carriers to adopt marketing as a philosophy of business. The following case study illustrates the process of transition from production- to marketing-orientation.

Case study: Sealink Stena and the market for ferry services

Until the 1980s, the ferries carrying passengers, cars, coaches and freight vehicles across the English Channel were not generally renowned for style or sophistication. The market was somewhat 'captive', and the fares/tariffs charged by the various ferry operators were fairly similar. In more recent times, however, real competition between ferry operators has developed. As well as conventional ferries, some routes have seen competition from 'fast ferries' – hovercraft, and more recently their successors, the wave-piercing catamarans. There is also a growing challenge from air transport. An even greater threat is posed by the Channel Tunnel. Since customers now have a fair degree of choice, ferry companies must respond with business strategies that are truly customer-oriented.

Until 1984 Sealink was a State-owned ferry operator which, for historical reasons, came under the aegis of British Rail. For some years, Sealink's management had experienced difficulties in obtaining finance for new and replacement assets, especially when compared to their main rival, the privately-owned Townsend Thorensen. Under the government's privatization programme Sealink was, however, sold to the Sea Containers group. The latter were able to put substantial investment into upgrading Sealink's services with new and refurbished tonnage, improved port and terminal facilities, as well as other support functions such as computerized reservation systems. When the bulk of the British Ferries subsidiary of Sea Containers was subsequently sold on in 1990 to the Swedish company Stena Line AB, the new owners were therefore able to enjoy the benefits from the progress which had been made.[7]

When the Stena group acquired Sealink, they had already gained a favourable reputation for quality and for efficiency as an international shipping operator. Lars-Erik Ottoson, the then President of Stena Line AB, has commented on the company's approach to improving profitability on its established services between Sweden, Denmark, Norway and Germany.[8] Cost cutting was not enough – with ferries there are very high fixed costs for the vessels, port operations and other overheads. Productivity was improved by using the ships for more sailings per day throughout the year, and by improving load factors – that is, the passengers and vehicles carried as a percentage of capacity available on each sailing. Thus, the standard turn-round time was reduced to 45 minutes, and new computer systems were introduced to improve the practical capacity to handle a larger volume of passengers with a maintained service level. New booking systems allowed new types of products, like conferences and package tours, to be introduced.

Stena's commercial strategy also focused on investment in luxurious 'cruise ferries', a new generation of vessels which have transformed the image of a ferry service from the customer's point of view. As well as providing the core product of short sea transport for passengers and vehicles, cruise ferries have a level of comfort and programme of on-board entertainment which have greatly enhanced their operators' competitiveness. The emphasis on retailing, high quality catering and other leisure facilities enhances their potential to generate revenue on routes where the customers have a high level of disposable income, and can treat the voyage as part of their holiday. It has offered greater scope to lengthen the summer season and to offer attractive reasons to travel. The range of products can also be expanded and packaged to include conferences, night cruises, mini-breaks, shopping trips and package tours.')

On the cross-Channel routes, Sealink Stena introduced two super ferries – the Stena Fiesta and Stena Fantasia – in 1990. Their on-board passenger facilities include 'sky dome' entertainment centres, bars, high quality retail outlets, lounges and entertainments for lorry drivers, and special facilities for children and parents with babies. The size of these vessels, which each have capacity for 1,800 passengers and 650 cars, offer economies of scale for the ferry operators, enabling them to offer excellent value for money for the basic product. In 1991, two further modern vessels – the Stena Invicta and Stena Challenger – were introduced on the Dover–Calais and Dover–Dunkirk routes. Sealink Stena's major rival, P & O European Ferries, also adopted a very market-oriented strategy and its fleet of cross-Channel cruise ferries includes two large vessels, the Pride of Dover and the Pride of Calais.

With marketing activity, ferry services on most routes across the Channel and North Sea have experienced steady traffic growth. Although the number of foot passengers declined somewhat during the 1980s, the increase in car passengers more than compensated for this loss.(An increasing number of UK residents take their cars to the Continent, enjoying the convenience and independence of their own transport. Coach travel to mainland Europe has also increased in popularity. The shorter sea crossings through the ports of Dover, Folkestone, Ramsgate and Newhaven account for some 70 per cent of passengers, with almost 60 per cent going through Dover alone.[10] With regard to freight traffic, the flexibility, security and other benefits of Roll-on/Roll-off facilities, and increased trade between the UK and European Community partners, have also encouraged traffic growth. Some of the 'wheeled cargo' loaded onto trucks and trailers is carried on lorry decks of passenger ferries, some is carried on freight ferries.)

Ferry operators are, however, facing a number of competitive threats and their marketing strategies for the 1990s must take account of these. Although the Sea Containers group sold Sealink, they retained their hovercraft services under the trading name Hoverspeed. The life-expired hovercraft have been subsequently replaced with innovative wave-piercing catamarans known as

'SeaCats'. Initially introduced on Hoverspeed's Portsmouth–Cherbourg route, in summer 1991 they began operating Dover–Boulogne (40 minutes) and Dover–Calais (35 minutes). These crossing times compare with approximately 1 hour 50 minutes and 1 hour 15 minutes for these routes by conventional ferry. SeaCats have capacity for 400 passengers and 80 cars.

Air transport also presents a challenge. During the 1970s and 1980s charter flights from the UK to mainland Europe showed dramatic growth. A high proportion of these were Inclusive Tours to Spain, Portugal and Greece, and these were not directly in competition with cross-Channel ferries. Nevertheless, the attractiveness of low-price packages will have influenced some holidaymakers in their choice of destination. Liberalization of scheduled air services within the European Community in the 1990s is, however, expected to encourage airlines to offer discounted fares especially aimed at leisure travellers on many routes.[11] This will create further direct competitive pressure for ferry operators.

The greatest challenge of all will, however, come from the Channel Tunnel. Eurotunnel, its operator, has a large debt burden to pay off because of the huge scale of capital investment. Nevertheless its running costs are estimated at only 10 per cent of those of ferry operators.[12] It will offer frequent 'Le Shuttle' services carrying cars, coaches and road freight vehicles in Roll-On/Roll-Off fashion through the tunnel itself, with a journey time of 35 minutes between the two terminals. In addition, international passenger and freight trains will run through the tunnel. Thus, for the first time, the UK railway system will be physically linked to those on mainland Europe. The Channel Tunnel will bring a massive increase in total capacity – almost twice the size of the 1990 car market by ferry, and a quarter of the Roll-On/Roll-Off freight market to all European destinations.[13] The impact of the tunnel will probably be felt on many cross-Channel and North Sea services but its greatest effect will be on short sea crossings closest to its route from Cheriton near Folkestone to Sangatte near Calais.

Segmentation, Targeting and Positioning

Market awareness should lead to an appreciation of the important principle that the demand for any product or service is seldom uniform. Rather, the market is made up of identifiable types of customer. The process of distinguishing these different customer groups is known as market **segmentation**. Thus, the concept of segmenting customer demand is a further refinement of market-orientation in that it focuses attention on the requirements of specific groups, rather than assuming a homogeneous market.

The specific variables used to segment the market will depend on the product or service under consideration. For transport operators in passenger markets, the criteria might include:

(a) **Age** – e.g. youth markets may have a relatively low average income but high propensity to use public transport, compared to adults in the middle age range.

(b) **Gender** – e.g. women may be more frequent users of buses and trains because of their lower level of access to private cars, in contrast to men.

(c) **Socio-economic groups** – e.g. higher managerial or professional groups on average commute longer distances and may be prepared to pay a higher fare than junior managerial or clerical staff.

(d) **Lifestyle** – e.g. with vacational travel, some people desire adventure and want to feel like pioneers or explorers, while others desire an undemanding, relaxing holiday.

(e) **Journey purpose** – e.g. passengers travelling to and from work, school or college, have very different requirements to those travelling on their employer's business during the working day, which will be different again to those going shopping or travelling for leisure.

For operators in freight markets, the criteria might include:

(a) **Size of customer** – e.g. a multiple retailer or large manufacturer may have considerable negotiating power and their buyers will probably demand volume discounts and high service specifications in contracts to transport their goods.

(b) **Urgency** – e.g. in some situations, such as a broken-down vehicle requiring a spare part, customers demand high priority express transport, other situations have far less urgency.

(c) **Handling characteristics** – e.g. some freight, such as grain and cereal, can be transported in bulk, others in unit loads of various shapes and sizes, some goods such as cameras and electronic hardware are delicate and fragile while some are hazardous and require special handling, subject to strict safety regulations.

(d) **Security** – e.g. high value goods require special arrangements to protect them against theft in transit or during handling operations, low value goods are less vulnerable.

(e) **National/international** – e.g. freight being imported from, or exported to, another country will generally require special documentation and will need to satisfy various government requirements concerning import/export licenses, duty payments and so on.

Having investigated the demand characteristics of the market as a whole, and distinguished the various market segments using appropriate criteria, a market-oriented supplier will examine its own internal strengths and weaknesses, as well as the opportunities and external threats. It should then have sufficient knowledge to select particular segments for prime attention. This process, known as **targeting**, enables a transport operator to concentrate its efforts on those groups of customers which it is well placed to serve and which appear to offer the best scope for profitable growth. Products can then be designed and developed to have specific attraction for these target markets. Through the process of **positioning**, the operator's services should appeal to these particular groups of customers who should be able to distinguish them from all others offered in the market-place.

Marketing Mix

In order to stimulate demand from target markets, a supplier should develop an appropriate blend of the **Marketing Mix**. This concept has been defined by Lancaster and Massingham as 'the set of marketing ingredients which a company can use to achieve its objectives'.[14] The ingredients, or variables, are often referred to as the 'Four Ps' of marketing: product, price, place and promotion. The principles of marketing mix can be applied both to physical products and services, including those provided by a transport operator.

The **product**, in marketing terms, is best understood as the set of benefits offered to the customer. In transport such benefits might include, for example, peace of mind. In public transport the benefit offered by a particular operator might be a feeling that one is not in danger from violent assault, especially when using the system at times when few other passengers are present. For women passengers in particular, the reassuring presence of staff, or surveillance of terminals and vehicles by closed circuit television, and emergency alarm systems with two-way voice communication, may be ways of creating peace of mind. In freight transport, the benefit might be reasonable certainty that one's possessions, entrusted to the carrier, will not be damaged, lost or pilfered *en route.* Some operators are able to supply this benefit by effective security systems and by using information technology to monitor the progress of individual consignments, informing the sender when they have been received.[15] In general, as far as the customer is concerned, transit is a means to an end. Thus, the benefits might include access to higher paid jobs in a city centre or access to distant export markets. In a few cases, however, transport provides benefits in its own right – such as the enjoyment of a sea cruise or scenic journey by coach or train.

The **price** is also an important tool in marketing, although transport operators do not always use it effectively. Some use 'cost plus' pricing, whereby the fare or tariff charged to the customer is worked out on the basis of how much it cost the operator plus a standard margin for profit, for example, cost plus 15 per cent. Some use 'single pricing', either through a flat rate or a fixed rate per mile. These two methods may be simple to calculate and may seem fair, but they may not bear much relation to how much a particular type of customer may be able or willing to pay. A third method, known as 'differential pricing' or 'price discrimination', aims to maximize revenue for the supplier. Thus, different rates may be charged to different segments of the market. In passenger transport, for example, optional leisure journeys may be stimulated off-peak when the operator has spare capacity. Thus additional journeys may be made, bringing in extra revenue. The approach recognizes that there is an optimum price which can be charged – customers of a particular segment may be prepared to accept a fare or tariff increase up to a certain level beyond which demand and overall revenue will fall off. The approach must also guard against 'down trading' whereby customers, who would have paid a higher price, take advantage of cheaper offers. Thus, 'inhibitors' such as restrictions on time of travel, or advance booking requirements, must be introduced.

The **place** or location element of the Marketing Mix is also important. It has several meanings or interpretations in the context of transport. The convenience of access points to a transport system (for example, the bus stop, railway station or airport) can be critical, especially where the customers have a choice of operator and/or mode. The routes, wider network of services, and exit points at the destination are also important from the customer's point of view. Ideally, transport would be 'door to door' and flexible – a major competitive advantage of private cars over public transport, and of road freight vehicles over freight railways, for example. Place may also be taken to include the convenience of point of sale locations. Thus travel agents enable airlines and other passenger transport operators to penetrate the wider market and gain a physical presence in many locations. Similarly, passes for public transport such as the London Transport 'Travelcard' can be made available in newsagents and other local retailers, for the convenience of customers. Yet another interpretation of place is the distribution of service information. Thus, details of the areas covered, arrangements for collection and delivery, rates and an- *EDI* cillary services such as insurance, can be sent to freight customers by post or even transmitted electronically – to the users' computer terminals.

This leads to the fourth 'P' of **promotion**, also referred to as the **Communications Mix**, because it represents the blend of techniques used for communication between suppliers and their various target groups. Some transport operators such as road hauliers, coach hire firms and airlines, use direct selling – sales staff go out to potential customers in order to persuade them to purchase their firm's services, to negotiate, and to take orders. Advertising is promotion using the various media – (television, radio, cinema, posters, newspapers and journals. 'Below the line' activities cover a wide range of non-media promotions, including leaflets, brochures, point of sale displays, direct mail, promotional videos, trade exhibitions and so on. Last, but not least, public relations involves building bridges between a firm and its public, so that each can understand the other better. Public relations is about creating and developing goodwill and mutual respect. The particular significance of public relations for transport operators is the subject of the next chapter of this book.

Conclusion

Marketing is fundamental to any business where the customers have a choice. Transport operators must be innovative and responsive to market demand if their business environment is competitive. They must also establish the requirements and spending power of different groups of customers through market segmentation. If the operator's objectives are commercial, they will then target the segments of demand which they are well placed to serve, and which offer scope for profitable expansion of their business. Transport services should be developed to appeal to these target groups through positioning. This is achieved through an appropriate Marketing Mix of product, price, place and promotion.

Notes

1   Hibbs, J. (1989) *Marketing Management in the Bus and Coach Industry*, chapter 5, pp. 49–53: Croner.
2   See chapters 17 and 18 in part IV below.
3   Definition adapted by Institute of Marketing in Thomas, M. (1986) *Pocket Guide to Marketing*, p. 81: Blackwell.
4   Lancaster, G. and Massingham, L. (1988) *Essentials of Marketing*, p. 9: McGraw-Hill.
5   Cottham, G.W. (1987) 'Identifying the Market – The Yorkshire Rider Approach', Chartered Institute of Transport Conference, 12 September.
6   Dear, D. (1986) 'Marketing a Change at British Airways' in *Transport*, April, p. 52.
7   Peisley, A. (1990) 'The UK – Europe Ferry Industry and Strategies for the 1990s' in *Travel and Tourism Analyst No. 2*, p. 6: Economist Intelligence Unit.
8   Ottoson, L. (1991) 'Efficiency and New Business' in *Transport*, May/June, p. 81.
9   Ibid.
10 'Ready for Tunnel Battle' (1991) *Transport* (editorial feature) January/February, p. 6.
11 Liberalized air fares and the Single European Market are discussed in chapter 14 below.
12 'Ready for Tunnel Battle', op. cit.
13 Sealink Stena Line (1992) *Funnel versus Tunnel*, p. 3, information pack.
14 Lancaster, G. and Massingham, L. op. cit. p. 71.
15 A description of such a system in express parcels operation is given in the case study of TNT in chapter 6 below.

5

Relating to the Public

Like marketing itself, the concept of public relations is often misunderstood. There is a common misconception that it is about 'image polishing' – putting a favourable gloss on any incident or shortcoming in an attempt to present an untarnished public face. The purpose of public relations is, however, to develop a genuine dialogue between an organization and its public. In a service industry such as transport it is a vitally important function.

The Purpose of Public Relations

Public relations (PR) has been defined as: 'the deliberate, planned and sustained effort to establish and maintain mutual understanding between a firm and its public'.[1] This rightly conveys the idea that it is managed and controlled. A strategy is carefully prepared. It also suggests that the communication is two-way. This should enable an organization, such as a transport operator, to understand its public and vice versa.

Roger Hayward stresses the importance of 'personality' for any organization – whether in the commercial, public or voluntary sector. PR is more than the projection of personality. Rather, it is the development of personality itself: 'The corporate personality is what the organization is, reflects what it believes in, determines where it is heading.' He then goes on to argue that once this has been agreed by the management of an organization, it becomes the central factor in building corporate reputation.[2]

As explained in chapter 4, PR is one element of promotion, also known as the Communications Mix. As such, the PR function should be planned and co-ordinated with the other key elements, which may include direct selling, advertising and below-the-line promotions. The promotion as a whole should, in turn, be blended with the other variables of the Marketing Mix – the product, price and place – in order to influence the organization's target market(s).

Audiences, Messages and Techniques

This leads on to the identification of the target audiences or 'publics' with which an organization may establish and maintain mutual understanding. The management of corporate reputation requires communication with various external audiences, as well as internal ones – the managers and other employees must also 'feel good about' the organization for which they work. The target audiences of transport organizations will vary a great deal according to form of ownership, size and scale of operation, mode of transport and so on, but an initial list may include all or some of the following:

(a)   Existing and potential customers.
(b)   The local communities in the areas served.
(c)   Shareholders and other investors.
(d)   Employees, trade unions, staff associations.
(e)   Trade associations and other employers' organizations.
(f)   Other transport operators who may, or may not be, competitors.
(g)   Government and its agencies at local, national, and international level.
(h)   Pressure groups.
(i)   User bodies.
(j)   The mass media – the press, radio and television.

To take the example of a bus company, good PR is essential to commercial success. The operator may encounter competition from other operators, as well as from private cars, taxis, and perhaps from other modes such as metros and Light Rapid Transit on parallel routes. For short journeys, some people may literally 'vote with their feet' and walk or cycle rather than take a bus. In such an environment, a bus operator can only survive and prosper if it can establish and maintain a good reputation for safe, reliable, regular services with drivers and other staff who are courteous and helpful. The company's relationship with residents and businesses along their routes is important, especially where new services are proposed – some will not want buses along 'their' road. A good relationship with local authorities is also useful, with regard to their highway, traffic management, and town planning powers as well as their responsibilities regarding public transport. The siting of bus stops, bus stations and interchanges, pedestrianization schemes, one way systems, banned turns, bus lanes and other priority measures clearly have important implications for the operator. Consultation at an early stage of proposals is much more likely to occur in a climate of trust and goodwill between operator and local authority.

Specific **techniques** can be used in a strategy to develop good PR. A bus company or other local public transport operator may, for example:

(a)　sponsor community projects, sports, arts and other cultural events in the locality;

(b)　organize depot open days with conducted tours, ideas and demonstrations;

(c)　give away or sell 'merchandizing' items such as T-shirts, mugs, pens and children's toys displaying the company's logo or emblem;

(d)　set up exhibitions in public libraries, schools, colleges and other places, and distribute company videos and pamphlets on request;

(e)　provide opportunities for individuals and local groups to meet the company's managers;

(f)　produce in-house publications such as house magazines and offer social activities and events for staff and their families.

The local media – local newspapers and regional radio and television channels – can have a significant influence on the company's audiences. Regular meetings with journalists, correspondents and editors can therefore play an important part in the PR strategy. Some General Managers of the privatized bus undertakings have established a high profile in their local communities through good media relations. Their discretion and freedom to comment is far greater than it was before the 1985 Transport Act. Unfortunately media-owners can be indifferent or actively hostile, and the reasons are not always rational. Nevertheless, with or without the goodwill of the media, it is important that the operator puts its case effectively. Press releases, briefings and conferences can, at least, reduce any misunderstanding of the message.

Visibility and Public Perception

It was noted in chapter 3 that in most forms of transport, the vehicles, terminals and other infrastructure are literally visible to the public's gaze. Operators may therefore distinguish or disgrace themselves in full view of the customers and other passers-by, photographers, film crews and journalists. Other industries enjoy greater privacy and may conduct their business behind factory gates, or within suites of offices from which the public can be excluded.

Where significant improvements are carried out – a new airport terminal, new rolling stock, the launching of a new ship – the benefits should be communicated to the target audiences. In a promotional campaign, such as that which led to the unveiling of the refurbished London Liverpool Street station in 1991, PR must be carefully managed and controlled. Such work is necessarily carried out on-site, and often involves months or years of inconvenience to the travelling public. James Abbott complimented British Rail's PR team on their work: 'The royal re-opening will set the seal on something the station's regular users have come to realise in recent months – the old Victorian station of inconvenient passageways and inadequate facilities has been transformed, through six years of muck and noise, into one of London's finest termini.'[3]

The mass media represent an important audience for transport operators, but some modes seem to stimulate media attention far more easily than others. In general, airlines benefit from the glamour and romantic appeal associated with foreign travel. It is the newest mode and is commonly perceived as a young and dynamic industry. A new airline route, a promotional fare offer or the introduction of new aircraft can all be newsworthy events, which receive coverage in the national daily newspapers, television and radio networks. Some Chairmen of airlines have been particularly skilled self-publicists, projecting their flamboyant personalities to great effect. Although his airline and the 'Skytrain' concept ultimately failed, Sir Freddie Laker received a great deal of favourable media coverage and emerged as a celebrity and popular hero.

Other modes have experienced much greater difficulty in capturing the public's imagination through the media. Chairmen and senior managers of railways, ferries and other shipping lines or bus and coach companies may find it much harder to convey a positive PR message. Often, they are portrayed in a defensive role, reacting to an incident or answering criticism of poor service or increased fares. Indeed, the prominent media coverage of transport problems in recent times may well have encouraged the belief that PR represents little more than an exercise in damage limitation. British Rail has faced particular difficulties in maintaining standards and meeting customer expectations with ageing rolling stock and infrastructure. As Professor Bill Bradshaw has commented, where investment and modernization has taken place, cost constraints have sometimes led to unsatisfactory compromises: 'pressure is exerted to provide less equipment and capacity than is required, so that late delivery, teething troubles, or traffic growth, lead to disappointment instead of celebration'.[4]

No aspect of transport causes greater problems for the management of corporate reputation than public concerns over **safety**. Unfortunately, during the 1980s in the UK nearly all modes of transport received adverse publicity through news coverage of one or more serious accidents. In the early 1980s, a number of motorway crashes involving coaches captured the headlines. In the mid to late 1980s, a series of major accidents raised further fears concerning the safety of ferries, air transport, underground and surface railways. The vulnerability of all modes of transport to terrorist attack added a further dimension adding to public anxiety despite increased security.

During the 1980s the membership and influence of environmental pressure groups grew, and a shift in public opinion brought a greater emphasis on 'green' issues in public policy in the UK and elsewhere. Each mode of transport creates its own particular set of problems for the physical environment. Some problems, such as noise and vibration of road vehicles, tend to be localized. Others, such as pollution of the atmosphere by jet aircraft, can be global.[5] Modes of transport such as railways and buses, which do relatively little damage to the environment, have managed to capitalize on their PR strengths, and have stressed green themes in their promotional strategies. No mode, however, is free from criticism. The proposed route for the Channel Tunnel Rail Link was vigorously opposed by well-organized pressure groups, and many believe that the latter had a strong influence in the government's intervention which forced British Rail to abandon its preferred route in 1991.

Front Line Staff

As stressed in chapter 4, the public is becoming increasingly discerning. In any service industry, the first point of contact with the organization's personnel is critical – it is an opportunity to offer reassurance and peace of mind as well as the human touch. Conversely, unfavourable initial impressions can aggravate anxiety. Either way, in transport, as in other sectors, the public's perception of an organization is strongly influenced by the actions and attitudes of front-line staff. In PR terms, the corporate personality is expressed by the drivers, conductors, guards, loaders, cabin crew, booking office clerks, telephonists and so on.

In some modes of transport the work of these front-line staff tends to be low paid, unglamorous and repetitive. They often work long and unsociable hours, and may not always feel motivated to please the public they serve. Transport is hardly unique in this respect – in the retail sector, for example, the pay and conditions for sales assistants and check-out staff are generally unattractive. Nevertheless, as noted in chapter 3, there are certain characteristics which distinguish transport. Commonly, it is round the clock, and in contrast to factories, shops and offices, the front-line staff are geographically spread out on the vehicles, along the way, and at the terminals.

Many work on their own or in teams, often without direct supervision. In freight transport, the person who collects or delivers the consignment has an important PR function: establishing and maintaining mutual understanding between a firm and its public. In 'own account' transport, where a supplier, wholesaler, or retailer uses his own vehicles to deliver his own products, the front-line staff are generally the main point of contact with the customer. In the case of breweries, for example, the drivers who deliver the beer are said to be the 'ambassadors' of the whole company. As far as the public houses and other customers are concerned, they are the firm's representatives. Indeed, they **are** the company. In the case of third party transport, such as road haulage, where the firm carries other people's freight for profit, the shipper must feel confident that the drivers and/or loaders will carry and handle his products with due care and deliver them to his customers in pristine condition.

In bus operations, the drivers and their supervisors have not always been recognized as the leading edge of PR. Yet, in a competitive market they have a very important role. Go Ahead Northern in North-East England gave special priority to a programme for training all their front line staff in customer relations. Furthermore, the inspectors took a new title as Group Leaders and new responsibilities. Formerly the 'police officers' of the company, nowadays they each lead a team of drivers dedicated to a particular route or small network. As David Hind's study of Go Ahead Northern has emphasized, their job is to maintain ridership through quality control and good customer relations, as well as to be proactive in looking for new business. Thus, they are 'required to forge links with the local community by, for example, giving presentations to schools, clubs and societies, and by looking for any unsatisfied public transport needs in their districts'.[6] The following case study shows how an international airline with a flair for innovation has developed a strategy for managing corporate reputation.

Case study: Virgin Atlantic Airways

Virgin Atlantic Airways was established in 1984 by entertainment entrepreneur Richard Branson.[7] Its corporate mission expresses the airline's unique aim: 'As the UK's second long haul carrier, to build an inter-continental network concentrating on those routes with a substantial established market and clear growth potential, by offering the highest possible service at the lowest possible cost.'

It offers three classes: Economy Class, Mid Class and Upper Class – 'first class service at a business class fare'. It operates a fleet of Boeing 747 aircraft with services between the UK and various destinations in the United States and Japan, with new routes to South Africa, Singapore, Australia and elsewhere planned for the 1990s. As a relatively small airline with a limited promotional budget compared to large carriers such as British Airways, PR, as defined in this chapter, is a vital function.

Virgin Atlantic puts a strong emphasis on added value through the personal service and attention to detail that a small airline can offer. After 15 years as a businessman and customer of many airlines Branson became frustrated with those which were 'run by large conglomerates who have two or three hundred other planes. Their definition of success has traditionally had much more to do with size than quality – let alone the idea of actually entertaining the person who is on the flight'.[8] A flight can be a time of stress,

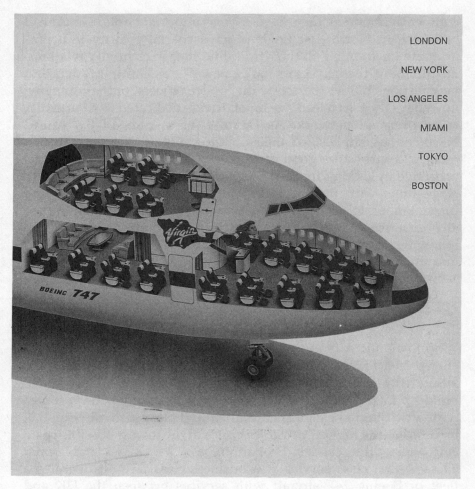

Plate 5.1 Virgin Atlantic Airways' 'Upper Class', courtesy of Virgin Atlantic Airways

worry or boredom. Yet it **should** be a time for relaxation, enjoyment, and perhaps for meeting fellow passengers. The approach with Virgin Atlantic has been to create a welcoming and sociable environment, somewhat like a private club or country home.

Cabin crew and other front-line staff play an important part in creating this atmosphere. Virgin Atlantic's policy is to select younger people with an outward-going personality and personal initiative, who are 'excited about the job and actually look forward to going to work in the morning'.[9] These are mostly recruited from outside the airline industry, and trained from scratch. In Economy

Class, Branson introduced live entertainment – performers with diverse talents ranging from mime artists to accordion players. The passengers also have the benefit of personal video players with a choice of six channels. Children can watch cartoons and pop videos, and are given ice cream and candyfloss. Upper Class customers have generously-sized seats which fold down and allow them to sleep if they wish to do so. They may also use the on-board lounge areas where they can converse with other business travellers, play chess, cards, backgammon and so on. There are also dedicated Upper Class lounges at the airport terminals, and free chauffeur-driven limousines at either end of the journey.

With regard to the formal management of PR, Virgin Atlantic is reluctant to use outside firms. Like many other carriers, it believes that such agencies seldom possess sufficient specialist, in-depth knowledge of the airline business. PR is therefore handled in-house by a team of three people. Virgin Atlantic's prime external audience is the travelling public – air passengers from the UK, United States, Japan and other destinations served by their routes. Good relations with the mass media are cultivated as a means of influencing this audience through opinion-formers who influence or actually write the copy, present documentaries and so on. The travel industry, including travel agents, tour organizers, hotel chains, tourist boards and convention bureaux, are another audience. They can be influenced directly, for example, through presentations and briefings or meetings at trade exhibitions, as well as indirectly through the travel industry's trade journals.

Thus, favourable reports by intermediaries can greatly assist promotional effort, for example with the launch of a new service or customer facility. Not only can this be highly cost-effective relative to other forms of promotion, but 'third party endorsement' is generally more convincing and persuasive than, for example, saturation advertising or direct mailing. A major disadvantage of over-reliance on these channels is the danger that the message becomes distorted through misunderstandings or simply through insensitive editing. Another disadvantage is that the airline has no control over the timing, emphasis or style of an article in a daily newspaper or other media coverage. A good, newsworthy story about an airline can easily be overshadowed by another item on the day in question.

Sympathetic and effective media coverage was particularly important for Virgin Atlantic in 1991 – a year of intense rivalry between carriers on the North Atlantic and many other routes. Airlines fought hard to win back traffic lost during the Gulf War, as a worldwide recession deepened. It was also the year in which Virgin Atlantic won an important victory in gaining access to London Heathrow Airport. Until then, it had been restricted to London Gatwick because of the UK government's 'Traffic Distribution Rules' for the major airports in South-East England. This was a significant relaxation of government policy, which also allowed two of the world's largest carriers – American Airlines and United Airlines – to operate from London's premier airport for the first time.

The lead-up to Virgin Atlantic's Heathrow launch was a comparatively long time in which to sustain media interest. The hardest PR campaign – gaining permission to fly from Heathrow – gained momentum in January 1991. During this period, the airline's public relations office made sure that the key opinion-formers – transport and aviation correspondents, city editors, journalists working for the 'heavyweight' daily newspapers and trade journals, **understood** the issues and Virgin Atlantic's position. Following the Secretary of State's decision two months later, the new services received widespread and favourable publicity. From March to July, attention turned to the airline's internal audience – the employees were given briefing sessions, a weekly newsletter, and a series of rallies attended by Richard Branson and the senior managers. These explained the implications for those who would be transferred from Gatwick to Heathrow.

Meanwhile, British Airways ran an impressive promotional campaign – 'the World's Biggest Offer' which gave away some 50,000 free seats on 23 April. To support this, their PR department organized 76 press conferences in 50 countries. The airline also spent a great deal on advertising.[10] *PR Week* reported that this campaign was intended to combat the general downturn in demand, rather than the carrier's new rivals. Nevertheless, another British Airways initiative, specifically targeted at business travellers through improvements to First and Club Class services, was launched just one day before the arrival of Virgin Atlantic and American Airlines at Heathrow. As British Airways' Chief Press Officer commented, the timing 'wasn't just coincidence'.[11]

Extensive media coverage for Virgin Atlantic has also been helped by its Chairman's larger-than-life personality and daredevil stunts. Richard Branson's spectacular feats by yacht, parachute and hot air balloon have particular appeal to younger people – an important audience who admire his lack of convention. It can also be interpreted as a return to the pioneering spirit of the airline industry. There have been some very tangible benefits:

'The Virgin Challenger crossings had made me well known enough to be invited to appear in a series of television commercials being run by American Express in the UK. The result was millions of pounds' worth of free television advertising for the airline. As far as the balloon trip was concerned, it did wonders in getting the name of the airline into the media.'[12]

Virgin Atlantic has achieved considerable success with its novel aim of 'putting the fun back into flying'. The airline's emphasis on value for money has been widely acclaimed and it has won a number of prestigious awards. It has capitalized on the advantages of being a relatively small carrier flying a carefully selected range of long haul routes – it can exercise tight control over service delivery and offer consistently high standards of quality. Yet its triumphs have inevitably caused jealousy within the airline industry. Despite its modest size, it is seen as a threat to its larger rivals. It erodes their revenue on prime routes. Airline competition in the 1990s is anything but 'gentlemanly', and as large carriers use questionable tactics in the battle for market share, the importance of good PR can hardly diminish.

Conclusion

PR is essentially proactive. It requires a strategy and good planning to develop a dialogue between an organization and its public, which is made up of specific audiences. Techniques can be used to facilitate this two-way communication, and ensure that the organization listens to what the public has to say. Transport tends to have a higher profile than many other industries, and some carriers have used this visibility to good effect. With rising expectations of service quality, the transport operator's front line staff have a major part to play in creating good PR, and it is they who express the organization's corporate personality.

Notes

1   Institute of Public Relations (1986).
2   Hayward, R. (1990) *All About Public Relations*, p. 4: McGraw-Hill.
3   Abbot, J. (1991) 'Liverpool Street Redeveloped' in *Modern Railways*, December, p. 639.
4   Bradshaw, W. (1992) 'BR at the Crossroads' in *Modern Railways*, January, p. 28.
5   For a fuller discussion of environmental issues in transport see chapter 19 below.
6   Hind, D. (1986) 'Working on the Buses' in *Marketing*, 9 October, p. 38.
7   As noted in chapter 2 Virgin Atlantic was set up as a private limited company, and is part of the Virgin Group.
8   Branson, R. (1989) 'A Vanguard Venture into the Airways' in *The Journal of the American Chamber of Commerce (UK)*, October, p. 30.
9   Ibid.
10 'Heathrow: Flying Into the Battleground' (1991) in *PR Week*, 18 July.
11 Ibid.
12 Branson, R. (1989) op. cit. p. 33.

Part II

Systems

6

The Systems Concept

The customers use transport as a system. They expect a well-connected network of services which is convenient and easy to use. This chapter introduces the 'systems concept' – an approach which emphasizes the relationship between the component parts which are necessary for any body or organization to function. It examines the practical steps which are necessary to put this into practice in passenger and freight transport.

Transport Systems

The systems concept is based on the philosophy that 'the whole is greater than the sum of the parts'. The component parts of a system are interrelated. Any change which is introduced in one part of the system will affect all others, through a chain reaction. Planning and co-ordination are therefore needed to ensure that the elements of the whole work together to the benefit of the user.

Firstly, transport systems can be analysed in terms of three basic elements:

(a) The **vehicles** are the means by which the traffic – that is, the passengers or freight – is carried. The term is used in a general sense to include road vehicles, railway rolling stock, vessels and aircraft.
(b) The **ways** are the tracks or media on which, or through which, the vehicles travel. They include roadways, railways, seas, rivers, canals, airspace and airways.
(c) The **terminals** provide the access and exit points along the way – the essential nodal points of any transport system. Examples of

terminals include bus stops and stations, loading areas and bays for vans and trucks, railway stations and goods sidings, seaports, riverports, wharves, airfields and airports.[1]

The vehicles are necessarily spread out geographically as they travel along the ways or stand at the terminals. The movements must be worked out with precision:

(a)   to satisfy the pattern of customer demand in space and time;
(b)   to take account of constraints such as the availability/duty hours of staff, necessary maintenance and refuelling, capacity of vehicles, ways and terminals, as well as to make the most efficient use of these human and physical resources.

In all modes of transport, the process of **routing** and **scheduling** the vehicles is a critical activity which brings together the demand factors (a) and supply factors (b). The planning of routes and schedules is no less important for a small haulage operation than for a major international airline. Nevertheless, in large transport undertakings there are many variables to consider.

Railways, for example, are complex systems. Furthermore, many are self-contained in that one operator owns and controls the vehicles, ways and terminals.[2] The scheduling of trains must take account of the programme for maintaining and upgrading of track, signalling, civil engineering structures, station facilities and so on. The introduction of new rolling stock, capable of higher speeds, may provide opportunities to improve running times and make more journeys with fewer trains. Yet many factors such as track speed, signalling capacity, rostering of staff and so on need to be evaluated. The periodic revision of a working timetable will therefore involve a complicated set of decisions in order to arrive at optimum solutions to keep pace with changing customer demand on the one hand, and to make the best use of resources on the other.

In any transport system, the **actual** movement of each vehicle must be constantly monitored against its **planned** route and schedule. A daunting set of factors – congestion, adverse weather, motive power failure and so on – may conspire to disrupt the planned operation. Transport therefore requires a **communication system** to keep the managers and other employees well informed as situations develop. This flow of relevant information is a prerequisite for swift corrective action to remedy or to alleviate problems as they occur. Furthermore, many operators now recognize that keeping the customer well informed is equally important.

Internal communication within the operator's system must therefore be supplemented by communication between the provider of transport and the customers.

The following case study examines a system which has been developed over the past decade to provide fast, secure and reliable transport for documents, parcels and freight.

Case study: The TNT Express System

From just one truck in Sydney, Australia in 1946, TNT has grown to become one of the largest and most diverse express transport companies in the world. It has established itself as a market leader in express deliveries and now serves over 190 countries.

TNT's UK domestic operation was established in the late 1970s and now provides a comprehensive range of services from guaranteed delivery next day before 9.0 a.m. or 10.30 a.m. for very urgent consignments, to less rapid and more economical delivery for less urgent items. Time-critical goods can also be delivered direct in the shortest possible time by TNT Sameday and TNT Supamail has been developed specifically to deliver urgent documents, business mail and small packages. The company services its customers through a network of more than 300 locations and provides a door-to-door delivery and collection service to any address in the UK.

Regular customers can now take advantage of TNT Despatcher, a microcomputer-based system that automatically processes and prints the necessary documentation for each consignment, removing the need to complete forms manually. This saves time, improves accuracy and helps to keep administrative costs to a minimum. The latest information technology programme, being phased in over the next two years, will revolutionize the industry. It will allow some customers access to TNT's computer network, providing real time information, and enabling the customer to request services directly through a terminal in their offices, allowing, for example, manufacturing companies to order deliveries that match their 'just-in-time' requirements.

In response to telephone requests, TNT Express will pick up consignments utilizing their nationwide fleet of over 3,000 vehicles – trucks, vans and motorcycles. Each vehicle follows a planned route within a given area, to optimize vehicle mileage and to make the operation as time- and cost-efficient as possible. Many of the

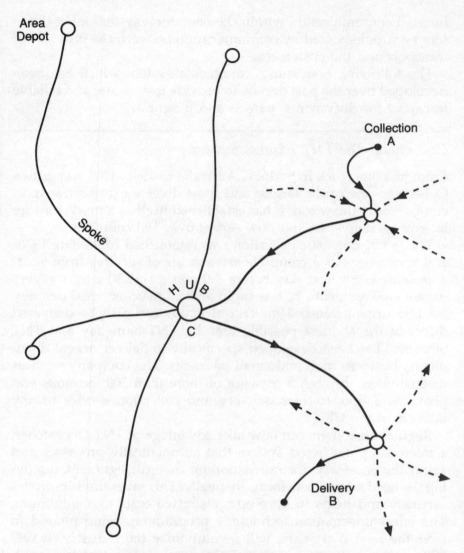

Figure 6.1 Principles of 'hub-and-spoke' operation for express deliveries. A consignment travels from collection point A to delivery point B via central hub C

company's vehicles are equipped with the latest in-cab technology, ensuring that drivers can be reached *en route* to service urgent collection requests. This link can also provide road traffic information to divert vehicles away from congested roads.

On completing their collections and deliveries, the drivers return to their base – one of 27 strategically located depots around mainland Britain. Items for local delivery are then sorted and delivered within the depot's territory. Consignments for Northern Ireland or the offshore UK islands are airfreighted to provide timed next-day delivery.

Over 90 per cent of the consignments are however, consolidated for onward distribution via TNT's central sortation complex – its hub – at Atherstone in Warwickshire. The system utilised is known as the 'hub-and-spoke' concept. A fleet of tractor units and over 1,000 articulated trailers are used for the nightly trunk movements from their depots to Atherstone. All the vehicles are routed from the regions via the motorway network to the geographical centre – a pattern resembling the spokes of a wheel. They are accurately scheduled to arrive at the hub at precise times during the night, ensuring the most efficient operation possible for unloading and sorting the consignments. Telex is used to advise management at Atherstone of the estimated time of arrival of all vehicles.

The hub at Atherstone covers 19 acres and the main rectangular building has a total of 90 loading bays. It is here the trailers are unloaded and the individual consignments checked and weighed and measured as they enter the sortation hall. A sophisticated materials handling system conveys each one to the correct loading bay for onward movement to its destination terminal.

The trailers are then loaded up again and return along the spokes, back to the 27 terminals. Back at these bases the trailer loads are broken down and sorted according to their urgency and final destination within the depot's territory. The vans and motorcycles then work in delivery mode, again keeping to planned routes and schedules.

As with any major operator in the express business, TNT Express has invested heavily in computer technology. Not only are the movements of vehicles and handling operations closely monitored, so are individual consignments, with electronic track and trace facilities ensuring that the whereabouts of any consignment is known at all times, from collection to delivery. This facility provides customers with a number of benefits:

(a) Instant status reports on the consignment's location whilst in transit.
(b) Immediate confirmation of delivery on request with exact time of receipt and the receiver's name.
(c) Written proof of delivery.

The new information technology being phased in will allow some customers to carry out these functions themselves by tapping into the TNT Express computer network from their own terminal, at the touch of a button.

Seamless Systems?

TNT's UK operation, described above, uses its own fleet of road vehicles – vans and motorcycles, tractors and trunk trailers. The company also possesses purpose-built terminals and a central sortation complex. The UK system links up with TNT's international network with its own fleet of aircraft and airfreight hubs. Thus, TNT can be described as a multi-modal **integrated** freight carrier.

In many other cases, however, the passenger journey or freight shipment cannot be made entirely within the system of one transport operator. The separate services of different carriers should therefore link up to provide a larger system for the benefit of the user. Ideally, the passenger who wants to get from A to B, or the shipper who wants a consignment of freight moved from A to B, would like a smooth and seamless system. How, then, can such a network be created?

If the entire system were designed rationally 'from scratch', a number of features could be incorporated:

(a) In the case of passenger transport, **interchange** facilities would be built to minimize time and effort in transferring from one service to another. For example, a commuter railway station interchange can have bus bays, with 'park-and-ride' and 'kiss-and-ride' facilities for car users. In freight transport, the **transhipment** facilities would be built on the same principle. For example, a cargo centre at an airport can be laid out for speedy and efficient handling of freight between aircraft, customs, temporary storage and road freight vehicles.

(b) Arrangements for **fare** or **tariff** payments would also be simplified for the convenience of customers. A passenger journey can involve changing between services owned by different operators, yet a through ticket or pass can be a significant advantage to the user. Similarly, freight movements can be made easier by a 'through bill of lading' – a shipping document which can be used when a transit involves more than one shipping line and onward movement by another mode of transport. In all cases, payment must be apportioned and allocated between the various carriers involved.

(c) Consideration would also be given to **timetable co-ordination** for connecting services. The aim would be to reduce waiting time for passengers and dwell time for freight. This would require discussion and co-operation between operators to plan their schedules. For example, express coach operators and railways can adjust their timetables to meet passenger ferries. Other situations can involve more difficult scheduling decisions – for example, holding a connecting service to satisfy one group of customers can delay and irritate another group.

The importance of **customer information** would also be recognized. It would be available where and when the users required it. It would be accurate and up-to-date, giving details of any delays or other problems, thus allowing customers to make alternative arrangements if they wished. Recent developments in information technology have brought great benefits in this respect and the quality of computer applications continues to improve relative to cost. For example, passengers can be offered real time information on seat reservations, arrival and departure times. Similarly, cargo shippers can be offered real time information on scheduled freight services and the physical progress of individual consignments.

In practice, however, truly 'seamless' systems are rare. Most transport services have developed incrementally, sometimes haphazardly. Few have been created according to any grand design or plan. Parts III and IV will consider the extent to which regulators and governments can help unify transport systems at local, national and international level.

Ways and Modes of Transport

Sea, air and rail transport tend to have relatively few terminals along the routes of their ways. In contrast, road transport may offer the advantage of door-to-door convenience. Except in the case of motorways, trunk roads, clearways and other roads where special restrictions apply, there is often a considerable choice of waiting or stopping places, i.e. terminals. Furthermore, there may be a relatively dense network of roadways, providing choice in the routing of vehicles. In short, road transport has a major advantage because of its inherent flexibility.

A major disadvantage of road transport, however, is that the vehicles must share a common way, available to all with the appropriate licence. Users generally gain access to the entire network through a single or periodic payment of road tax. In many areas, this freedom has resulted in serious problems of congestion, discussed in chapter 20. Although traffic lights and other methods are used to regulate the flow of road traffic, the controls are generally less sophisticated than those used in other modes, such as railway signalling and air traffic control.

In the UK, road transport **competes** directly with other modes, for example private cars and express coaches against railways and domestic airlines for inter-urban travel. Nevertheless, it may also **complement** other modes by providing necessary feeders. Roadways are therefore essential to the overall transport system of a country, and important for the development of economic sectors and geographical areas within the country. The recent government White Paper *Roads for Prosperity* justified a 10-year programme of expenditure of £12 billion, involving over 2,700 miles of new or improved roads for the national network. This will provide: 'Key routes for industry . . . widespread benefits for regions by providing better links . . . improved roads to seaports, airports, and the Channel Tunnel to help industry in the Single European Market after 1992'.[3]

The Role of Transport Terminals

Transport terminals have three main functions:

(a)   To allow **access to vehicles** along a way.
(b)   To permit **easy interchange** between vehicles operating on different routes, and between different modes of transport.
(c)   To facilitate **consolidation** of traffic, grouping together passengers or freight consignments into a larger unit for onward movement.[4]

The interrelationship between different carriers and modes of transport is illustrated in the following examples, where efforts have been made to put the systems approach into practice. Stansted Airport and the Port of Felixstowe both illustrate the pivotal role of transport terminals for passengers and freight respectively. The aim is to allow through traffic to be handled smoothly, satisfying customer requirements with regard to service quality and cost.

(a) Stansted Airport
Stansted in Essex is being developed as London's Third Airport. It is owned by Stansted Airport Limited, a subsidiary of the

privatized BAA plc, formerly British Airports Authority. In 1991 its new terminal was opened, raising capacity to 8 million passengers per annum and, subject to Parliamentary approval, it will be further expanded to 15 million. Its development will help ensure that London has the capacity to meet the projected increase in demand for air travel into the next century. It caters for holiday-makers as well as business travellers, and there are domestic, short haul, and long haul services. Air UK, this country's third largest scheduled airline, is based at Stansted. Charter carriers include Air UK Leisure, Britannia and Monarch Airlines.

The airport's advertising slogan, 'Easy Come, Easy Go', reflects its aim to offer passengers a stress-free journey. The new passenger terminal is designed to minimize the length and complexity of passenger movement. Outbound international passengers, for example, walk in a straight line through check-in, security and immigration and on to the departure lounge on the same level. Glazed walls provide natural light, creating an open and airy environment. Integral to the design are the automated 'People Movers' which transport passengers between the terminal and the satellite served by nine aircraft stands. Under the initial phase of development, the vehicles work a 'run-and-back' system, but as further satellites are added, they will operate along a continuous loop of track. A two-minute frequency is possible for peak periods.

Stansted is located 35 miles North-East of London. The M11 motorway comes close to the airport boundary, providing access to London and links to the national motorway network. Short-stay parking and a coach station are sited immediately in front of the new terminal. Long-stay parking is provided near the airport perimeter with a connecting shuttle coach. It is anticipated that a third of airport users will travel by rail. The 'Stansted Express' offers a dedicated service to London's Liverpool Street stopping only once to connect with London Underground's Victoria Line – a total journey time of 41 minutes. A new railway station has been constructed directly under the airport terminal with access by ramp, lift and escalator.[5]

(b) Port of Felixstowe

Felixstowe in Suffolk, established over a hundred years ago, has maintained its international reputation through an ambitious programme of expansion and modernization. It is now owned by the UK Port Operations of Huchison Whampoa Limited. Geographical location has been a major factor in its success, presenting minimum deviation for worldwide deep-sea services calling at North-West European seaports and the UK, and convenient short-sea connections to the Continent. In 1990 its new container facility, Trinity Terminal, was completed, enabling the port as a whole to handle over 16 million tonnes of freight annually. Felixstowe has attracted some of the world's leading container lines such as Cosco, Maersk Line, NYK Line, P & O Containers and Yang Ming Line. Its customers also include Roll-on/Roll-off lines such as Fred Olsen Lines and P & O European Ferries and general cargo lines handling forest products and other freight.

Trinity Terminal's ship-to-shore cranes can each handle 60 containers per hour. The terminal is serviced by a fleet of dedicated vehicles including rubber-tyred gantry cranes, giant forklift trucks and tractor units. These enable road trailers to be loaded and unloaded away from the apron area. The rapid physical handling is backed up by powerful computers for processing the documentation. Since 1984 Felixstowe has provided its forwarding agents and other authorized customers with access to HM Customs' Departmental Entry Processing System (DEPS), with computer terminals in their own offices. Today the Port of Felixstowe's 'community computer system' FCP80 is augmented by in-house systems including Container Control, Colour Graphics ship-planning and others – all designed to provide accurate and up-to-date information on cargo passing through the port, improve efficiency and reduce or eliminate paperwork.[6]

The road and rail system serving Felixstowe's hinterland must match the seaport's fast handling methods and keep up with the pace of traffic growth. Hauliers carry the containers on trailers via the A45 road and on to the national motorway system. A new trunk road is being completed to improve East-West links, especially between Felixstowe and the industrial and commercial centres of the Midlands. About 30 per cent of Felixstowe's containers move by rail. A new spur links Trinity Terminal with the main London–Ipswich line and Railfreight Distribution's trunk services. Within the seaport itself, the layout has been planned so that container cranes can feed the flatwagons without intermediate handling, further speeding the physical handling. The track bypasses the central port area, minimizing conflicting movements and thus avoiding congestion.

Conclusion

Transport functions as a system, whose interrelated elements are the vehicles, ways and terminals. Routing and scheduling of vehicles plays a central role in the process of relating customer demand to the supply of human and physical resources. Careful planning and precision of execution is required to co-ordinate a large, integrated transport system such as an express parcel operation. It is unusual, however, for a large-scale transport system to be planned afresh. More commonly, separate operations grow up incrementally and independently. In some circumstances operators may be willing to co-operate with one another. Different services and modes may play a complementary role in a larger system. Yet, it can sometimes be difficult to weld together the disparate elements. The planning and design of a new passenger or freight terminal may provide an excellent opportunity to create a more satisfactory whole to the benefit of customers.

Notes

1 See Benson, D. and Whitehead, G. (1985) *Transport and Distribution*, pp. 16–18: Longman.
2 In some cases two or more railway operators share the same ways and terminals. The European Commission's proposals to allow free access to European Community railways for any authorized operator are discussed in 'Splitting Track from Trains' in *Modern Railways*, May 1991, pp. 238–40.
3 Department of Transport (1989) *Roads for Prosperity*: HMSO.
4 Benson, D. and Whitehead, G. op. cit., p. 31.
5 See *Easy Come – Easy Go* (1991) BAA Stansted.
6 *Port Journal* (1992), Port of Felixstowe.

7

Transport and Tourism

This chapter examines the management of tourism, in which transport itself is considered as part of a wider system which takes people away from their normal surroundings – for leisure, business, social and other purposes. Transport operators serving tourism markets need to gain an understanding of how their own services relate to other components of the total 'package', which may include accommodation and catering, as well as visitor attractions and facilities at the destination. Furthermore, in view of the concerns of many host communities, and some of the tourists themselves, operators need to be aware of the social and environmental implications of tourism development.

Tourism Management

Tourism has been defined as 'the temporary short-term movement of people to destinations outside where they normally live and work, and activities during their stay at these destinations; it includes movement for all purposes, as well as day visitors and excursions'.[1] This definition embraces international tourism (across national frontiers) and domestic tourism (within the tourist's own country). It includes visits with or without an overnight stay; and by independent travellers as well as organized groups.

The definition covers trips made for a variety of purposes:

(a) **Leisure** travel, including day trips, holidays and visits to friends and relatives (VFR).
(b) **Business-related** travel, including conferences, trade fairs, and conventions.

(c) **Other** categories of travel, including study tours, convalescence, and pilgrimages.

The product consumed by the tourist generally involves three main elements which can be supplied separately or combined. The major components of tourism are:

(a) **transport** – travel by aircraft, ship, train, coach, car etc., often a combination of modes e.g. fly-drive, fly-cruise;
(b) **accommodation** – overnight stay with or without catering, e.g. hotel, apartment, villa, campsite, caravan park etc.;
(c) **attractions** – natural or built features of the destination, e.g. beach resort, skiing resort, historic town, theme park, commercial/shopping centre etc.

These may be supported by a range of services provided by other businesses and organizations. In the UK **public** sector support includes promotion by Tourist Boards, education and training for people employed in the industry, and Tourist Information Centres, many of which offer guidebooks, maps and computerized databases which are continuously updated. **Private** sector services include insurance, banking, currency exchange and reservation systems for booking travel and accommodation. **Voluntary** organizations also play an important role, especially in raising standards of service. The latter include trade associations such as the Bus and Coach Council[2] and professional bodies such as the Institute of Travel and Tourism.

Some tourism products may be sold direct to the public, for example, car hire, hotel accommodation and theatre tickets. Yet they may also be sold through intermediaries. **Travel agents** offer a wide range of tourism products normally on a commercial basis, often providing customers with the convenience of a high street location and 'one-stop shopping'. **Tour operators** buy tourism services in bulk and combine them as a single product. In vacational travel this is sold as an Inclusive Tour or package holiday.

Features of Tourism and Role of Transport

Tourism is unusual in that the customer must be taken to the product, rather than the other way around. In vacational travel in particular, prospective tourists may have little clear idea of what the travel experience will be like until they depart and little knowledge of the destination until they arrive. It is often said that 'those who sell holidays are selling dreams'.[3] Thus, as well as the tangible elements discussed above, the tourism product generally includes a host of intangible elements such as a sense of fun, sociability, excitement, style and so on, which contribute greatly to the customer's enjoyment of the holiday.

Another feature is that the tourism 'industry' in most countries is highly fragmented. The different elements of the product are supplied by a range of different businesses and organizations who play a complementary role yet generally take decisions quite independently. Given their strong interdependence as a system, bottlenecks may occur. For example, inadequate supply of air transport to a developing resort will depress demand for hotel bed-spaces and vice versa. Without adequate planning one sector of the tourist industry may be unable to keep pace with another, perhaps leading to dissatisfaction with the product as a whole.

Despite this general fragmentation, however, a process of **integration** has been a notable feature in recent years.[4] This includes vertical integration, for example tour operators acquiring airlines, travel agencies and so on. It also includes horizontal integration where mergers and take-overs occur within one sector, for example tour operators acquiring other tour operators in order to increase their market share and reduce competition. From the customer's point of view this process may bring some benefits from better co-ordination and quality control. Economies of scale may reduce price. On the other hand it may lead to bland standardization and a reduction in consumer choice.

It was noted in chapter 3 that transport cannot be stored. This characteristic can also apply to other elements of the tourism product. From the operator's point of view, unsold seats on an aircraft, train or coach are wasted as soon as the vehicle departs. Likewise, hotel bed-spaces are wasted if rooms remain vacant on the night concerned. Seats at sporting, entertainment and cultural events are similarly perishable. Suppliers of tourism products must therefore take into account the pattern of demand, which will typically show strong **peaks** and **troughs** over time: seasonal, weekly or daily cycles. Vacational travel by the UK population, for example, is highly concentrated in the months of July and August because of school holidays and the climate in European resorts. Since the product cannot be stored, capacity must be geared up to the peak, yet overheads must be covered during the slack period off-season.

These regular cycles of demand are generally fairly predictable. Other upswings and downturns are more difficult to anticipate. Motivation to visit a particular destination may be influenced by a wide range of factors from favourable exchange rates to fashion. Conversely, cataclysmic downturns have been caused by fears of terrorism, war and social unrest, concerns over environmental pollution and so on. It is hard, perhaps impossible, for tourism providers to respond to such volatile demand, so investment may involve a high level of risk.

The success of transport operators who carry tourists thus depends not only on the other elements or sectors of the tourism industry, but also upon a pattern of consumer demand which is often irregular and unstable over time. Victor Middleton has commented that, in general, transport operators perform a 'functional' role in the overall transport product: 'modern transport is not normally a part of the motivation or attraction of a destination visit . . . a functional element which is essential to the existence and growth of tourism but not of itself, a sufficient reason to travel'.[5]

There is a danger, then, that tourist transport becomes simply a means to an end, with an overall emphasis on cost reduction, perhaps at the expense of service quality. Nevertheless, some tourism providers have adopted a different strategy. An alternative approach recognizes that from the customer's point of view, the transport may be part of the whole experience and enjoyment of a trip, rather than something to be endured. The following case study shows how this can be achieved through co-operation with other sectors of the tourism industry and a detailed understanding of the needs of the tourists as customers.

Case study: London Coaches' Sightseeing Tours

London Transport gained considerable experience operating sightseeing tours. In 1951, during the Festival of Britain, they initiated a non-stop circular itinerary using double decker buses, the tops of which offered an excellent vantage point, enabling visitors to enjoy the sights of the capital. As London's tourist industry expanded with increasing numbers of overseas visitors, such tours provided a modest but useful source of income. Yet, a period of nearly 30 years when competition was restricted seems to have engendered a degree of complacency, and the tour was not really developed to its full potential.

In 1980, market entry was opened up, and rival operators, large and small, now compete for the custom of London's tourists. At peak season, as many as 100 double decker buses, run by six or more competing firms, offer sightseeing tours, most of which have an itinerary lasting one and a half hours. With an adult fare of around £9, payloads of £350 or more are quite common. Thus, despite the inherent seasonality of demand, and the vagaries of the English climate, the market opportunity has been described by some as 'a licence to print money'![6]

London Transport's response to the erosion of their former monopoly was to establish London Coaches (LC) in 1986 as a profit centre to operate and market sightseeing tours, private hire, charters and other services such as commuter coaches. In 1988 LC became a limited company in its own right – responsible for managing its own employees and assets, and for its costs and revenue. In 1992 it was privatized through sale to its senior managers, and thus split away from London Buses and the London Transport group of companies.

The tour provides an example of transport which must offer far more than simply a means of conveyance. As discussed in chapter 4 above, the product must satisfy a number of benefits, which must be considered from the customer's point of view. For a visitor to London, these might include the following:

(a) A means of gaining familiarity with the geography of London and its famous landmarks such as Buckingham Palace, the Houses of Parliament, St Paul's Cathedral and so on.
(b) An opportunity to view these and to take photographs as souvenirs of the visit.
(c) An entertaining and enjoyable experience which provides relaxation and, at the same time, informs and stimulates interest in the capital city, its history and its contemporary culture.

The company philosophy of LC emphasizes 'comfort, style and reliable services'. Some of their competitors have considerably lower overheads and LC do not wish to undercut their rates. Competing on the basis of high service quality does, however, demand commitment from all their employees. As their staff newsletter stresses, success depends upon 'a friendly and efficient response to an enquiry, letter or telephone call, and when travelling with LC, a smart, courteous and helpful driver and guide supported by a well presented, clean and reliable vehicle'.[7]

LC's marketing strategy has been to build on the familiar image of a red Routemaster bus – a vehicle popularized throughout the world in films, guidebooks and picture postcards. They acquired a fleet of over 50 Routemasters, some of which were converted to 'open toppers' for fine weather, and later some to 'convertibles' with a removable hood. All have been refurbished to a high standard. The tour has been branded and promoted as 'The Original London Sightseeing Tour' (TOLST), in a distinctive red livery to differentiate its vehicles from those of competitors.

The method of commentary posed something of a dilemma. Until 1990 LC used 'Blue Badge' guides on all TOLST trips. These are qualified people who must meet the London Tourist Board's stringent requirements, including the ability to care for passengers with particular needs such as children, the elderly and mobility handicapped. The guides provide a live commentary as the tour passes well-known sights. They also point out the less familiar, more bizarre and amusing features of the capital. An important advantage of using such guides is that they can improvise according to passenger response, and the circumstances of the day, especially traffic conditions and route diversions.

Some of LC's competitors had, on the other hand, installed taped commentaries. Although somewhat expensive to install, they have the advantage of being fairly cheap to run. Furthermore, multi-track systems with headphones enable passengers travelling on the same tour to listen to a commentary in their own language. The disadvantage is that tapes can be rather impersonal. Nevertheless, LC decided to convert some TOLST vehicles to offer multi-track commentaries, thus helping them to improve their penetration of the growing market of visitors from mainland Europe, Japan and other non-English speaking countries. Nevertheless, they retained other tours with English-speaking guides, which have a particular appeal to tourists from elsewhere in the UK, North America and Australasia. They also retained some other guided tours in French and German.

Other customer benefits were introduced. The TOLST product was augmented by offering an optional extra – tickets to certain tourist attractions on the route, enabling passengers to enter without queueing and to benefit from discounted prices. Following a successful venture in joint ticketing with Madame Tussauds, similar arrangements have been extended to London Zoo at Regents Park and to the Rock Circus. In August 1991 LC launched a new service, branded 'London Plus'. This combines a 'London Passport' book of vouchers giving discounts on visitor attractions, restaurants and so on, with a guided 'hop-on, hop-off' tour. A frequent service enables customers to alight at any of the stops and to rejoin the tour as often as they please. Thus, by offering a two-day pass, London Plus provides an alternative to TOLST with the added benefit of flexibility.

Many people wrongly assume that buses and coaches represent the 'cheap and cheerful' face of tourism – leisure travel for those who cannot afford anything better. The case study suggests, however, that through attention to the needs and wants of customers, the operator can develop a premium travel product which can gain a distinctive presence in the market-place. A well designed itinerary and an intelligent interpretive commentary is a form of entertainment. Thus, an appreciation of the total leisure product can lead to a successful formula which provides the customer with a satisfying and sophisticated experience.

Sustainable Tourism

Tourism is now one of the most important industries in the world in terms of turnover and the number of people employed. In many countries it has been encouraged and supported by governments and their agencies as a source of foreign exchange, wealth-creation and new jobs. Nevertheless, in most cases, the growth of tourism has been driven by the commercial decisions of the private sector. Most tourism markets are highly competitive, and tourism entrepreneurs have generally been given a loose rein. Few governments have attempted to regulate the supply of inbound tourism. Yet nowadays, some express concern over the 'unacceptable' face of tourism which may do serious and irreversible damage. Adverse effects on the physical environment, and on the society and culture of the host population, may destroy the very qualities which make a place attractive as a tourist destination.

From the consumer's point of view, the opportunity to travel can greatly enhance the quality of life. As people become more affluent and gain more leisure time, they often have a strong urge to travel. Tourism entrepreneurs respond to this demand. In the mid-nineteenth century, Thomas Cook pioneered escorted tours from the UK to continental Europe by rail and sea. He held a strong belief in the educative role of tourism, and hoped that it would play its part in promoting understanding between different societies and cultures. Nevertheless, there has always been a hedonistic side of tourism, as people seek pleasure and entertainment in novel surroundings away from home. A tour becomes a commodity, to be bought and consumed like any other product. Today's beach-bars, hotels and discotheques on the shores of the Mediterranean and elsewhere may, if unsympathetic in scale and character, create friction, rather than promote harmony between visitor and host.

The huge growth in international tourism since the 1960s has been made possible by developments in transport technology, especially by high capacity jet aircraft which have greatly reduced the cost and journey time of foreign travel. In the UK and other Northern European countries, large operators have used their bargaining power to obtain volume discounts on air charters and hotel accommodation in the resorts of Southern Europe, especially Spain, Portugal and Greece. **Mass tourism** grew very rapidly indeed during the 1970s and 1980s as major tour operators battled for market share by offering very low prices for Inclusive Tours. With little planning, some resorts have become grossly overdeveloped. The physical ugliness of towering concrete hotel blocks has been compounded by pollution of the sea, the noise of aircraft and heavy traffic, overloaded electricity and water supply, thefts, violent crime and the bad behaviour of 'lager louts'. Local customs often become self-conscious shows put on for the visitors, and traditional crafts debased to produce souvenirs and trinkets. Understandably, such problems have sometimes overshadowed the economic benefits, and caused ill-feeling towards the tourists.

They have also given rise to dissatisfaction from many of the tourists themselves. Alan Snudden, Chairman and Managing Director of Monarch Airlines, has commented on the decline in quality of the products offered by some large tour operators. From a peak of 13 million package holidays from the UK in 1988, the market subsequently declined to about 10 million per annum. Mass tourism was becoming unfashionable and boring: 'we are now beginning to carry the third generation of passengers, for whom the existing resorts do not generate the same feeling of excitement'.[8] Many prefer to move on to less commercialized destinations where the welcome from the host population is more genuine.

Many have gained the confidence to go independently, making their own arrangements for transport and accommodation. Some have invested in timeshare premises. There has been an even more dramatic growth in long-haul charters to more exotic locations – Florida, the Caribbean, Mexico, East Africa, Thailand, Malaysia and so on. In the case of Monarch Airlines, long-haul charters grew from almost nothing in 1987 to represent some 50 per cent of revenue by 1990.[9]

The high capacity jet aircraft have also facilitated the growth of **inbound tourism**. This includes the arrival of high-spending visitors from North America, whose absence during the Gulf War and its aftermath was a serious blow to the tourism industry in the UK. It is anticipated that the Channel Tunnel will encourage more visitors from Continental Europe who will be able to travel on the international trains or use the rail shuttles for private cars and coaches. **Domestic tourism** – movement by UK residents within their own country – is also important. Unfortunately for many UK seaside resorts, traditional 'bucket-and-spade' holidays have been in decline, mainly because of competition from the Inclusive Tours to Southern Europe described above. Nevertheless, there has been a welcome growth in the 'short break' market. Coach operators and British Rail have negotiated with hotels to offer attractive packages for long weekends off-season. This trend, which helps to even out the peaks and troughs in demand in both transport and accommodation, has also brought economic benefit from visitors who spend money in the locality. Destinations range from established centres such as York and Chester to towns such as Bradford and Halifax, which have actively promoted tourism as a catalyst for economic development to compensate for the decline of traditional industries such as woollen textiles.

In developed countries such as the UK, the economy and employment base is reasonably diverse and tourism has grown at a less frenzied pace than in the Costa Brava, Majorca or Corfu. Furthermore, firm control is generally exercised through town and country planning, and pressure groups at national and local level provide a powerful lobby to protect the amenities of valued townscapes and landscapes. Nevertheless, the growth of tourism can sometimes compromise the quality of the environment. For example, the expansion of airports near **major cities**, to increase capacity for airborne tourists, may cause noise disturbance and road traffic congestion. Tourist coaches may park or stop in places where they cause obstruction and danger to other road users and pedestrians. They may also be visually intrusive and contribute to noise and atmospheric pollution. In residential and public areas tourists may receive blame for an increase in litter, vandalism, rowdy behaviour, prostitution and kerb-crawling.

In **smaller towns and villages** tourism may also be regarded with a certain ambivalence. In addition to the income- and employment-generation, investment in accommodation and other facilities for tourists may provide new uses for older buildings which might otherwise become derelict. In many **rural areas** throughout Europe income from farming has been depressed by reductions in subsidy. Farmers and landowners are being encouraged to diversify into new business ventures, and some are developing farm holidays, sporting facilities and other sidelines. Nevertheless, at weekends and other times in the summer, local residents may resent the traffic congestion, parking problems, crowds, noise, and general loss of privacy. Some **National Parks**, such as the Lake District and Snowdonia, suffer particularly intense pressure from visitors who arrive by private car or by coach, and it is sometimes difficult for the Park Authorities to reconcile their twin policy aims – to preserve and enhance natural beauty, and to provide for open air recreation.

The English Tourist Board, Countryside Commission and Rural Development Commission have published a joint report addressed to people involved in running tourism businesses, including those in the transport sector. Entitled *The Green Light: A Guide to Sustainable Tourism*, it concludes that tourism can bring many benefits such as helping to maintain historic buildings, improving degraded landscapes and allowing an exchange of cultures. Yet, like other economic activities it can create a range of unwelcome effects on the environment, including overdevelopment, overcrowding, pollution and erosion. It stresses the growing awareness within the industry that fragile and beautiful places continue to prosper from tourism in the long as well as the short term. It advises tourism providers of the advantages of 'going green': 'you will be harmonising your own activities with what is best for the environment while at the same time building a solid basis for long-term growth; you will be offering your visitors a better product and projecting a responsible and credible image; you could also be saving money and attracting new visitors, guests, passengers and customers'.[10]

Conclusion

The worldwide growth of tourism has provided business opportunities for passenger transport operators of all modes. It is important for such carriers to relate their own services to the larger
system which supplies tourism products to markets which become increasingly diverse, segmented and sophisticated. High
volume/low price mass tourism has become discredited and seems
to be experiencing structural decline. Host communities and many
tourists are growing aware of the need to conserve the valued
qualities of the destinations visited. Tourism itself can thus be
understood as **a part of** still larger social, economic and environmental systems, not separate from them. Some tourism providers
are now expressing support for the concept of 'sustainable tourism' which seeks to maintain the delicate balance of such systems
in the interest of future prosperity, but only time will tell if this
can be translated into reality.

Notes

1   A definition adopted by The Tourism Society (1977).
2   See discussion of the Bus and Coach Council in chapter 18.
3   Holloway, J.C. (1989) *The Business of Tourism*, p. 11: Pitman.
4   Ibid. p. 57.
5   Middleton, V.T.C. (1988) *Marketing in Travel and Tourism*, p. 242:
    Heineman.
6   Ryall, T. (1988) 'A Licence to Print Money?' in *Bus Business*, 24 August,
    p. 10.
7   'On the Road' (1989) *London Coaches Courier*, February, p. 2. Staff
    Newsletter.
8   Snudden, A. (1990) 'Success in a Package', in *Transport*, January/
    February, p. 21.
9   Ibid.
10 English Tourist Board, Countryside Commission and Rural Devel-
    opment Commission (1992) *The Green Light: A Guide to Sustainable
    Tourism*, pp. 1–5.

8

Transport and Logistics

This chapter examines the management of logistics – a concept which treats transport as part of a wider system for distributing freight from supplier to consumer. Operators should be aware of the interrelationships between transport and the other elements which may include warehousing, inventory management, order processing, packaging and materials handling. As with transport and tourism discussed in the previous chapter, operators should be aware of the social and environmental implications of freight distribution.

Logistics Management

Logistics, or physical distribution management, has been defined as: 'the management of the supply chain, from the raw material right through to the point where the end product is finally used or consumed'.[1] This definition conveys the idea that logistics is about goods in **transit** as well as goods in **storage**. It also takes an overview of the entire physical distribution chain: upstream to where the raw materials are obtained, and downstream to the final point of sale. Along this chain, the goods may change hands several times from producers, through intermediaries, to consumers.

Distribution of raw materials such as coal or timber may be relatively simple, involving bulk transport and storage of commodities which are of low value relative to their weight and volume. As value is added and a greater variety of stock lines is manufactured, however, the distribution system becomes more complex. Retailers, at the end of the distribution chain, may handle thousands of different lines of consumer goods, many of which will be of high value.

The role of the Distribution Manager is to ensure that enough stock can be made available where and when the customer needs it. The goods must also arrive in an acceptable condition, without damage or loss. This service must be performed at the minimum cost consistent with the standards required. Thus, logistics is about getting the right goods safely to the right place, at the right time, at the right cost.

The main elements of logistics management are:

(a) **transport** – the inward movement of supplies and outward movement of deliveries;
(b) **warehousing** – the storage of goods at various stockholding points along the distribution chain;
(c) **inventory management** – the management of the value of the goods held, optimizing the level of stock held;
(d) **order processing** – the use of information systems to handle orders upstream from suppliers and downstream to customers;
(e) **packaging and materials handling** – the design of packages and the equipment used to handle items individually or as unitized loads.

Suppliers, wholesalers and retailers may carry out such functions themselves as an 'own account' operation. A large bakery, for example, may have its own fleet of delivery vehicles, its own warehouses and so on to distribute bread to its customers. Alternatively, all or some of the five main distribution activities may be contracted out. The bakery may decide to use a haulier, third party storage and so on. It may, indeed, decide to contract out the whole operation to a distribution company who can offer a comprehensive service. During the 1980s, in the UK, there was a significant shift away from own account operations towards the use of contract distribution. The Tibbett and Britten Group, for example, greatly expanded its hanging garment distribution services – its 'Fashion Logistics' operation provides shared transport, warehousing and so on for many well-known clothing suppliers and retailers. Its 'Transcare' operation provides a bespoke distribution service for Marks and Spencer.

Features of Logistics and the role of Transport

The integration of logistics activities has brought benefits, both in terms of overall cost reduction and in better service quality to the customer. The term 'total distribution concept' has been adopted. As Rushton and Oxley have explained, the aim is 'to treat the many different elements that come under the broad banner of distribution as one integrated system. It is a recognition that the inter-relationships between different elements, say, transport and storage, need to be considered within the context of the broader scheme of things.'[2]

Information technology has helped to put these ideas into practice. Computer systems used in distribution can handle vast quantities of data quickly and accurately, providing continuously updated or real time information which can be made available to authorized personnel in distant locations, such as headquarters, offices, factories, warehouses, transport depots and retail outlets. The various specialists involved in providing the distribution services may therefore monitor the movement and storage of goods along the entire distribution chain.

The information can therefore be used to guide decisions on a day-to-day basis. Furthermore, it can be built up over time to identify patterns and trends. This can be used as a basis for assessment and forecasting. Thus, computer applications can be used in physical distribution:

(a) **operationally** – e.g. to optimize the routing, scheduling and loading of delivery vehicles;
(b) **tactically** – e.g. to estimate storage requirements for seasonal peaks;
(c) **strategically** – e.g. to plan entire warehousing networks with regard to the number, size and optimal location of stockholding points.

In the manufacturing sector, information technology is being used to help plan and control their material flow from the sourcing of raw materials and components, through work-in-progress to the delivery of finished products. Many car manufacturers, for example, are using just-in-time (JIT) techniques which aim to eliminate waste and provide a smooth, continuous flow through the production process. Stock levels are kept to an absolute minimum, yet replenished in time to feed the production line.

In the retail sector, information technology is similarly used to help plan and control the flow of consumer goods so that the retailer neither overstocks nor runs out of stock. Multiple retailers selling groceries, for example, must respond to shoppers who expect wide choice, freshness and value for money. Some supermarkets now offer more than 10,000 product lines, many of which have a limited shelf life. Freezer foods, dairy products, fresh fruit and vegetables are distributed in temperature-controlled conditions in transit, in storage and intermediate handling: the 'cold chain', which must be organized on JIT principles in order to restock the supermarket shelves.

Production and supply, then, must be precisely matched to the pattern of demand. All along the distribution chain, stock levels are being reduced, yet a complete range of products must be made available to the customer who represents the next link in that chain. Perishable goods such as newspapers and fresh milk are, by definition, time-sensitive, and cannot be stockpiled in advance of customer demand. Yet the adoption of JIT has made many other items time-sensitive. The customers of distribution services, that is the suppliers, wholesalers and retailers, do not wish to hold large quantities of stock if they can possibly do without it. They would rather have their suppliers deliver small quantities of stock frequently. They would like their orders to be processed and executed speedily. They would like complete reliability so that deliveries are made at an agreed time just when they need it – neither too early nor too late. JIT systems have gone a long way towards satisfying these demands.

There are important implications for transport operators serving distribution markets. Account must be taken of fluctuations in demand over time. Some flows of goods may be fairly even, yet many show strong seasonal, weekly and daily peaks and troughs. The customers of distribution want flexibility – the facility to make changes at short notice. Demand will also be influenced by upswings and downturns of the economy which affect purchasing levels of both industrial and consumer goods. All this often means that the vehicle fleet is heavily used for limited periods, with considerable spare capacity at other times. Careful attention must therefore be paid to efficiency, yet this should not be to the detriment of the quality of service offered to distribution customers. In the past, many companies regarded freight transport as a burdensome overhead: 'a means to an end', rather like the tourist transport discussed in chapter 7. The exacting standards now demanded of suppliers in making goods available has led, however, to greater recognition that the transport can **add value** to the products sold. The following case study illustrates how this can be achieved through integration of the various elements of distribution:

Case study: The Role of Logistics in Sainsbury's Retail Growth

J. Sainsbury (JS) was already a well-established retail chain selling groceries to shoppers in South-East England when, in the 1960s, it embarked on an expansion programme, the momentum of which continues into the 1990s. Their core business is selling food and other Fast Moving Consumer Goods (FMCGs), but the vital contribution of logistics support has long been recognized by the owners of the company. The Board includes a Distribution Director with overall responsibility for the integrated system of logistics activities – transport, warehousing inventory management, order processing, packaging and materials handling. Careful planning, coordination and implementation of these is essential to supply the retail stores with the wide range of quality items marketed to the customers at prices which offer good value for money in a highly competitive business. Thus, logistics plays its part in ensuring that the retailer lives up to its slogan: 'Good Food Costs Less at Sainsbury's'.

During the 1960s, the company built a series of Regional Distribution Centres (RDCs) to service its retail outlets in South-East England. These large, purpose-built warehouses are strategically located for motorway access. Each has an operating depot for a fleet of delivery lorries. This strategy enabled the company to pioneer the concept of 'retailer consolidation' giving it very tight control over the distribution chain which had previously been dominated by the manufacturers. In order to bulk sell products to JS, the majority of suppliers are required to trunk to the RDCs where JS takes over the entire logistics operation. The 'supplier-controlled' distribution which it replaced had meant that the delivery vehicles of many different manufacturers queued up at 'the back door' of the retailer's stores. This often led to delays, unreliable delivery schedules, multiple handling and inefficiency. It created problems for the store manager who had to keep excess 'safety' stock which took up valuable retail floorspace. The new system meant that the products of various suppliers could be consolidated into one high-capacity vehicle which could deliver to just one or perhaps two shops with accurate arrival times and minimal handling.

Retailer-controlled distribution brought improvements to the freshness and presentation of the goods sold. Furthermore, there are inherent cost advantages in the economies of the new system compared to the old. In a retailer-controlled system trunk vehicles are used by the suppliers to bring their goods to the RDC. Then, through consolidation, trunk vehicles are also used to deliver in bulk to the store. Thus, JS tends to carry out store deliveries using articulated lorries – tractor units with 40 foot trailers – except where poor physical access to a particular shop necessitates the use of smaller rigid vehicles. Retailer consolidation gives JS the necessary flexibility to respond to rapid changes in volume and distribution, in order/delivery cycles, and in seasonal patterns and external factors such as supplier problems.[3]

Basingstoke RDC, one of the original company-owned warehouses, has good access to the M3 motorway and services a territory which covers about 70 stores to the South-West of London. Its layout is divided into four major sections – for goods held at four different temperatures:

(a) **Ambient** – e.g. tinned and bottled goods, breakfast cereals, toilet rolls.
(b) **Produce** – e.g. fruit and vegetables which are kept at about 10°C to ensure freshness.
(c) **Chilled** – e.g. butter, cheeses, bacon, fresh meat, fruit juices, yoghurt, kept at about 3°C.
(d) **Deep frozen** – e.g. freezer foods kept in cold storage at about –20°C.

As at other RDCs, the incoming suppliers' goods are generally unitized on pallets which must meet JS specifications. The outgoing goods, consolidated for delivery to the retail stores, are generally assembled into 'roll pallets'. These are large caged containers or temperature-insulated units on wheels, which can be easily rolled from the trading dock into the delivery vehicle and, using a tail lift, rolled out at the other end of the journey into the retail store. Thus, the whole operation is streamlined to allow quick turn-round of the vehicle during loading and unloading. This allows optimum utilization of the vehicles and of the drivers' time.

As JS expanded by opening new retail outlets northwards and westwards of their original territory in South-East England, the company opted to use contractors rather than build more company-owned depots. This enabled the company to concentrate effort and resources on their core retail business. Nevertheless, computer technology has enabled them to exercise the same tight control over the supply chain. Contractors such as NFC Exel Logistics and Christian Salvesen, who provide dedicated distribution for JS, use the 'DISCO' system, JS's own stock management computer system, which is installed and controlled by them. Upstream, the manufacturers who supply the goods must use compatible Electronic Data Interchange (EDI), which enables JS buyers to order stock through paperless communication – computer to computer. As David Quarmby, Joint Managing Director and former Distribution Director of JS, has explained:

> The decline of own account operation, perhaps more than anything, reflects the power of information technology to substitute 'control by information' for 'control by doing it yourself'. Systems used by Sainsbury's for branch ordering, depot replenishment, stock control and branch order picking and assembly means that effective control of activity in one of its contract depots is exactly the same as that in a Sainsbury-owned depot.[4]

Logistics continues to play a vital role in the retailer's business strategy for growth, and the Distribution Director is closely involved in many decisions. When new supermarkets and superstores are proposed, the distribution system to supply them with goods must be carefully planned in relation to the network of company-owned and contractors' warehouses and transport. The road access, site layout and unloading facilities of a new retail outlet must be designed to accommodate the delivery vehicles and allow quick and easy turn-round. Similarly, the promotion of a new product or special offer must be planned and co-ordinated with regard to the logistics support to get the goods to the stores.

Effective and efficient logistics can give a multiple retailer such as JS a strong competitive advantage. As well as ensuring consistent freshness and good presentation, it can facilitate the important benefit of customer choice. Thus the shopper can select, according to taste and household budget, from a very wide selection of items indeed. A large superstore may offer as many as 15,000 or more different product lines, which include some very specialist 'niche market' products. Many perishable items have very short shelf-lives, especially since health-consciousness has led to the reduction of additives and preservatives in recent years. It is the responsibility of the distribution function to make sure that the retail stores are kept stocked up with the right quantities of the complete range of products that the customers require, and that they are replenished on time. Developments over the past few decades have brought enormous improvements to the sophistication of logistics operations. Not only have these brought economies which have been passed on to the consumer, but they have also added value to the products sold.

Sustainable Logistics

Commercial decisions concerning logistics operations are made with a view to reducing costs and/or increasing revenue. Developments in logistics may bring additional benefits to customers and to the economy. In a competitive market, more efficient distribution will help bring down prices charged for the end product. And, the quality and availability of goods will also improve. Nevertheless, as with tourism discussed in the previous chapter, there may be adverse effects on society and on the physical environment. Again, distribution operators have a high profile, and need to be aware of the effects of their actions on public relations, as defined in chapter 5. Those adversely affected may well protest and make their views known. This may influence opinion-formers, the media, and decision-makers in government at local, national and even international level.

Without the distribution activities carried out by and for retailers such as J. Sainsbury, described in the case study above, our standard of living would suffer. As consumers become more affluent, they come to expect a wide range of goods from all over the world to be conveniently available throughout the year in high street and out-of-town stores. Yet, increasing affluence also tends to bring an increased awareness of environmental issues and an ability to organize and lobby. As Cooper, Browne and Peters have commented: 'Concern for the environment has long ceased to be a preoccupation of fringe lobby groups; it has moved into the mainstream of government and business interests. Neither governments nor companies can now afford to be negligent towards the environment . . . .'[5]

In most advanced economies, the nature of the **mode of transport** used for distribution provides cause for concern. Road vehicles predominate because of the inherent door-to-door convenience and flexibility of the mode, described in chapter 6 above. In the UK, some 82 per cent of the goods lifted are transported by road, compared to only 7 per cent by rail, 7 per cent by water and 4 per cent by pipeline.[6] Published in 1980, the report of the Armitage Committee into lorries, people and the environment provided a wide-ranging discussion of the adverse effects of road freight vehicles on the amenity of residential areas, historic centres and the countryside. Whilst it proved impossible to combine these nuisances into a single measurable index, the various costs included noise disturbance, vibration damage to buildings and other structures, atmospheric pollution, danger and visual intrusion. The possible policy responses to these problems could be categorized broadly into:

(a) improvements to **vehicle design**;
(b) **segregation** of goods vehicles from people and sensitive environments wherever possible, e.g. by constructing bypasses;
(c) **suppression of demand** for road freight transport by quantity licensing or by increased taxation.

Since there has been no desire to return to quantity licensing, and taxation of hauliers in the UK is already considered high by European standards, the emphasis has been on (a) and (b).

There is an important trend in distribution towards **centralized warehousing**. In advanced economies, where motorway systems are well developed, suppliers of many consumer and industrial goods find it an advantage to build very large national distribution centres (NDCs) to service demand in an entire country. In Europe, many are building distribution centres to serve the whole Single European Market and its 12 Member States.[7] It does, however, increase the demand for trunking movements. In commercial terms, these increased transport costs are more than outweighed by the savings made elsewhere. In environmental terms, however, it adds to the total number of vehicle miles run, the demand for fossil fuels, atmospheric pollution and so on.[8]

The trend towards JIT deliveries to industry can also generate more transport movements. There are clear advantages for the customer who can hold less inventory, yet have faith in the supplier's ability to replenish the required stock reliably – for example a vehicle manufacturer receiving components for assembly on their production line. Such economies can be passed on to the final customer. Yet, JIT tends to necessitate more frequent deliveries of smaller quantities of stock in smaller vehicles. There is also a general trend towards round-the-clock distribution. This brings better utilization of both warehouses and vehicle fleets. And, by running vehicles at night when the roads are generally clear of private cars, savings can be made in vehicle operation costs and in fuel. If however, the vehicles are routed through, or deliver within, residential or mixed use areas, sleep disturbance and ill-feeling can result.[9]

Many environmentalists would like to see a modal shift away from road freight and towards rail and water transport. It is important to emphasize that the latter two modes are generally more suited to the movement of bulk commodities such as coal, metal ores and aggregates, and to longer distance transits, especially over 300 miles. The convenience and flexibility of road freight has already been stressed. Nevertheless, there are signs that distribution strategies are being reappraised with regard to modal choice. In more affluent countries, increased numbers of private cars bring increased congestion and less reliable transit times for road haulage. Operational costs will tend to rise. 'Combined Mode' operations, using containers or other unit loads, may offer significant benefits by using railways, and in some cases inland waterways and coastal shipping, for the trunk haul. Road haulage is used at either end for collection and delivery. Much depends upon the speed and cost-effectiveness of transhipment at the terminals. In the United States and elsewhere in recent years, there has been considerable investment by the private sector in such facilities and in rolling stock to carry containers, or 'piggyback' operations where the loaded road vehicles themselves are carried by rail on flatwagons.

In the UK, in contrast to other European countries, the drive to profitability for rail freight operations has encouraged British Rail to focus very closely on those segments of the freight market which it is well placed to serve – for example, over 50 per cent of its revenue has came from moving coal. In summer 1991 its loss-making Speedlink operation for general less-than-trainload freight was abandoned. Although 75 per cent of Speedlink's traffic was retained, some freight went back on to the roads, for example the bulk liquid distribution from Taunton Cider in Somerset.

The **Channel Tunnel** provides new opportunities to send freight by rail, since for the first time British Rail's network will be physically joined to railways in Continental Europe. As a result, there will be many more long-distance transits where Combined Mode operations should be able to compete with road-only haulage. A major constraint is presented, however, by the UK loading gauge – the width and height profile of rolling stock which is smaller than that which is standard for much of Continental Europe. Considerable investment has gone into the design and construction of special rolling stock such as small-wheeled flatwagons, freight terminal facilities and other works. Nevertheless, the prospects for large-scale upgrading of routes, through structure clearances (including tunnels and bridges), to Continental standards are very uncertain because of the enormous cost implications.[10]

Conclusion

Logistics provides yet another example of systems thinking. Here, transport is treated as one element which is combined and co-ordinated with others to offer a total distribution service. As economies develop, the flow of materials, parts, and finished inventory becomes increasingly complex, as suppliers respond to the more sophisticated demands of affluent consumers who want a wide range of specialist products, many of which have to be moved considerable distances to the point of sale. Furthermore, in order to improve efficiency of distribution, and to maintain product quality, the timescales become more critical. As a result, the function of logistics management requires increasing ingenuity. Road freight has developed as the dominant mode of transport, but its adverse effects have received much criticism. The challenge of satisfying the pattern of customer demand in an environmentally-acceptable fashion adds a further dimension to logistics management in the 1990s.

Notes

1   Institute of Logistics and Distribution Management *The Facts About Logistics Management*, p. 1: ILDM.

2   Rushton, A. and Oxley, J. (1989) *Handbook of Logistics and Distribution Management*, p. 14: Kogan Page.
3   Quarmby, D. (1987) 'Road Improvements – Identifying the Wider Benefits of Freight Distribution', in *Transport Economist*, summer, p. 14.
4   Ibid. p. 16.
5   Cooper, J., Browne, M., and Peters, M. (1991) *European Logistics – Markets, Management and Strategy*, ch. 13, p. 270: Blackwell.
6   Department of Transport (1989) *Transport Statistics Great Britain 1975– 1988*, figures for 1988 table 1.13: HMSO.
7   See discussion of distribution in the Single European Market in chapter 14.
8   See Cooper, J. et al. (1991) op. cit. pp. 272–7.
9   Ibid. pp. 277–9.
10   See Abbot, J. (1992), 'Railfreight Distribution Prepares for the Chunnel' in *Modern Railways*, April, pp. 192–6.

Part III

Regulators

9

Quantity Licensing: Road Transport

Road carriers can be regulated by granting or denying them a licence which gives them authority to operate. 'Quantity' licensing regulates the **supply** of transport. It may limit the number of operators permitted to enter the market. It may also control the price charged to the customer, and the frequency/capacity of the service. In the UK, and some other countries, quantity licensing has largely been abandoned in favour of a deregulated or liberalized market. This chapter examines the reasons why it was first introduced and discusses the implications where it has been abolished.

Forms of Quantity Licensing

Quantity licensing, also known as 'economic regulation', has been used to control the free play of market forces in both road passenger and road freight transport in various countries, at various times. In essence, a regulatory body or agency is set up by the State to exercise controls over the supply or quantity of transport. Such intervention, by definition, blunts commercial competition, since it may determine some, or even all of the following factors:

(a) The **number of operators** allowed to trade in a particular geographical area, or along a particular route, may be limited. In some cases a single carrier is granted a monopoly. As well as controlling market entry, it may also refuse carriers permission to leave, obliging them to continue operating services which, in themselves, are unprofitable.

(b)   The **price** charged for passenger fares and freight tariffs may be fixed by the regulatory body, or floors or ceilings set. In the case of monopoly, this is to prevent the operator abusing their privileged position by raising the price unjustifiably. Where there are two or more carriers, it prevents one undercutting another's rates.

(c)   The **frequency** of a scheduled service, and/or the **capacity** of the vehicles used may also be controlled.

The justification for economic regulation, and the methods used, have differed according to the type of road transport operation. The following examples show why and how it has been applied.

Taxis

London taxis, or rather their horse-drawn predecessors, provide a very early example of economic regulation in road passenger transport. They are still subject to a stringent licensing system. Hackney carriages (named after the horses which pulled them) began to ply for hire in the streets of London in the 1620s. Following their rapid growth in popularity as a form of public transport for the well-to-do, their owners were required to obtain a licence to operate, and to pay duty to the Crown. Today's 'black cabs' are required to comply with laws and regulations, same of which date back to the last century. These licensing requirements not only include the range of quality standards for taxis discussed in the next chapter, but also regulate the **fares** which their drivers can charge. A digital metre clearly displays the correct fare. Thus, the hirer is protected from opportunist operators who might charge more in any situation when taxis are in short supply and demand is great, or where customers are unaware of the appropriate fare – for example visitors to London. Nor is it possible for one licensed taxi to undercut another's fare to win customers.

In London, the regulatory body for taxis – the Public Carriage Office – does not fix a limit to the **number** allowed to operate. Although taxis carry only a small proportion of the total passenger journeys, they do satisfy a specialized particular market demand for convenient, door-to-door transport in privacy and comfort. In 1903 there were 11,500 taxis in London, but after the First World War their numbers dropped, and that figure was not reached again until 1976. By the late 1980s there was a rise to about 15,000[1] – a situation which led to some excess demand during the Gulf War and economic downturn of the early 1990s, as taxi drivers waited patiently for customers.

Outside London the regulatory framework is substantially different. District Councils have a duty to license taxis under the 1985 Transport Act. Although they can exercise some discretion over the number of taxis they are prepared to license, they can only impose such a limit if it can be established that 'no significant unmet demand' would remain.[2]

Buses and Coaches

It is interesting to note that, long before any form of economic regulation by the State, bus operators got together to establish their own order through 'associations' governing scheduled services on particular routes. Theo Barker reports that, as early as 1831, just two years after George Schilibeer's pioneering horse-drawn omnibus started operating in London, various rival carriers had formed an association to limit the number of vehicles on a route, to agree fares, and to allocate times to each bus. Inspectors were posted along the route to make sure that this was being done. Furthermore, if another operator from outside the association attempted to make an entry, vehicles belonging to association members were run in front of the intruder to deny him customers. The allocated time-slots could, however, be exchanged and traded within the association.[3]

By about 1910 motorbuses began to prove themselves as a reliable mode of public transport. Cheaper to operate per passenger-mile than their horse-drawn predecessors, they offered greater flexibility than electric trams. Technology further improved, and many operators entered an expanding market for local transport. In addition to the demand for work and school journeys, an increasing number of shopping and leisure trips were made by bus. Entrepreneurs, both large and small, saw bus operation as an attractive business proposition. Market entry was relatively cheap, and the end of the First World War in 1918 brought in growing numbers of owner-drivers, as ex-servicemen acquired vehicles and started running their own bus services.

During this period, the State made no attempt to intervene in market forces. In the 1920s some operators, with a degree of enlightened self-interest, published timetables and made every attempt to keep to schedule. They often provided regular services from early morning until late evening, as well as operating on Sundays. They also ran feeder services on the more lightly-trafficked routes. Unfortunately, some others were less scrupulous, and showed little responsibility. The so-called 'pirate' operators never tried to offer a regular, timetabled service throughout the day. Rather, they 'creamed off' the traffic on busy routes at busy times. The worst of them even turned passengers off, and reversed in the street, if they saw a queue waiting to travel in the opposite direction.[4]

Before long, there was growing support for some form of public intervention to regulate local bus operations. Firstly, there was mounting evidence that such unbridled competition contributed to traffic congestion, and worse still, caused accidents. Rival bus operators were sometimes reckless as they overtook and raced each other to pick up at bus stops. Secondly, established operators argued that if they were to continue operating a stable network of timetabled services, they would require protection, especially from the pirates who were eroding their most lucrative traffic.

In response, economic regulation was introduced, firstly in London from 1924 and then elsewhere in the UK from 1930. Initially, limits were set on the number of buses allowed to ply on certain busy streets. Then, a system of route licensing was brought in whereby 'Road Service Licences' were issued by the regulatory body, the Traffic Commissioners. Existing operators had priority in objecting to new applications, making market entry virtually impossible. Fairly quickly, a series of mergers and take-overs resulted in territorial monopolies – networks operated by one company, free from other bus competitors. Tours sold to the general public were also subject to licensing requirements. Only private hire and charters remained outside quantity licensing.

In return for this unusual degree of commercial protection, the bus companies had to apply for permission from the Traffic Commissioners to vary their services, including changes to the routes and frequency of service, as well as for any fare increases. In economic terms, bus operators maintained unprofitable services within their own network through **cross-subsidy**. This provided a fairly stable system until the mid-1950s when increased car ownership began to reduce the viability of many bus services. The operators applied to the Traffic Commissioners for approval for shrinking networks, reduced frequencies and increased fares. This made buses less attractive to their customers, and so the downward spiral continued.

The 1968 Transport Act created the National Bus Company – a public corporation. Thus most bus operations in UK were in public ownership, either in the nationalized sector or as municipals. The 1972 Local Government Act empowered local authorities to subsidize bus services through 'network support' which met an operator's overall deficit. The creation of Passenger Transport Authorites[5] led to high levels of subsidy in some metropolitan areas where the Authorities had a strong commitment to low fares and encouraging greater use of public transport. Nevertheless, with a rather unsatisfactory combination of cross-subsidy within a bus operator's territory, and blanket subsidy from local authorities or PTAs, it was hard, if not impossible, to pin down costs and revenue with any precision. The question of value for money became an important issue as operators demanded more finance to maintain services. Since neither the local authority providing the subsidy, nor the fare-paying passenger, had any choice of bus operator, it was difficult to say whether they were receiving the standard of service they deserved.

The 1980s brought a complete reversal of public policy. Following Labour's defeat in 1979, a Conservative government, deeply committed to free market principles, took the radical and controversial step of abolishing economic regulation after over 50 years of quantity licensing. Firstly, under the 1980 Transport Act, controls over market entry and pricing were lifted for scheduled long-distance express coach services as well as for tours (both over 30 miles). Ending the near-monopoly of the National Express scheduled network, the effects were encouraging for free marketeers – improvements in service quality and fare reductions on many routes resulted in increased ridership. Nevertheless, National Express remained a dominant force, responding well to the challenge of competition. Using high-specification coaches on its branded 'Rapide' routes, journey times were substantially reduced. Their on-board toilets eliminated the need for 'comfort' stops and full use was made of the national motorway network. Hostesses and stewards, trained in customer care, were brought in to sell light refreshments and to attend to passengers. Other novelties such as videos, previously associated with airline travel, were also introduced.

A wide range of operators did, however, gain market entry on particular routes and sustained their challenge. Some were privately-owned independents such as Stagecoach which operated services between Scotland and England.[6] Others were municipal, PTE, and National Bus Company subsidiaries. Better, cheaper coach services on certain routes also provided a serious challenge to British Rail on some of its inter-urban routes. Thus, the deregulation of express coaches created much greater competition between the **two modes** for the leisure market. In South-East England the pattern of long-distance commuting into London provided opportunities for some to introduce commuter coaches. Though some proved unreliable due to traffic congestion, others expanded, for example those operated by King's Ferry, London Coaches and Maidstone and District from Kent. For some commuters these provide a useful alternative to British Rail Network SouthEast and the private car.

Meanwhile, attention turned to the future for local bus operations. As Peter White has commented,[7] the early 1980s saw significant drops in ridership in some areas, resulting from rising unemployment which reduced demand for work journeys, though by the mid-1980s this had stabilized. In some areas the vicious circle of higher fares and lower service levels continued, yet in others there was a welcome reversal of this trend. In the metropolitan areas, Labour authorities elected in 1981 renewed their policy commitment to low fare levels. In the capital, the Greater London Council's short-lived 'Fares Fair' policy was followed by the popular Travelcard providing inter-modal transfer between bus and rail.

Bus operators were well aware of the government's intention to deregulate and privatize local bus services, the details of which were set out in the 1984 *Buses* White Paper. The impending new order provided a spur to better marketing and customer relations. In 1984 Devon General introduced an innovative network of minibuses in Exeter. The high-frequency services, penetration of new areas with narrow roads and tight corners, opportunities for 'hail and ride' – stopping anywhere on certain sections of route, and perceived friendliness of the service proved popular with passengers, including higher income groups which had previously shown reluctance to use buses. Minibuses also provided the opportunity for a fresh start in negotiating drivers' wages and conditions of service. There was scope for part-time working and greater flexibility. Drivers were trained from scratch and selection criteria included a positive attitude to customer care. Minibuses and larger midibuses were subsequently introduced by many other operators to replace selected big bus services and/or provide new routes.

During this period leading up to deregulation there was an emphasis on efficiency, not only in running the buses, but also in engineering and administrative functions. Municipal bus operators, for example, achieved an increase in bus miles per staff hour of about 9 per cent between 1980 and 1984.[8] There was an increased willingness to decentralize operating, engineering, marketing and other functions to divisional managers, as discussed in the case of Busways in chapter 2. Thus, by the time bus deregulation was actually implemented, there was already an encouraging trend towards a more market-led approach, and towards greater efficiency. Nevertheless, the legislation which swept away quantity licensing brought fundamental change in the bus industry.

Under the 1985 Transport Act, the government deregulated local bus services outside the London area (though their intention to deregulate the latter was reaffirmed in 1991). With effect from 26 October 1986, Road Service Licences were abolished, opening up scheduled bus operations to competition. From that day, both new and existing operators have been free to run local bus services wherever they perceive a commercial opportunity, simply by registering their intention to do so, and details of the proposed route, timetable and so on with the Traffic Commissioners.[9]

In introducing the new legislation, the Secretary of State expressed his belief that the deregulation, along with its privatization, would revitalize the bus industry.[10] By encouraging a new commercial awareness, operators would be more responsive to the passengers' requirements. The new approach would help arrest the decline in service levels and reduce the amount of public subsidy required to support bus services. Under the new system, the process of registering commercial services would serve to identify the 'viable network' – services not in need of financial support.

Thus, the County Councils and Passenger Transport Authorities – who formerly played an important role in service planning and co-ordination of public transport, have no influence over the provision of registered, commercial services. They are, however, required to consider any needs which are not being met, and empowered to subsidize services which they believe to be necessary for social reasons. This might include, for example, a service to an isolated village community, a Sunday service to a hospital and so on.[11] If they decide to support such services they are also required to follow a statutory procedure for **competitive tendering**. The authority will then set out the service specifications, including the route, timetable and other matters such as vehicle capacity, and design features to conform with the recommendations of the Disabled Persons Transport Advisory Committee (DPTAC). This will be in the form of an invitation to tender. Having established the specifications, the tendering authority will normally accept the lowest tender.

Opinion is still divided concerning the benefits, versus the disadvantages of bus deregulation. To some extent, this reflects the perspective of different interest groups, for example bus passengers in different geographical areas, bus operators large and small, employees of bus operators and their trade unions, bus manufacturers, local authorities, taxpayers and Council Tax payers. Amongst these, there are winners and losers. The major arguments for and against can be summarized.

In Favour of Deregulation

Those in favour tend to emphasize the following points:

(a) Commercial pressures to gain and retain customers encourage bus operators to be market-oriented, as defined in chapter 4. Competition, or the threat of it, focuses attention upon:
  (i) cost control so as to keep fares to a reasonable level;
  (ii) enhancement of service quality, putting customer requirements first.
(b) Deregulation encourages innovation, rewarding bus operators with a flair for creative thinking, who are bold enough to take risks. This new spirit of entrepreneurship has ended many years of stagnation and poor response to the changing pattern of customer demand. These new demands, and the tendency to decentralize, provide more responsibility and challenge for managers in the bus industry.
(c) Competitive pressures through tendering should also reduce the level of public subsidy from central and local taxation. The system also allows financial support to be targeted more accurately. The local authority should therefore obtain better value for money, provided there are sufficient local bus opeartors willing to tender.

Against Deregulation

Those against deregulation tend to stress:

(a) Competing bus operators are unlikely to co-operate with one another. Indeed illegal agreements may lead to action under legislation governing restrictive trade practices. Deregulation therefore jeopardizes various aspects of integration which have previously benefited the passengers:
   (i) through ticketing valid on different services within a network;
   (ii) comprehensive information about a service network, including timetables and route maps;
   (iii) co-ordination between routes, schedules and facilities for easy interchange

(b) With a climate of uncertainty, and a scarcity of capital for investment, some bus operators have found it hard to maintain a reasonable age profile for their vehicles. Planning ahead for phased fleet replacement has often been abandoned. Similarly, budgets for personnel training and development have tended to suffer.

(c) Intensive competition between operators on particular routes, colloquially known as 'buswars', can result in excessive mileage and low load factors – a wasteful use of resources. Timetable frequency is seldom equally spaced. Rather, competing services tend to leave within a few minutes of each other, with little benefit to the customer. In some urban areas competition has exacerbated traffic congestion.

(d) In general, however, such buswars tend to be shortlived. The victors are generally larger operators, with the resources to fight off smaller rivals by putting on additional buses and cutting fares.[12] A series of mergers and takeovers has gone ahead and some very large groups have emerged. By 1989, seven large groups each had an average of 1,200 vehicles, and the largest had between 2,000 and 3,000.[13] There are therefore fears that the end result will be the re-emergence of near-monopolies, yet without the controls which formerly existed through economic regulation.

Road Freight

As with road passenger transport, intense competition between road freight operators in the 1920s suggested the need for quantity licensing. From 1933, a regime of economic regulation was administered by the regulatory bodies, the Licensing Authorities (LAs). This regime served to protect the commercial interests not only of established hauliers, but also of the railway companies, then privately owned. As Edmund Gubbins has commented: 'In many ways, the system was a reflection of the perceived importance of the railways and was used as much to protect the railways from competition as to regulate the industry'.[14] In those pre-motorway days, road freight operations were seen primarily as feeder services to rail transport.

The LAs could issue three types of licence to operators:

(a) **'A' Licence** – A category which entitled the haulier to carry freight for hire and reward, that is, to transport shippers' goods for commercial gain.

(b) **'B' Licence** – A category which entitled the operator to carry for hire and reward as well as own account traffic, that is, his own goods. There were, however, restrictions on the geographical area covered and on the commodities which could be carried.

(c) **'C' Licence** – This entitled the operator to carry own account traffic only. It was the only type of licence which the LAs granted automatically, provided the safety and other quality regulations were met.[15] In the other categories, existing road freight operators and the railways could object.[16]

By the mid-1960s, such economic regulation seemed anachronistic. Technological improvements had greatly improved the speed and reliability of goods vehicles, and the national motorway programme was well under way. Thus, road haulage provided a viable means of transporting freight across the UK. The Labour government of the day, therefore, decided to liberalize the road freight industry. The 1968 Transport Act had the effect of opening up market entry. Thus, the UK haulage industry has well over two decades' experience of operating in a highly competitive market without quantity licensing. This contrasts with other European countries such as Germany and France where economic regulation has prevailed until very recently. Such conditioning to the rigours of a free market should stand UK hauliers in good stead in the liberalized market for road freight within the Single European Market.[17]

Although its carriers often transported freight over far greater distances, the haulage industry in the United States followed a similar course. During the 1930s, there was intense competition which resulted in rate wars. The trucking industry asked the federal government to intervene to limit the number of operators, and to establish minimum rates.[18] This request was granted, and from 1935 the trucking industry was subject to quantity licensing. Frederick Stephenson explains that by the 1970s, the trucking industry was receiving criticism on the grounds that profits were **too healthy**. A former Chairman of the regulatory body expressed his belief that relaxation of entry rules would improve trucking services, lower rates and provide more innovative pricing. The entry of lower cost operators would encourage the less efficient ones to curb their costs and improve productivity.[19]

Governments in the UK, the United States and other countries have recognized that quantity licensing for road haulage serves little useful purpose, yet blunts competition. Deregulation was justified on the grounds that it would benefit shippers of freight, and thus the customers who receive and consume the goods. Unlike the local bus industry described above, new haulage firms, varying in size from owner-drivers with one vehicle to very large companies, have managed to gain market entry. After more than 20 years, competition on price and service quality remains keen in general haulage and in specialized road freight markets such as hanging garments, bulk liquids, temperature controlled food and so on.

Conclusion

Economic regulation suggests that transport should be treated differently from other industries. It was introduced in the UK and elsewhere in the belief that unrestricted competition was not serving the best interest of the public. Yet, in practice, protected markets can also be harmful, since they tend to foster inefficiency and complacency. Free marketeers argue that wholesale deregulation offers the best solution. Others argue, however, that the various modes of transport have different types of market structure and that, in some cases, checks and restraints on open competition are fully justified.

Notes

1 'Seminar Addresses Key Issues' (1989), in *Transport*, January/February, p. 14.

2   Faulks, R. (1987) *Bus and Coach Operation*, p. 100: Butterworths.
3   Barker, T. (1990) *Moving Millions*, pp. 17–18: London Transport Museum.
4   Op. cit. p. 87.
5   See explanation of public corporations, municipals and Passenger Transport Authorities in chapter 2.
6   Although the Stagecoach express coach operation was subsequently sold on to National Express.
7   White, P. (1986) 'What Future has the Bus Industry?' in *Transport*, June, p. 99.
8   Ibid.
9   The Traffic Commissioners' powers with regard to quality regulation are discussed in chapter 10.
10 HMSO (1984) *Buses*, White Paper.
11 See discussion of supported local bus services in Devon in chapter 15.
12 See discussion on the role of the Office of Fair Trading in chapter 13.
13 Robinson, D. (1989) 'Where will it all End?' in *Transport*, September p. 198.
14 Gubbins, E. (1988) *Managing Transport Operations*, p. 174: Kogan Page.
15 For discussion of quality licensing in road freight, see chapter 10.
16 Gubbins, E. op. cit., p. 174.
17 See discussion of the liberalization and harmonization of road freight within the European Community in chapter 14.
18 Stephenson, F.J. (1987) *Transportation USA*, p. 81: Addison Wesley.
19 Ibid. p. 87.

10

Quality Licensing: Road Transport

Through quality licensing road carriers can be regulated to ensure that they comply with minimum requirements and various safeguards. These include standards concerned with safety, competence and protection of the environment. Again, control is exercised by granting or denying a licence.

Regulation of Standards

Quality licensing is used to ensure that road passenger and road freight carriers observe certain specified standards. These requirements are established as benchmarks, and individual road carriers must comply with them. The standards may apply to:

(a) the operator;
(b) the vehicles;
(c) the drivers and other personnel.

As with quantity licensing discussed in the last chapter, a regulatory body or agency is set up by the State to exercise control. Yet, unlike some forms of economic regulation, it must **not** discriminate, for example, in favour of an existing carrier against a newcomer. With quality licensing, the regulator must make sure that the statutory requirements have been met. If the regulator is satisfied, the licence must be granted. The main areas of concern are:

(a) **Safety** issues, so as to minimize danger to passengers, the operator's employees, and any third parties such as other road users.

(b) The **competence** of the operator's managers, drivers and other employees with regard to the knowledge and skills which are deemed necessary for the job in question.

(c) **Environmental** issues, so as to minimize noise, atmospheric pollution and other adverse effects on amenity and health.

Principles of Regulation

A road carrier has important responsibilities. The operator must ensure that the business is run safely at all times and all places, that tasks are performed by competent personnel, and that due care is taken to minimize damage to the environment. As in other industries, the best operators establish a 'culture of quality' – procedures and practices designed to achieve high standards, relevant training and support to update the knowledge and skills of employees and so on. Bearing in mind the importance of public relations emphasized in chapter 5, no carrier actually wants a poor safety record, a reputation for incompetence or to damage the environment. Nevertheless, circumstances such as pressures to reduce costs, or to increase output without adequate resources, may force an operator to adopt bad practices, and to compromise standards.

To a certain extent, standards can be raised by **self-regulation** within the transport industry, especially through the trade associations discussed in chapter 18. These organizations for employers and operators provide a very useful function in disseminating information on best practice, and some provide training, consultancy, and other services for their members. Nevertheless, trade associations are voluntary, and their members are under no obligation to make use of the support they offer, or follow their advice. Furthermore, there are many operators who choose not to join. Unfortunately, there are some who operate at the margins of the law, or outside it. As Brian Colley of the Road Haulage Association has commented:

> There have been calls from within the industry for better self-regulation. One must ask why self-discipline doesn't work now when the essential rules are already in place. If managers now choose to condone speeding, hours and records irregularities, or turn a blind eye to vehicle defects, all of which have a bearing on safety, what form of self-regulation is going to change matters?[1]

Thus, where the self-discipline of individual operators or self-regulation within the transport industry fails to secure acceptable standards **external controls** are required. As Professor John Hibbs has commented in the context of bus and coach operators, such regulation is needed 'so as to ensure safety, reliability and a certain standard of business behaviour, including an increased stress on the environmental consequences of its operations'.[2] As in other industries, an agency is set up by the State to protect its citizens against danger, nuisance and other hazards. Regulators with relevant professional and technical expertise are thus given authority to enforce the standards in accordance with the rules set out in legislation, regulations and other statutory instruments.

In road passenger and road freight transport, there are thousands of operators, many of which are sole traders and other small firms. Indeed, many are owner-drivers with only one vehicle. Furthermore, they share a common way – the public highway. Thus, a licence is required to run most types of haulage operation, to drive a particular category of bus or coach and so on. It is beyond the scope of this chapter to provide a detailed account of quality licensing for the various types of road carrier. The laws and procedures are inherently complex, and the regulations are frequently updated. Nevertheless, the following examples are used to illustrate the principles and to explain how and why the various forms of quality licensing have been applied.

Taxis, Hire Cars and Minicabs

The regulatory framework for taxis requires high standards, and both the vehicles and their drivers must be licensed. This is to protect the passengers who hire the taxis with regard to their personal safety, and to guard against possible misconduct such as overcharging or taking unnecessary detours. In London, the distinctive 'black cabs' have a number of safety features such as special door locks. They clearly display their function, their availability for hire, meter and a number by which they can be identified. Their standardized design provides ample space for passengers and luggage. It has an advantage in access provision for people with severe mobility handicaps – wheelchairs can be accommodated as a standard design feature in the MCW Metrocab, or through modifications in the FX4W model.[3]

The competence requirements of 'green badge' London taxi drivers ensure that they are well acquainted with the roads and sites of the centre and inner areas through the 'knowledge' test. As noted in the last chapter, no ceiling is placed on the number of operators, but this special requirement tends to restrict market entry. A less stringent knowledge test applies to 'yellow badge' drivers, whose operation is confined to specified suburban areas. Any passenger with a complaint concerning the conduct of a taxi driver in London may take their grievance to the Public Carriage Office. Outside London, District Councils must license taxis and their drivers and may apply appropriate quality licensing requirements.

Taxis are licensed to ply for hire. Thus, the customer may hail one at a taxi rank or in the street. In contrast, hire cars or minicabs are vehicles which may only be hired by a booking made personally or by telephone to the base office. Again, the situation in the capital is quite different to the rest of the country. In London, minicabs, which started operating in the 1950s, are subject to virtually no controls beyond the normal licensing of private cars.[4] Some estimates put their number as high as 40,000, or $2\frac{1}{2}$ times the number of licensed taxis.

Many people in London are understandably concerned about the potential danger to the passenger, and some believe that a form of quality licensing should be introduced to provide some assurance concerning safety and other standards of service. Furthermore, the tendency of some minicab drivers to flout the law and openly ply for hire has angered licensed taxi drivers. Outside the capital, District Councils have the discretion to license hire car and minicab drivers as well as their vehicles. Thus some control may be exercised over quality – for example checks concerning any previous criminal convictions of the driver and over the age and suitability of the car.

Buses and Coaches

Quality licensing is also used to protect bus and coach passengers who might otherwise be vulnerable, for example to operators running unsafe, unroadworthy vehicles, or employing drivers who might be unqualified or tired through working excessive hours without a break. It also reduces any danger to other road users.

Other powers can be used to ensure that bus routes and stopping places have regard to public safety considerations. It was noted in chapter 9 that quantity licensing has been abolished in the UK, except in London (for the time being). The regulatory bodies which carried out the economic regulation prior to the 1985 Transport Act – the Traffic Commissioners – now function solely as authorities for quality licensing. The country is divided into Traffic Areas, each with a Traffic Commissioner appointed by the Secretary of State for Transport.

The buses and coaches to which these licensing laws apply are known as Public Service Vehicles (PSVs). Services involving the use of these vehicles must be run with the authority of an appropriate Operator's Licence (O Licence), or permit for exemption.[5] To obtain such a licence, the operator must apply to the Traffic Commissioner in the area where his operating centre is located.[6]

The major categories of the O Licence are:

(a) The **Standard National Licence** which is required to carry passengers for hire and reward within the UK, that is, to operate public services for commercial gain.
(b) The **Standard International Licence** to carry passengers for hire and reward internationally, as well as in the UK.
(c) The **Restricted Licence** where the operator only runs vehicles with up to 8 seats or up to 16 if not used as part of a hire and reward passenger-carrying business, for example a nightclub which provides a courtesy coach for its customers.

The Traffic Commissioner must be satisfied that the applicant can fulfil certain requirements. All must be:

(a) 'of good repute', meaning that account must be taken of any previous convictions of the applicant, or the applicant's employees or agents;
(b) 'of appropriate financial standing' meaning that the applicant must show evidence that there is sufficient money for the vehicles to be maintained safely, and to administer the business properly.

In the case of a standard O Licence, the applicant or his/her manager must hold the relevant qualification as proof of 'professional competence' to carry out national or international work, as appropriate. Other matters for consideration by the Traffic Commissioners include the applicant's facilities for proper maintenance of the vehicles, and the arrangements for ensuring compliance with drivers' hours regulations.

Police authorities and local authorities both have the right to object to an O Licence application if they consider the would-be operator unsuitable.[7] If the Traffic Commissioner grants the licence, they will include a condition specifying the number of vehicles permitted to operate from the base(s), and may specify particular categories of PSV.

The applicant has a right of appeal. Any subsequent breaches of the law may lead not only to prosecution, but, in some cases, to suspension or revocation of the O Licence. Proposed services must be registered with the Traffic Commissioner and, having done so, the operator is obliged to run them responsibly. As Rex Faulks has commented 'passengers must be protected from any unscrupulous operator who might make false promises by publishing timetables to which little or no effort is made to observe'.[8]

Quality licensing also regulates:

(a)   the **drivers** who must hold an appropriate Passenger Carrying Vehicle (PCV)[9] licence, and abide by the regulations which govern their working hours and rest periods;

(b)   the **vehicles** in the various classes of PSV, the requirements for which include a valid Certificate of Initial Fitness and conformity with Construction and Use Regulations. The vehicle must also pass its annual Department of Transport test, and may be inspected at any time, at any place, with or without passengers on board.

As explained in chapter 9, other PSV operations can no longer object to a proposed **route** in areas where deregulation has come into effect. The Traffic Commissioners may, however, impose conditions in order to prevent severe traffic congestion or danger to other road users, following representations from a local authority.

Road Freight

In the case of road freight, the main objects of concern are the safety of other road users and the effects on the environment. Quality licensing is used to exercise control over road freight carriers. The regulatory bodies which were responsible for economic regulation (before the 1968 Transport Act) – the Licensing Authorities (LAs) – now function solely with respect to quality licensing. Again, the country is divided into Traffic Areas, each with an LA appointed by the Secretary of State for Transport. The underlying principles of regulation are very similar to those for buses and coaches described above.

Road freight vehicles which exceed 3.5 tonnes permissible maximum weight must be run with the authority of an Operator's Licence (C Licence), except in the case of certain exempted vehicles.[10] There are three categories:

(a) The Standard National Licence which is required to carry goods for hire and reward within the UK, that is, where a shipper's freight is carried for commercial gain.
(b) The Standard International Licence to carry goods for hire and reward internationally, as well as in the UK.
(c) The Restricted Licence where the operator only carries goods in connection with his own business. It can be used within the UK and abroad for its intended purpose.

The LA must be satisfied that the applicant can fulfil a number of key criteria, which again include the requirements to be:

(a) 'of good repute'
(b) 'of appropriate financial standing';
and, except in the case of the Restricted Licence, to be
(c) 'professionally competent'.

The competency requirements are equivalent to those for operating buses and coaches. However, there are some road freight operators who possess 'grandfather rights'. People who were in responsible positions in the haulage industry before 1975 were deemed to be competent, and were issued with a certificate of proof.

As with road passenger transport, the LA must ensure that the applicant's arrangements for drivers' hours and records regulations are adequate. Also, that the vehicles are not overloaded. They must also assess the suitability of the operating centre where the vehicles are normally kept. With road freight transport, the list of statutory objectors includes the police authority and local authority, trade unions and trade associations. In addition, since 1984 it has been possible for representations to be made by owners and occupiers of land in the vicinity. Thus, neighbours and residents along the roads used by the operator's vehicles may object on environmental grounds.

If the LA decides to grant an O Licence to the applicant, conditions may be attached. If any environmental objections are considered valid, appropriate conditions might include:

(a)   a limit on the number and class of vehicle at the operating centre;
(b)   restrictions on the times when the operating centre may be used, for example not on Sundays;
(c)   the specification of routes by which vehicles may enter or leave the centre;
(d)   provision for off-street parking and loading/unloading of vehicles.

As with road passenger transport, an aggrieved applicant has the right to appeal.

Quality licensing also regulates:

(a)   the **drivers**, who must have a licence appropriate to the category of Large Goods Vehicle (LGV), and comply with the regulations for drivers' hours and records;
(b)   the **vehicles** which are subject to Constriction on Use Regulations, the annual Department of Transport test, and inspections at the roadside or on the operator's or other premises. Regulations govern important matters of public safety, including the weight, distribution and secure restraint of the load carried. In addition to the general requirements, specific regulations govern the carriage of particular types of freight such as food, livestock, dangerous substances, explosives and radioactive materials.

The environmental problems associated with road freight vehicles – noise, vibration, atmospheric pollution, visual intrusion and so on – have caused a great deal of public concern in the UK and elsewhere.[11] There has been a shift towards the use of larger vehicles, especially since 1983, when the maximum permissible weight limit was raised from 32.5 tonnes to 38 tonnes.[12] This has allowed some operators to consolidate loads and thus to reduce vehicle movements. Nevertheless, the impact of large goods vehicles in residential and other noise-sensitive areas has led some highway authorities to exercise restrictions in order to protect local amenity. Under the Heavy Commercial Vehicles Act 1973 they are empowered to prohibit freight vehicles above a specific weight at specified times (or at all times) by imposing lorry bans. They may also implement other traffic management schemes which affect road freight carriers, including waiting and loading restrictions to reduce congestion or possible danger to other road users.

Conclusion

Quality licensing provides a method of regulating the operational standards of the many road passenger and road freight carriers who use the public highway. The reasons for control, and the aspects of operation so governed, vary according to the type of service: taxis or hire cars; bus and coaches; road freight operations. Nevertheless, the underlying principles and methods are basically the same. In the UK, quality licensing has hitherto been governed by legislation from Parliament, and by directives from the Secretary of State for Transport, who has certain delegated powers to update the standards used. The different standards which have been used in each of the 12 Member States of the European Community are, however, in the process of harmonization – the implementation of common rules and regulations as explained in chapter 14 below. The shift away from economic regulation in the UK and elsewhere has been noted, yet the justification for quality licensing has never been in question. Indeed, the tendency has been to make controls more stringent, in order to reduce accidents, improve competence standards, and lessen damage to the environment.

Notes

1 Colley, B. (1990) 'Looking for Acceptance by all' in *Transport*, May, p. 121.
2 Hibbs, J. (1987) *The Bus and Coach Operator's Handbook*, p. 153: Kogan Page.
3 White, P. (1989) 'Fighting off a Mini Challenge' in *Transport*, January/February, p. 13.
4 Ibid.
5 Such permits apply to purposes which include education and certain non-profit making activities, and to community buses run without profit.
6 If the operator has centres in more than one traffic area, he must apply to the Traffic Commissioners for each one.
7 This is with regard to certain specified criteria – the requirements of good repute, financial standing, compliance with the law, maintenance ability, or professional competence.
8 Faulks, R.W. (1987) *Bus and Coach Operation*, p. 95: Butterworths.
9 The term PCV has replaced PSV with regard to driving licences.
10 Such exemptions include, for example, certain local authority vehicles

such as those used for road cleaning, refuse collection and disposal, agricultural machinery and trailers, road rollers and so on.
11　Chapter 19 discusses the impact of road freight and other modes of transport on the environment.
12　Dearden, S. (1990) 'Road Freight Transport; Social Costs and Market Efficiency' in *Royal Bank of Scotland Review*, December, pp. 28–41.

11

International Regulation: Air Transport

Civil aviation is still a young and expanding industry. Its development has reflected international politics in the twentieth century. This chapter examines the economic regulation which has resulted from the bilateral agreements between governments, and the commercial agreements between airlines. It reviews the process of liberalization on routes between countries whose governments favour a more free market approach. Quality regulation and its effectiveness at national and international level is also examined, with regard to air safety and other standards.

Freedom of the Air?

An important principle was established in 1919, when civil aviation was in its infancy. It was decided, under the Paris Agreement, that every nation has sovereignty over its own airspace. That is, all foreign aircraft require permission to fly over that country and/or land at its aerodromes and airports. Thus, the world's first international scheduled daily commercial service, which started between London and Paris in that same year, required a bilateral agreement by the UK and French governments. The Havana Convention of 1928 reaffirmed the principle of national control over airspace.

Since the government of each country has the ultimate sanction of refusal, there is considerable scope for international bargaining for the privilege of picking up and setting down traffic – passengers, freight and mail. This has resulted in a complex web of reciprocal agreements between pairs of countries, known as **bilaterals** or **Air Service Agreements** (ASAs). Traffic rights are usually traded between countries on a like-for-like basis. Concession is traded for concession. There are also some **multilateral** arrangements between groups of countries.[1]

Each nation generally nominates a 'flag carrier' for a given route. In many cases, this is a State-owned airline, for example, Air France, Air India or Nigeria Airways. In some cases, there is a government-owned airline and one or more independents. For example, Ireland has the State-owned Aer Lingus, and the privately-owned Ryanair. Such airlines have generally gained access to international routes through **multiple designation** – the nomination of two or more airlines by each government in a bilateral agreement.[2] In some cases, all the international airlines registered in a country are privately-owned. For example, American Airlines, Delta Air Lines, United Airlines and others are nominated as flag carriers by the United States on particular routes. And, since the denationalization of British Airways, all UK airlines are in private ownership. Other UK flag carriers include Air UK, British Midland Airways and Virgin Atlantic Airways.

In 1944, an unsuccessful attempt was made to liberalize international air services through multilateral reform. Representatives of the United States government argued the advantages of free market competition. This would allow the following **Five Freedoms**:[3]

1 **Firstly**, the privilege to fly over the territory of another country, without landing.
2 **Secondly**, the privilege to land in another country for non-traffic – that is for technical reasons, e.g. crew change, refuelling.
3 **Thirdly**, the privilege to carry traffic from the country of registry to another country.
4 **Fourthly**, the privilege to carry traffic from another country, back to the country of registry – the opposite direction to the third freedom.
5 **Fifthly**, the privilege to carry traffic between two other countries, provided the flight originates or terminates in the country of registry.

In addition to these Five Freedoms, the expression **Sixth Freedom** is sometimes used to describe the carriage of traffic between two other countries, via the country of origin – the home base of the airline. This arrangement may be used in an international hub-and-spoke system.[4] There is also the privilege of **cabotage** – the carriage of traffic between points within another country.

Whereas the first two Freedoms have been accepted almost universally, the others have been resisted by many governments in order to protect their national flag carriers, particularly with regard to scheduled services. In general, civil aviation has been very tightly regulated through the intergovernmental ASAs, although there have been some notable exceptions in recent times. These have resulted from the co-operation of like-minded governments prepared to liberalize international routes. The political and diplomatic developments which have promoted this pro-free market approach, and the implications for air carriers and their customers, are discussed below.

Charters and Scheduled Services

Air charters are non-scheduled flights which operate according to demand. Thus, an aircraft may be chartered for the exclusive use of a group of passengers or for a consignment of freight. In some cases, an aircraft is chartered jointly by several parties who share the cost, but such consolidation – for passengers or freight – may involve some inconvenience, since the timing and route taken may be a compromise. Light aircraft may be chartered for the convenience of a party of executives on international business. The most spectacular growth of charter operations from the UK, however, has been in the leisure market.

From very small beginnings in the early 1950s it has grown to a point where charter traffic now exceeds that on scheduled services. Such phenomenal expansion has been facilitated by the multilateral agreement covering 'the Rights of Non-Scheduled Services in Europe', signed in 1956. This has allowed a mutual exchange of traffic rights, based on an Inclusive Tour (IT) principle – the charter flight plus accommodation as a minimum requirement. The purchasing, organizational and marketing skills of tour operators such as Thompson have exploited the use of high capacity jet aircraft and inexpensive accommodation, particularly in Spain, to provide low-cost package holidays for a mass market.[5] In more recent years, the IT principle has been relaxed to facilitate a growing number of seat-only charters which now represent a substantial market segment for some charter airlines. These are particularly attractive for customers who wish to travel independently and those with time-share accommodation.

Elsewhere in the world, chartered aircraft carry different types of traffic – for example, religious pilgrimages. In the United States, 'supplemental airlines' have played an important role in carrying troops and equipment to combat zones in times of war. Some countries have had a restrictive policy towards inbound charters, usually to protect their national airlines' scheduled services. In more recent years, however, some have adopted a more liberal approach, particularly in order to encourage the expansion of tourism, where their carriers have insufficient capacity. In the late 1980s there was a substantial growth in long-haul charters from Northern Europe to other continents such as the 'winter sunshine' coastal resorts of Goa in India, Florida, and other destinations in North America.

An international scheduled service operates to a published timetable, as a fixed route. They have generally been far more tightly regulated than charter flights. As a result of intergovernmental negotiation through bilaterals, and commercial agreements between the airlines concerned, economic regulation has often determined all of the following:

(a) **Market entry** – The number of airlines allowed to fly a scheduled service on a particular route is specified through the nomination of flag carriers as described above. The use of particular 'gateway' airports is usually specified.

(b) **Price** – The fares and the freight tariffs charged may also be agreed. There is no possibility of one airline undercutting another on price.[6]

(c) **Frequency/capacity** – The frequency of service established in the schedule and the capacity of the aircraft used may also be agreed so as to limit competition between the airlines concerned. This is known as 'capacity sharing'.

(d) **Pooling** – Under pooling agreements two airlines pool the total revenue collected and share it, generally on a 50:50 basis. Thus, competition between the airlines is completely eliminated.

Until comparatively recent times, the worldwide airline trade association,[7] the **International Air Transport Association** (IATA) played a dominant role in setting fares and tariffs on scheduled services between countries. IATA performs a number of functions which are very useful to airline customers, for example, the through-ticketing system, which allows passengers to make one payment in their own currency for a multi-sector journey on different air carriers. Nevertheless, its role as a cartel, facilitating the negotiation of fares and tariffs through its Traffic Conferences, brought criticism from consumer groups and some pro-free market governments as well as from some airlines which wanted more commercial freedom.

IATA's Traffic Conferences divide up the world into broad geographically-based markets. Each serves as a multilateral forum of airlines, which negotiates in order to agree rates for scheduled services operated by IATA members. These price proposals then require approval from the governments of the countries concerned. IATA's influence was, however, beginning to wane somewhat in the 1970s. Group charters, outside the trade association's sphere of influence, were undercutting IATA rates for some market segments on certain routes. Since IATA membership is voluntary, some international airlines chose not to join, and to set their rates independently. Furthermore, some of IATA's own members were discounting some fares on some routes, especially to compete with non-IATA carriers.[8]

Matters came to a head in 1978, when the United States government's regulatory body, the Civil Aeronautics Board,[9] formally questioned why United States flag carriers participating in IATA's traffic conferences should remain immune from the Anti-Trust laws against restrictive commercial practices. Then, Delta Air Lines and Pan Am resigned from IATA, allowing the carriers greater flexibility in facing a changing competitive environment.[10] Following lengthy international negotiations, IATA eventually responded with a major reform, whereby airlines would henceforth be allowed to opt out of the price-fixing Traffic Conferences if they wished. In other words, such airlines can join the trade association, and not participate in the cartel. Thus, of the 166 Active Members of IATA in 1991, 72 (43 per cent) were non-participants in 'tariff co-ordination'. The latter include airlines such as Cathay Pacific, Malaysian Airlines System, Singapore Airlines and many smaller carriers.[11] As a result of the increased flexibility allowed to airlines, customers are being offered a wider, sometimes bewildering array of fares.

As with deregulation of the local bus market in the UK, discussed in chapter 9, opinion is still divided over the merits of liberalizing international air transport. Again, the reader is urged to consider both points of view. Firstly there are a number of arguments which can be raised in defence of economic regulation:

(a) **Stable prices** – Fares and tariffs remain at an agreed level for a period agreed by the Traffic Conference, in contrast to deregulated markets where prices may fluctuate wildly.

(b) **Regular year-round services** – Governments may use economic regulation to insist upon regular, reliable year-round services. In contrast, liberalized markets may allow airlines to alter schedules, or even abandon routes altogether with little or no notice to the customer.

(c) **Cross-subsidy of thin routes** – As with the former regulation of local bus services in the UK, 'thin' routes – uneconomic air services to remote communities – may be cross-subsidized as feeders by the airlines, provided their more lucrative routes are protected from open competition. Deregulation may result in the loss of some thin routes, and the closure of local airports serving such communities.

(d) **Efficient use of scarce resources** – In many parts of the world, there are serious problems of excess demand for airspace, runways and terminal facilities. Regulated services, avoiding 'wasteful competition', should make better use of infrastructure.[12]

(e) **Anti-competitive behaviour** – Unrestricted competition may lead to predatory pricing, especially by well-financed established carriers wishing to eliminate rivals. Given the resources required to run an international scheduled airline, market entry by a new operator may prove very difficult. After a period of time, take-overs, mergers and strategic alliances between airlines may reduce the choice available to customers, presenting them with an oligopoly of 'megacarriers', dominating global markets. Thus, some controls are necessary to prevent anti-competitive behaviour.

There are, however, some important criticisms of economic regulation of the kind which has prevailed in air transport on many international routes. Those in favour of the free market argue that deregulation would provide a clear incentive for air carriers to reduce prices, and provide a level of service appropriate to their various markets. It should provide the more **competitive, innovative and customer-centred** approach to business, discussed in chapter 4. The pro-deregulationists gained ascendency in the United States in the mid-1970s, setting off a process of liberalization that sent shock waves around the airline world. The debate continues in the 1990s with the measures to create 'freer skies' in Europe – to be discussed in the wider context of the **Single European Market** in chapter 14. The following section introduces some major issues which have been raised by airline deregulation.

Competition and Innovation

In the mid-1970s in the United States, the case for airline deregulation was something of a crusade – pro-consumer, and against the big business cartels of established airlines as well as the bureaucracy of government agencies. As Louis Gialloreto has explained,[13] in 1978 the time was right. Reaching the mid-point of his term of office, President Carter was keen to raise his government's popularity. The creation of an 'open skies' regime for domestic airlines would result in lower fares. New entrant carriers would improve service and offer a variety of different air travel products. This was at a time when inflation was running high and the cost of air travel was increasing faster than the usual pace. Furthermore, there was a need to reduce public spending. Abolition of the Civil Aeronautics Board would receive popular acclaim.

Thus, the **Deregulation Act 1978** ended 40 years of strict quantity licensing. Domestic airlines, provided they satisfied the safety and other quality requirements for being 'fit, willing and able', would be free to enter the market-place. They could establish new routes, and pull out again if they wished. They would be able to charge whatever price they considered commercially appropriate. The dissatisfied customer would have the option of taking his/her custom elsewhere. But, as Gialloreto points out, the issue of which consumers would be getting the lower fares was never quite fully explained to the travelling public. He stresses that in a free market system the only markets where one has to compete on price are those where there are other competitors who are doing the same thing. In many of the smaller US markets, competition did not increase. Deregulation was a signal to some carriers that they could now abandon the less profitable markets.[14]

Nevertheless, the initial results of the bold, unprecedented experiment were encouraging on many of the heavily-trafficked routes. Deregulation was also to allow the entry of new carriers such as People Express, which offered low priced fares on 'no frills' services, employing staff on very flexible conditions of service – a strategy which proved highly successful during the deep economic recession of the early 1980s.[15] Some air fares on trunk routes even dropped below those of rail or express coach operators. Suitably encouraged, the United States government promoted new liberalized agreements with other governments by renegotiating bilateral agreements.

The 'Bermuda II' bilateral between the UK and the United States, signed in 1977, received criticism from free marketeers for being too restrictive. Nevertheless, greater competition on transatlantic services resulted from the opening up of new routes by younger carriers such as British Caledonian and Delta. Furthermore, Laker Airways, a new entrant from the UK, launched the innovative 'Skytrain' concept targeted at budget leisure traffic. Entrepreneur Sir Freddie Laker anticipated that a substantial latent demand for transatlantic travel would materialize – if the price was low enough. Thus, the no-reservation 'walk on' service was introduced, using wide-bodied jets with near-maximum seating and high load factors.

The subsequent collapse of Laker Airways in 1982 was the subject of protracted litigation, but may commentators attributed its financial collapse, at least in part, to the aggressive response of the much larger rival transatlantic airlines which offered heavily discounted fares. Nevertheless, independent competition from the UK side was to re-emerge with the launch of Richard Branson's Virgin Atlantic Airways, described in chapter 5. Furthermore, the United States reached relatively liberal agreements, with certain other European governments such as Holland.

During the 1980s, the development of **Computer Reservation Systems** (CRS) demonstrated the significance of capital investment in information technology as a competitive weapon. CRS provide real time information – continuously updating details of flight times, seat availability and fares. CRS began before 1978 but deregulation accentuated its importance – given the minute-by-minute changes in price, printed fare tables were no longer appropriate. Furthermore, CRS terminals installed in travel agencies and other retail outlets provided airlines with powerful tool, enabling them to penetrate the market geographically.

Between 1976 and 1986 the number of ticket agency locations in the United States more than doubled from 12,000 to at least 25,000. The proportion of airline tickets sold through agents grew from about 40 per cent to nearly 85 per cent.[16] The use of CRS became a controversial issue, since it seemed to give a big advantage to the large carriers which could invest in such systems. Initially each of the five CRS displayed flights operated by its airline owner more prominently than those of its competitors. This practice was subsequently prohibited, but not everyone is convinced that today's CRS are fair to some of the smaller airlines.[17] American Airlines' pioneering CRS – SABRE – is the largest privately-owned, real-time computer system in the world. Yet, Robert Crandall, the airline's Chairman, has strongly refuted criticism that it has given them an unfair advantage, commenting that the creation of CRS 'was a business response to the need for an efficient distribution mechanism for a rapidly growing industry'.[18]

Deregulation in the United States led airlines to develop, **hub-and-spoke** systems. These are based on the same principles as the express parcel systems, such as TNT, described in chapter 6. The essential difference is that passengers in transit have more demanding requirements than parcels! Nevertheless the logistics are basically the same. Thus, a pair of locations, A and B, are connected by routes resembling the spokes of a wheel, via a central hub, C. Large carriers such as American Airlines developed very big domestic hub airports, feeding passenger traffic between dozens of city pairs. With regard to **costs**, if can be argued that the additional expenses associated with extra take-offs, landings and facilities for passenger interchange are more than offset by savings achieved by using larger aircraft with high load factors and centralizing operations. From a **marketing** point of view, the inconvenience for passengers of changing aeroplanes and loss of direct flights is generally outweighed by a more frequent service and scope for lower fares on some routes. Furthermore, the inbound/outbound flights are synchronized, so as to minimize waiting time at the hub.[19]

This increasing use of hub-and-spoke and the commercial desirability of synchronizing 'waves' of scheduled flights has, however, exacerbated problems of congestion at peak times. Excess demand for infrastructure at major airports has inevitably caused delays, causing frustration to passengers and the airlines themselves. Particular problems of increased flight delays occurred at the large hubs such as Newark and Chicago O'Hare.[20] The capacity constraints have also created difficulties for new entrants to the market, unable to get suitable slots for departures. The response of established airlines has been to demand more infrastructure provision by the government – air traffic control, terminals and runways. Thus Robert Crandall has argued that much of the complaining one hears about deregulation is a consequence of the lack of capacity and the need for slot allocation. The best way to solve the problem is not to create even more rules, but to provide the necessary facilities so there is enough room for everyone who wants to compete.[21]

Deregulation in the United States has also raised the important issue of the **consolidation of the airline industry** into a few very large carriers. While some carriers such as American Airlines chose a strategy which emphasized internally-generated growth, others did so by mergers and acquisitions.[22] As Donald Pickrell has shown, there was a flurry of growth in the number of competitors in the early 1980s to 19 carriers on national or important regional routes, nearly double that before deregulation. Yet by 1988 only 10 survived.[23] In the adverse climate of the early 1990s, even Pan Am succumbed and filed for bankruptcy. Bailey Morris concluded, 'the results of US airline deregulation have been the opposite of what was expected: a few big sharks have gobbled up all the small fish . . . it is feared that the price advantage will disappear as a few dominant airlines push through fare increases and cut back service to smaller cities'.[24]

The experience of deregulation in the United States – the biggest airline market in the world – has considerable relevance for international services, as liberalization gathers momentum on important routes in various parts of the world, particularly in Europe. The use of CRS becomes increasingly significant in gaining access to international markets. Airports throughout the world are developing and marketing their facilities as international hubs. There are also fears of a global airline oligopoly. An aviation conference held by the Chartered Institute of Transport posed the question: 'Can airline competition survive the 1990s?' In reply, transport consultant Ray Colegate commented that competition 'is by its very nature self-extinguishing because the ambition of the players is to put their competitors out of business'. The European Community has established rules to protect customers, and to prevent large suppliers dominating their markets – 'as traditional forms of regulation that have applied to airlines are progressively dismantled, these wider principles of fair competition become increasingly relevant to them'.[25]

Quality Regulation

Given the international nature of civil aviation, as a mode of transport, it is appropriate and necessary to standardize safety and other aspects of quality regulation on a global basis. Anticipating the huge growth in air transport after the Second World War, the **International Civil Aviation Organisation** (ICAO) was set up in 1947 as an intergovernmental agency to perform this co-ordinating role. Its aim is to develop the principles and practices of international air navigation and to foster the planning and development of international air transport. Thus, it has supervised the safe and orderly growth of civil air transport, worldwide. In recognition of the importance of its role, ICAO has been given the status of an agency of the United Nations.

The objectives of ICAO[26] are to promote international civil aviation through the development of airports, airways, and air navigation facilities; to promote safety; to develop techniques for international air navigation; and to ensure that the rights of member countries are fully respected so that every member country has a fair opportunity to operate international air carriage. Its structure is democratic. Over 140 nations belong to ICAO, and all are represented on its governing body – the **Assembly**, – which meets at least every three years. This in turn elects the **Council** with representatives of 30 countries, to supervise ICAO's activities between meetings of the Assembly. Much of the work of the organization is necessarily of a highly technical nature, and is carried out by its specialist Committees who report back to the Council.[27]

ICAO establishes detailed specifications for standards and procedures, but it is not an enforcement agency. Thus, as Edmund Gubbins comments, its effectiveness depends on the willingness of the nations of the world to make concessions and work together to reach agreement. ICAO recommendations must be translated into legislation by each member country in order for them to become effective.[28] ICAO has also been much involved in the United Nations' Development Programme, where it has assisted less developed countries to set up air services, infrastructure, and their own regulatory agencies.[29]

In the UK, the regulatory body is the **Civil Aviation Authority**. Established in its present form under the Civil Aviation Act 1971, it is a multi-purpose agency, with a wide range of responsibilities. As set out in its mission statement,[30] the CAA's primary purpose is to maintain and where possible improve existing standards of safety'. Thus, it will:

(a) provide and manage a safe air traffic control system in the UK;
(b) set standards for and monitor the airworthiness and operational safety of all UK-registered aircraft;

(c)   ensure the maintenance of high levels of safety in:
 (i) the operation of UK aerodromes;
 (ii) the licensing of UK aircrew, air traffic controllers and maintenance engineers;
 (iii) the UK design, manufacture or overhaul of aircraft, engines
  and equipment.[31]

The Civil Aviation Authority is both a public service enterprise
and a regulatory body. Its responsibilities include:[32]

(a)   The National Air Traffic Services, both air traffic control and telecommunications, in conjunction with the Ministry of Defence.
(b)   The economic regulation of the civil aviation industry, including air
transport licensing, the licensing of air travel organisers and the
approval of air fares and certain airport charges.
(c)   Air safety, both airworthiness and operational safety, including the
licensing of flight crew, aircraft engineers and aerodromes, and the
certification of UK airlines and aircraft.
(d)   Advice to the Government on civil aviation matters, both domestic
and international.
(e)   Consumer interest; private aviation requirements; economic and
scientific research; the collection and publication of economic and
scientific data; and consultancy and training for overseas adminis-
trations.
(f)   The CAA also owns a subsidiary company, Highlands and Islands
Airports Ltd, which operates eight aerodromes in Scotland.

The Chairman and Board of the CAA are appointed by the
Secretary of State for Transport. Its duties are set out in legislation.
Nevertheless, the CAA is constitutionally independent of government, and its 7,400 staff are not civil servants. Furthermore, it
is financially independent – it does not receive subsidy from the
taxpayer. The philosophy behind this is that the cost of providing
essential services to civil aviation ought to be paid for by the user
(in the main the air traveller) and not by the general public, many
of whom do not use air transport.[33] The CAA will oversee the major
developments in air transport anticipated for the 1990s – growth
in air traffic and technological progress in aircraft and infrastructure, such as Air Traffic Control systems.

The airlines of the world will also continue to play their role in
maintaining and raising standards through their trade association.
IATA's constitution includes the important aim: 'to co-operate with

the International Civil Aviation Organisation and other international organizations'. In practice, IATA and ICAO liaise closely on a number of key issues, for example – air safety, security and combating terrorism and protection of the environment. With regard to the latter, IATA has recently set up an Environmental Task Force (ETAF) to 'co-ordinate activities in this field, identify measures to reduce pollution, develop common industry positions, and provide information on the industry's contribution to environmental quality and protection.'[34]

On the issue of aircraft noise, IATA recognizes the reasons why governments wish to introduce more stringent regulations. In its annual report for 1990 IATA comments that the airline industry has strongly advocated that such measures should 'only be introduced on a co-ordinated world-wide basis through ICAO'.[35] This is greatly preferable to the piecemeal adoption of different noise regulations in different regions and countries, which makes fleet planning by airlines extremely difficult. Nevertheless, it should be borne in mind that the interests of the two organizations are not identical. Essentially, ICAO is an organization of the world's **governments**, whereas IATA is an organization of international **airlines** and, like any other trade association, must promote and defend the interests of its members.[36]

Conclusions

International air transport has developed in a tightly regulated environment. For many years, economic regulation has been closely controlled by intergovernmental bilaterals and commercial agreements between airlines – with prices negotiated and fixed through the Traffic Conferences of the International Air Transport Association. Since the late 1970s, however, there has been much more flexibility and commercial freedom on some important international routes. Within the European Community in the 1990s, there will be 'freer skies' for airlines of member states – an important development to be discussed in chapter 14. Quality standards are regulated within a worldwide framework, established by the International Civil Aviation Organisation, translated into laws and rules by governments, and enforced by the agencies of individual countries.

Notes

1   As in the 'third package' agreement between European Community Members States discussed in chapter 14.
2   Multiple designation may be route-specific, or relate to a pair of countries. In some cases a specified number of airlines may be designated, whereas in others any number is allowed.
3   This was agreed at the Chicago Convention of 1944.
4   See explanation of hub-and-spoke systems in chapter 6.
5   See discussion of Inclusive Tours in transport and tourism in chapter 7.
6   As explained below, fares and tariffs are negotiated through the Traffic Conferences of IATA, and then submitted to the relevant governments for approval. Under the 'double approval' system, both governments have to approve before a price change can come into effect. Thus one government, unwilling to allow its national flag carrier's prices to be undercut by a foreign airline, can exercise its power of veto.
7   See general discussion on trade associations in chapter 18.
8   See Stephenson, F.J. (1987) *Transportation USA*, p. 442: Addison Wesley.
9   The Civil Aeronautics Board was eventually wound up in 1984. Its remaining duties being transferred to the Department of Transportation.
10   Stephenson F.J., op. cit. p. 442.
11   From IATA membership table, in *IATA Review* (1991), no. 3, p. 6.
12   See discussion of congestion and air transport in chapter 20.
13   Gialloreto, L. (1988) *Strategic Airline Management: The Global War Begins*, pp. 19–20.
14   Ibid. pp. 20–21.
15   When the economy picked up, however, the strategy proved less appropriate and People Express was absorbed by the Texas Air Group, after experiencing severe financial difficulties.
16   Pickrell, D. (1991) 'The Regulation and Deregulation of US Airlines' in Button (ed) *Airline Deregulation*, p. 23: MacMillan.
17   Ibid. p. 14.
18   Crandall, R. (1991) 'Crandall: Industry Outlook Gloomy' Interview by Kimberley Smeathers in *IATA Review*, No. 3, pp. 5–6.
19   Pickrell, D., op. cit. pp. 10–12.
20   Stephenson, F.J. (1987), op. cit. p. 376, see also discussion of airport congestion in chapter 20.
21   Crandall, R., op. cit. p. 5.
22   Gialloreto, L., op. cit. p. 41.
23   Pickrell, D., op. cit. p. 17.

24 Morris, B. (1992) 'Competition Leaves US Airlines on Critical List' in *The Independent on Sunday*, 13 January.
25 Chartered Institute of Transport (1991) 'The Ins and Outs of Competition' in *Transport*, January/February, p. 19.
26 Taneja, N.K. (1976) *The Commercial Airline Industry*, pp. 280–1: Lexington.
27 See Gubbins, E. (1988) *Managing Transport Operations*, pp. 145–6.
28 Ibid.
29 Bell, G., Bowen, P. and Fawcett, P. (1984) *The Business of Transport*, p. 296.
30 Civil Aviation Authority (1991) *Safe Journey: The Work of Britain's Civil Aviation Authority*, CAA document No. 535.
31 Ibid.
32 Ibid. p. 2.
33 Ibid. pp. 5–6.
34 International Air Transport Association (1990) *Annual Report*, p. 13.
35 Ibid. p. 14.
36 See discussion of the role and function of trade associations in chapter 18.

12

International Regulation: Sea Transport

In contrast to civil aviation, discussed in the previous chapter, merchant shipping is a very ancient mode of transport. It has inherited many trading practices from previous centuries. Nevertheless, technological and commercial developments since the Second World War have transformed it. This chapter reviews the various forms of economic regulation which have developed, and their relevance for international sea transport today. The various forms of quality regulation are also examined. The effectiveness of the latter in setting common standards for the merchant fleets of different nations is assessed.

Tramps, Tankers, Dry Bulk and Liners

Tramps are freight vessels which sail neither to a fixed schedule nor to a fixed route. Thus a tramp may be hired or chartered, usually to carry a dry bulk cargo such as coal, phosphates, grain, wool or ores such as bauxite and alumina. Traditionally they have been versatile, multi-purpose ships. Ease of market entry has allowed a large number of small firms as well as larger companies to operate them.

Freight rates are negotiable. They vary according to the availability of supply – the number of other tramp vessels and other transport – and the strength of demand at the time. It should be noted that the demand to carry these commodities may show strong seasonal peaks and troughs in different parts of the world. The demand pattern may also reflect upturns and downturns in the industries which consume these raw materials.

The market for tramp shipping has therefore shown many of the characteristics of the economic ideal of 'perfect competition'. It has followed the free market model, requiring the operator to develop a sound, market-oriented approach to business as outlined in chapter 4. There are still many tramp vessels, owned and operated by individuals and family firms. In recent years, a trend towards larger tramp vessels has encouraged mergers in order to raise the necessary finance. There has also been a trend towards longer-term charters of five to ten years' duration.[1]

Since the Second World War, however, the transport of bulk freight by sea has been revolutionized by the development of very large, specialized vessels. These include **tankers** which carry bulk liquids – oil, Liquified Petroleum Gas (LPG) and other fluids. The development of **supertankers**, in the 1950s, brought considerable economies of scale, both in construction and in operational costs – especially in crews and fuel. Similarly, very large **dry bulk** vessels carry ores, grain, coal and other solids. Both tankers and dry bulk vessels also save labour costs through highly mechanized systems for handling and discharging their cargoes. In sharp contrast to the classic tramp shipping described above, the huge capital investment required for these very large vessels clearly limits market entry.

Liners operate to a fixed schedule of sailings between ports, on a fixed route. They may carry general cargo, – mixed freight sent by numerous shippers on the same vessel. They may also carry semi-bulk cargo – commodities such as flour, sugar, cotton in bags, bales and so on, where a single consignment may take up a considerable part of the hold. Liner shipping developed in the nineteenth century, when the new steamships began to offer more reliable sailing times.[2] Then, as now, liner operation generally required a fleet, rather than a single vessel. It also needed shore facilities and administrative offices.

Ocean-going passenger liners used to be the only mode of intercontinental travel. But, with the development of reliable long-haul air services in the mid-twentieth century, they continued only for luxury cruises. Passenger ferry lines are important, however, in waters such as the English Channel, the Irish Sea, the Baltic and other short sea crossings.[3] **Roll-on/Roll-off** (Ro/Ro) ferries not only carry passengers, but also private cars and/or 'wheeled freight' loaded on trucks. Articulated vehicles have particular flexibility, since they may be sent either accompanied, with a driver and

Plate 12.1   P & O container ship and transhipment operation, courtesy of P & O

tractor unit as well as the semi-trailer, or else unaccompanied, where the semi-trailer goes alone, to be picked up by another driver and tractor unit at the destination ferry port.

Deep sea liner services have been transformed by **unitization** – assembling cargo into standard loads, which can be handled ship to shore by mechanical means. In particular **containerization**, discussed in chapter 6, facilitates inter-modal freight transport by road, rail and sea. The system was commercially pioneered by American entrepreneur Malcolm McLean, whose Sea Land company began in 1956. It was later adopted worldwide under the specifications of the International Standards Office – as ISO containers. At container ports such as Felixstowe,[4] the boxes, loaded with many types of cargo, can be lifted on and off the cellular container vessels with speed and efficiency.

Since the 1960s, an increasing amount of liner traffic has been containerized, rather than being shipped as loose cargo on 'break bulk' vessels. The major advantages of containerization are:

(a) greatly reduced loading/unloading time at ports;
(b) similar gains in speed and labour cost for other transhipment between modes;
(c) reduction in 'shrinkage' through pilfering;
(d) less packaging required to protect cargo from damage;
(e) lower insurance rates, because of the better security and physical protection in handling and transit;
(f) simpler documentation;
(g) freight can be consolidated and sealed by customs at Inland Clearance Depots (ICDs), away from congested ports.

Containerization has, however, required very large-scale capital investment in cellular vessels, as well as in the seaports and other infrastructure such as road-rail transhipment depots. As with the development of tankers and dry bulk vessels, economies of scale have been gained by constructing and operating container ships of great size. The carrying capacity of cellular vessels is measured in Twenty-foot Equivalent Units (TEUs) – a standard unit of length for container boxes. Typical vessels built in the late 1960s had a capacity of about 1,500 TEUs. In the 1990s, there are vessels of 3,000 TEUs or even more. Recent years have also seen the development of giant liner vessels which may take a combination of different cargo types, including containers, bulk liquid, dry bulk, break bulk and deep sea Ro/Ro. From the beginning, the acquisition of container ships stretched the finances of even the largest of the world's shipping lines, which have often formed consortia.

Liner Conferences Versus Independents

Since the 1870s, shipping lines have combined to establish cartels, known as shipping 'Conferences'. These are specific to certain routes or **trades**. At first sight, the existence of such Conferences may seem to be against the interest of the customer, the freight shipper, and therefore the consumer of goods carried. A Conference will certainly blunt competition between its members, and in some cases Conferences have had a dominant position over the trade. Nevertheless, the power of such cartels is curbed by a number of important checks, not least of which is the presence of shipping lines known as 'independents', which remain outside the Conference and may compete for their share of the market. Thus the shippers have a choice.

Conferences have ranged from loose agreements to highly formalized structures, with permanent secretariats. The scope of such agreements also varies, but may cover some or all of the following:

(a) **Price** – The freight rates for particular commodities (or passenger fares/vehicle tariffs in the case of ferries), may be fixed. In other words, Conference members agree to charge a uniform price, rather than trying to undercut one another.
(b) **Frequency/capacity** – In an attempt to reduce excess tonnage on a particular trade – too many vessels chasing too little traffic – the Conference determines the total number of sailings to be made by its members. It may then apportion them between the various company lines. The Conference may also specify the capacity of the vessels to be used. Thus, there is an attempt to even up demand and supply – a form of economic regulation by private enterprise.
(c) **Pooling** – In some Conferences, the traffic carried and revenue earned may be pooled and shared out between members on a negotiated formula. In some cases the costs are also shared. Sometimes the Conference will make an overall loss. This can occur during a tariff war between the Conference and independent lines. At such times the loss can also be pooled – a tactic which could be considered anti-competitive, depending on the relative power of Conference and independent lines.

How then have liner Conferences retained the loyalty of freight shippers and discouraged them from using independents? A traditional method is called the **deferred rebate** – where a shipper may claim a rebate (usually 10 per cent) if he has exclusively used the Conference lines during a specified period (usually six months). This money will generally be paid after a further six months, only if he continues in his loyal use of the Conference. A second method, known as the **dual rates** system, offers the shipper an immediate discount (usually $9\frac{1}{2}$ per cent), under a contract agreement (usually one year), subject to three months' notice of termination by either party.[5] Negotiation between individual shippers and Conference lines can involve a great deal of hard bargaining. The former enhance their negotiating strength by organizing themselves into user bodies known as **shippers' councils**.[6]

The Conference system is not without its advantages to the customer. It has provided a certain measure of regulation in a potentially volatile and uncertain market for international sea transport. In particular, it offers:

(a) **Stable rates** – The Conference lines guarantee that freight tariffs will not fluctuate wildly. At least rates will not go above a specified level for the period of the Conference agreement. This enables the shipper to quote a delivered price to overseas customers with confidence, and to budget more accurately.

(b) **Regular sailings** – The Conference lines guarantee to work a schedule – sailings in accordance with a published timetable between particular ports. These will operate regardless of any sudden fall in demand. This enables a shipper to plan and schedule his export consignments with the certainty of regular, year-round sailings.

Aggressive rate wars may nevertheless take place between a Conference and independent lines. Predatory pricing is often used as a weapon, the intention being to force the rival side into submission. Douglas Blackstock[7] has described the rivalry which took place in the early 1960s, when the UK/North Continent – East Africa Conference was faced with fierce competition from two Eastern European independents: DSR and POL. The Conference lowered its rates to match those quoted by the two State-subsidized lines. The latter were, however, able to withstand this retaliatory action and managed to secure valuable backloads of tea and coffee. Finally, the Conference had to negotiate terms. The outcome was that DSR and POL were admitted as Conference members.

In another example,[8] Sea Land left the Trans-Pacific Conference in the early 1980s, when profits had been reduced to an unacceptable level by independent lines. Sea Land was the largest container operator in the world, yet it had less than 10 per cent of the market share of the important Trans-Pacific trade. Numerous shipping lines, many with strong national ties, competed for a limited volume of traffic: 'Sea Land's strategy was to cut prices below Conference levels, and meet the competition head-on'.[9] As a result, Sea Land regained market share, weakened many of the rival independents, and forced the Trans-Pacific Conference to allow its members greater flexibility over pricing.

In general, Conferences have not been affected by government intervention. But trades which enter United States ports are a notable exception. Elsewhere, Conferences are 'closed' in that shipping lines have no automatic right to join. The United States has declared such an exclusive arrangement illegal,[10] requiring them to be open, – membership must be available to any line who wishes to join. There is also a **Liner Code**, concerning the allocation of traffic between countries under the United Nations Conference on Trade and Development (UNCTAD). This has been interpreted to mean that Conference traffic should be distributed on the following basis:

(a)   40 per cent to each of the two countries where mutual trade is carried on Conference ships;
(b)   a considerable part, e.g. 20 per cent, to third country liner companies (if any).

Known as the '40:40:20 Rule', opinion is still divided concerning its practicality.[11]

The Conference system originated as a desperate response by shipping lines to problems of oversupply on particular routes. Over a hundred years ago, John Squire, founder of the China Conference (now known as the Far Eastern Freight Conference) explained its rationale: 'We are trying to work a combination for the China Freight trade so that P & O, MM, OSS, Glens and Castles may not ruin each other.' Commenting on a court case which threatened the legality of liner Conferences, Squires said that if the decision went against them, shipping owners had better 'sell out as there is no use in continuing in business if the law decides we must cut each others' throats and ruin ourselves'.[12] Cartels are, by definition, **anti-competitive**. Yet, the degree to which Conferences blunt competition between their members varies according to the nature of the agreement. Pooling agreements can be highly restrictive. But, many Conferences, whilst agreeing uniform rates and fixing schedules and capacity, allow competition between member lines on quality of service – in particular speed and reliability of arrival time. Furthermore, there is always some outside competition from independent lines, and in some cases, from other modes of transport, such as 'land bridges' and 'sea-air' freighting services, discussed below.

Thus it can be argued that conferences have allowed the **orderly expansion** of international shipping, and created the right conditions for **investment** in new tonnage, especially during the container revolution in the late 1960s and early 1970s. As Sir Kerry St Johnson has concluded:

Any Conference ought to be a force for stability and to provide, if you like, a series of benchmarks against which standards of performance and competitiveness can be judged. Remove that force for stability and remove those benchmarks, and one can foresee the

introduction of immediate elements of confusion and hints of uncertainty, as much in the minds of shippers as amongst the lines
themselves.[13]

Competition and Innovation

Nevertheless, a number of innovations and developments in the
1970s and 1980s brought shippers wider choice and affected
Conferences on well-established trades. As intermediaries between
the shippers (customers) and transport principals (operators),
freight forwarders have played an important role in this process
of change. These are agencies which organize the through transport of shippers' consignments. They are therefore skilled, not only
at managing the complexities of inter-modal transport, but also
the documentation including customs clearance, insurance, and
increasingly the use of information technology.

Forwarders are able to take advantage of discounted tariffs for
consolidated freight which may be offered by transport principals.
Yet, as far as international shipping is concerned, their function is
to obtain the best service for their shippers in terms of **quality and
value for money**. They therefore owe no loyalty to any particular
line or Conference, or even to sea transport as a mode. In the short
to medium term, forwarders may make tactical decisions such as
the routing of freight to avoid congestion at a particular port, or
to avoid a zone affected by war or natural disaster. In the longer
term they may make strategic decisions such as the service, or
mode, which best suits the needs of a particular type of shipper.

One example of forwarders exercising such strategic choice was
the decision to send certain types of container traffic all the way
across Europe and Asia using the **Trans-Siberian Land Bridge**. In
response to relatively high freighting costs by sea for traffic between
Western Europe and the Far East, forwarders took advantage of
low rates offered by the State-subsidized railways which reflected
the former Soviet authorities' desire to earn foreign currency.

An even more dramatic development of the 1980s was the
establishment and rapid expansion of express **Round The World**
(RTW) shipping lines. As outsiders, they have presented a dramatic
challenge to Conferences, notably to the Far Eastern Freight Conference, which had previously enjoyed a very large share of the
trade. Partly in response to the rapid growth of exports from the

newly-industrialized countries of the Pacific Rim, container services were established, setting a new trend. As the term RTW suggests, their routes circumnavigate the world, via the Suez and Panama Canals, rather than following the routes of established trades. RTW is particularly associated with two shipping companies from Taiwan – Evergreen and Yang Ming, but shippers and forwarders can now use a range of RTW services offered by lines from various countries.

The main features of RTW services are that they:

(a) make only a **limited number of calls**, picking up and setting down containers at only a few ports per continent;
(b) tend to use **very large vessels** which can only be accommodated at deep water ports with appropriate handling equipment;
(c) require fast turn-round in physical handling as well as processing of documentation;
(d) negotiate **port dues** aggressively, so as to ensure value for money;
(e) need **good transport connections** for inward/outward movement of containers on **long feeder services**, using a variety of modes – smaller ships for coastal and short-sea feeders, inland waterways such as the Rhine system, railways such as British Rail's Freightliner services and road trailers.

The cost-effectiveness of RTW enabled these shipping lines to quote rates substantially lower than those of established Conferences. Furthermore, they were able to prove a satisfactory record of regular, reliable sailings comparable with those of Conferences. A number of forwarders therefore chose to use their services. Nevertheless, the Far Eastern Freight Conference fought back. Gillian Gutman of Freight Forwarding Journal reported: 'Conference lines, far from being the pushover that was assumed two years ago, marketed aggressively, matching rate for rate with the outsiders, while still maintaining enviable frequency.'[14] This intensive competition has inevitably led to excess capacity, and some believe that some accommodation or agreement between RTWs and Conferences will follow.

Another innovation of the 1980s was the establishment and expansion of 'sea-air' freight services. These have been developed by specialist companies and forwarders such as MSAS, ASG and Livingstone Freight.[15] Offering a lower cost alternative to pure airfreighting, such services provide greater speed than pure seafreighting, sometimes avoiding congested seaports. One such service called 'Australasia Express' was set up in 1987 to ship containerized cargo by sea from Felixstowe to Singapore, and then onward by air to over 30 Far East and Pacific Rim destinations, with rates some 35 per cent below pure airfreight tariffs.[16]

Quality Regulation

For over two centuries, a form of quality regulation has been exercised by **Classification Societies**. Originating as a service to owners and insurers of merchant vessels, they continue to oversee the construction and maintenance of ships classed in their name. Lloyd's Register of Shipping, the oldest Classification Society, provides a worldwide network of qualified naval architects and surveyors, with a wealth of knowledge and expertise. Thus, they carry out periodic inspections of hulls, boilers, engines and other equipment, in accordance with their rules and standards. Classification Societies have helped to raise and maintain quality in the building and operation of ships. Yet, the system is essentially independent of nation states, and not directly concerned with the wider aspects of quality regulation which are controlled by government legislation.

There is an important international agency which establishes quality standards for the merchant fleets throughout the world – The **International Maritime Organisation** (IMO), functions as an agency of the United Nations, dealing with maritime matters and essentially serving as a consultative and advisory body.[17] It was set up in 1948 in recognition of the need for international action to improve **safety** at sea, co-ordinated and promoted by a permanent body. Its role was subsequently expanded to include the prevention of **marine pollution**. The IMO is based in London with a Secretariat of international civil servants headed by a Secretary General. Its structure is very similar to that of ICAO, described in chapter 11. Nearly 130 nations belong to the IMO as members or associates. Its governing body, the Assembly, elects an executive, the Council, which has 32 representatives. Again, much of the work is carried out by IMO's various committees. The Maritime Safety Committee (MSC) is its most senior, and has a number of sub-committees concerned with matters such as safety of navigation, radio communications, life-saving appliances and so on. The Marine Environment Protection Committee (MEPC) is responsible for co-ordinating activities in the prevention and control of pollution from ships.

In order to achieve its objective, the IMO adopts Conventions which are mandatory. It also adopts Codes and Recommendations which are not binding, but which may be carried through into the legislation, and regulations, of member countries. The Convention on 'Safety of Life at Sea' (SOLAS) covers a wide range of issues designed to improve the safety of shipping. Another important convention for the 'Prevention of Pollution at Sea' (MARPOL) deals with pollution by oil, chemicals, refuse, sewage and other harmful substances.

As with ICAO, discussed in chapter 11, the effectiveness of the IMO depends on the willingness and ability of individual countries to legislate and enforce the standards established through the international Conventions and recommendations. Ships registered under the UK flag are subject to the Merchant Shipping Acts and vigorously inspected and monitored with regard to safety and other matters through the Department of Transport's Marine Division. In order to qualify for UK registration, a ship must be owned by a company incorporated under British law.[18]

The Marine Division thus enforces standards which have been established through the framework of Merchant Shipping law, for ships registered in the UK. The standards include:

(a)   all aspects of safety;
(b)   accommodation of crew;
(c)   competence and qualifications of Merchant Navy officers;
(d)   manning levels;
(e)   prevention of environmental pollution at sea.

The Marine Division also investigates accidents and carries out checks on both foreign and UK-registered ships. In this latter capacity, it now pools information with other European maritime countries.

Particular problems arise in international shipping, however, through the existence of 'flags of convenience'. Liberia, Panama and certain other nations do not require ships to be owned in those countries in order to qualify for registry. Some have very substantial tonnage, since they enable foreign owners to escape the more stringent controls which would apply if they registered ships in their own country. They may escape restrictions which would otherwise add to their costs. For example, United States flag ships must be crewed by United States citizens, and repaired in United States shipyards, or else be subject to duties on the cost of repairs in foreign shipyards.[19]

Conclusions

Historically, shipping developed from free market conditions, with little or no intervention from governments. From the late nineteenth century, liner Conferences provided a form of voluntary self-regulation through cartel agreements, but these have always faced competition from independent lines and sometimes from other forms of transport. Conferences now face an unprecedented level of external competition on a number of important trades, particularly through the development of Round The World shipping services. Quality regulation also began on a voluntary basis, through Classification Societies. Today, the International Maritime Organisation seeks worldwide standards for safety and anti-pollution measures, but its usefulness is undermined where governments fail to enforce them, and where shipping lines register under flags of convenience.

Notes

1 Branch, A. (1981) *Elements of Shipping* Fifth Edition, p. 43: Chapman and Hall.
2 Chrzanowski, I. (1985) *An Introduction to Shipping Economics*, p. 25: Fairplay.
3 See discussion of the development and marketing of Sealink Stena Ferries in chapter 4.
4 See discussion of containerized handling at the Port of Felixstowe in chapter 6.
5 Chrzanowski, I., op. cit. p. 91.
6 See discussion of shippers' councils and the Freight Transport Association in chapter 17.
7 Blackstock, D. (1985) 'The Conference System v Independent Lines – A Freight Forwarder's View' in *Freight Forwarding*, November, p. 56.
8 Stephenson, F. (1987) *Transportation USA*, p. 239.
9 Ibid.

10   Under the 1984 Shipping Act.
11   Beth, H.L., Hader, A. and Kappel, R. (1984) *25 Years of World Shipping*, p. 181: Fairplay.
12   Jennings, E. (1979) *Cargoes: A Century of the Far Eastern Freight Conference*, pp. 21–2: Meridian Communications.
13   St Johnson, Sir K. (1989) 'Conferences can be Competitive' in *Freight Forwarding*, May.
14   Gutman, G. (1987) 'Slicing up the Far East Cake' in *Freight Forwarding*, May, p. 27.
15   MacLeod, M. (1989) 'Orient Express, Market Spotlight Far East' in *Freight Forwarding*, May, p. 24.
16   Gutman, G., op. cit. p. 30.
17   Gubbins, E. (1988) *Managing Transport Operations*, p. 155.
18   Ibid, p. 152.
19   Stephenson, F.J., op. cit. p. 241.

Part IV

Government

13

Central Government

Transport plays an important part in the life of any nation. Central government may therefore intervene in various ways to influence the pattern of transport infrastructure and operations. Nevertheless, governments differ greatly in their approach. In the UK and some other countries, there has been a shift away from direct intervention towards *laissez-faire*, allowing much greater scope for the free play of market forces. This chapter outlines these important changes in the role of the State.

The Free Market Versus State Intervention

In a pure **free-market** system, the means of production, distribution and exchange would all be in private hands. Entrepreneurs would provide the essential driving force for the economy, bringing together capital, labour and land to establish transport and other businesses, as described in chapter 2. Prices would be allowed to find their 'natural' level, these being regulated by the interplay of supply and demand. The eighteenth century economist Adam Smith explained these principles in his famous book *The Wealth of Nations*.[1] The **effective** demand for any commodity is defined as that which purchasers are actually able or willing to pay for it. This is distinguished from **absolute** demand – a need or desire to acquire it. Interestingly enough, Adam Smith used a contemporary transport example to illustrate this point. He commented that a 'very poor man may be said in some sense to have a demand for a coach and six; he might like to have it; but the demand is not an effectual demand, as the commodity can never be brought to market in order to satisfy it'.[2]

At the opposite extreme, in a **planned** or **command** system, the 'commanding heights of the economy' are vested in the State. In the People's Republic of China, for example, resources are centrally allocated to sectors of the economy and regions of the country. Five- and ten-year plans set out the programme of priorities for transport and other key industries. Most transport is under direct Ministerial control, and prices are determined by the State planning agency. For example, a manager working for a State bus or urban railway undertaking has output targets, but little discretion with regard to revenue and costs. The fares are generally kept low. Indeed, they are sometimes almost free to the customer at point of sale. Furthermore, the manager must pay fixed wages and purchase vehicles, spares, fuel and so on at fixed prices.

In most countries, however, there is a **mixed economy**, which combines private enterprise and public intervention. Some transport is owned and run by the private sector, some by the State. There may also be some quantity licensing in particular modes of transport,[3] and public subsidy where the government's economic, social and environmental objectives cannot be satisfied by the free market. In the UK, during the period 1945–79, changes of government brought changes of emphasis and degree, yet both Labour and Conservative governments accepted the principles of a mixed economy. Neither questioned the premiss that national assets such as airlines, railways and other public utilities such as gas, electricity and water should remain in the public sector. Nor did they dispute that major infrastructure projects, such as the Channel Tunnel, international airports, motorways and railways should be financed and run by the State.

Rolling Back the State

In 1979, the election of a pro-free market Conservative government committed to 'rolling back the frontiers of the State' heralded a very different era – a sudden break with the 'postwar consensus'. It is accepted that 'some activities of government must always be provided in the public sector.[4] Nevertheless, **privatization** (see table 13.1), has occurred on a dramatic scale. The sale of transport undertakings has been part of a larger programme which, by 1992, had privatized two-thirds of the businesses once owned by the State, employing in total about 900,000 people. It has also provided a significant source of income for the Treasury.

Table 13.1 UK privatization programme of major transport undertakings

Undertaking	Year	Method
Hoverspeed (formerly Seaspeed hovercraft operation of British Rail)	1981	Private sale to Hover Lloyd (subsequently sold to Sea Containers)
NFC (formerly National Freight Corporation)	1982	Management and staff buy-out
Associated British Ports (formerly British Transport Docks Board)	1983–4	Public share issue
Sealink (formerly ferry operations of British Rail)	1984	Private sale to Sea Containers, (subsequently sold to Stena Line)
National Bus Company	1986–8	Sale of over 70 local subsidiaries, management buy-outs or private sales
British Airways	1987	Public share issue
BAA (formerly British Airports Authority)	1987	Public share issue
British Rail Engineering	1989	Sale to management-led consortium
Scottish Bus Group	1990–1	Sale of subsidiaries as with National Bus Company
London Buses	1992–	Sale of the London Buses subsidiaries, beginning with London Coaches Ltd
British Rail	1993–	Piecemeal, gradual sell-off starting with freight, and franchising arrangements for passenger services

Source: Transport, June 1986.[5] Adapted by the author.

'Setting the economy free' through **deregulation** of transport and other sectors has been the second major theme. It is accepted that 'some regulations may have been adopted in answer to legitimate concerns, but without proper regard to their overall impact on businesses and individuals. A proper balance needs to be struck between essential protection for the public, and over-zealous and intrusive controls aimed at the elimination of all conceivable risk.'[6] Thus, the liberalization of transport markets should encourage competition between operators, and choice for the customer – the passenger or freight shipper. It is argued that deregulation restores a 'contestable' market.

The third major theme has been the Conservative government's aim of **reducing the public sector's share of national income**. 'We believe that government should not gobble up all the proceeds of growth, and that those who create prosperity should enjoy it, through lower taxes and more opportunity to build on personal wealth'.[7] Reductions in the level of income tax have already been made, and the objective is to reduce the basic rate to 20 pence in the pound. The government is keen to stress that this does not necessarily mean a reduction in public expenditure. For example, capital expenditure on motorways, trunk roads and railways was raised in the early 1990s.[8] Nevertheless, operating subsidies have generally been brought down, and in some cases eliminated altogether. The process of privatizing British Airways, for example, turned a State-subsidized industry into a profitable enterprise, albeit with substantial debts written off by the government. Governments of some other countries which once had a strong commitment to the public sector have followed the UK's example, and are at various stages of reducing State intervention in transport. Notable examples are Australia and New Zealand.

In recent years, there have been examples of very large-scale schemes where private finance has been invested in public infrastructure. These include the Queen Elizabeth Bridge across the River Thames at Dartford in East London, which was wholly financed by a private consortium. The latter designed, built, and now operate it as a toll bridge. They will continue to do so for 20 years, which will provide an acceptable payback period, before it is returned to the public sector. A similar arrangement is sought for two further projects – a second crossing of the River Severn, and a new relief road to the north of Birmingham.[9] The proposed fast rail link to London Heathrow airport will be 80 per cent funded by the privately-owned Heathrow Airport Limited. As David Robinson has commented, the 'key to attracting private capital is to set these infrastructure schemes up in such a way that investors can see that the financial returns are judged sufficient to cover the risks.'[10] This philosophy is not confined to the UK – Europe's biggest transport project, the Anglo-French Channel Tunnel, has been funded without subsidy from either government. In Holland, private capital is being sought for a freight railway line into Germany, and the German government has approved, in principle, a massive programme of privately-funded motorway construction.[11]

Safeguarding the Customer

Some transport undertakings in the UK will remain in public ownership, for the time being, at least. In 1991, Prime Minister John Major introduced a special programme intended to help safeguard the customers' interests in transport and other sectors where there is a monopoly or near-monopoly. Known as the **Citizen's Charter** initiative, it 'addresses the needs of those who use public services, extends people's rights, requires services to set clear standards, and to tell the public how those standards are met'.[12]

Rail users already receive some degree of consumer protection through the official user bodies – the Transport Users' Consultative Committees.[13] Nevertheless, British Rail and London Underground have been required to produce their respective Passenger's Charters. British Rail's charter sets out service standards, including punctuality and reliability objectives. These vary between different types of service and different routes, to reflect the age and condition of the equipment. British Rail pledge with regard to Network SouthEast commuter services: 'if we fail by more than a small margin to meet our punctuality and reliability standards, you will be entitled to a discount when you renew your monthly or longer period season ticket'.[14] With regard to freight transport, the Royal Mail have also prepared a Citizen's Charter statement.[15]

Supporters of free market principles believe that liberalization of the economy is the best way to ensure that suppliers respond to effective demand. Nevertheless, it is generally accepted that some safeguards are needed to ensure that competition between suppliers is fair, and to protect the customers against a commercial monopoly, near-monopoly or cartel. Such controls are particularly necessary where privatized utilities have a dominant position in the market. Thus telecommunications, gas and water companies are subject to specialized **regulators** (OFTEL, OFGAS and OFWAT respectively). Likewise, the privatization and restructuring of British Rail will be accompanied by the creation of rail regulator.[16]

Privatization of the bus industry did not result in the establishment of an equivalent 'bus regulator'. Nevertheless, the 1985 Transport Act has brought them within the remit of the **Restrictive Practices legislation**, administered through the Office of Fair Trading (OFT) – a government department set up under the 1973 Fair Trading Act to protect consumer interests. The Director General of Fair Trading has responsibility for encouraging fair competition throughout the UK economy: 'because lack of competition in business may be against the public interest, the Director General has a duty to keep a watch on monopolies, mergers, and trade practices in the UK which may be restrictive or anti-competitive. In some instances the issue can be referred to the Monopolies and Mergers Commission for deeper investigation.'[17]

As in other industries, proposed agreements between bus operators must be placed on the Register of Restrictive Trading Agreements. The OFT may then advise the removal of any significant restrictions to fair trade. If, however, bus operators get together in secret, in order to draw up anti-competitive agreements and fail to register them, action may then be taken through the Restrictive Practices Court. The Director General has, indeed, followed this procedure against particular pairs of bus operators who fix fares and timetables on shared routes, and who agree **not** to compete on other routes. It can be argued that much prima facie evidence exists for many other such 'understandings' between operators. Nevertheless, the task of tracing them and proving that they exist may be beyond the capabilities of the OFT with its limited number of staff.[18]

Action has also been taken against bus operators for predatory behaviour – reducing fares and running extra buses with the deliberate intention of forcing a competitor to withdraw. The question of predation does however, pose some difficulties, since deregulation is supposed to encourage competition on price and service. At what point, then, does aggressive competition become predatory? The Director General has commented that the line between desirable competitive behaviour and predatory behaviour is sometimes hard to draw.[19]

Another important issue is the emergence of several, very large-scale operators. Just one year after privatization had been completed, one-third of the 72 former National Bus Company subsidiaries were controlled by just four large holding groups.[20] Some takeovers have been referred to the Monopolies and Mergers Commission, and some specific conditions have been imposed. For example, the purchase of Bristol City Line by Badgerline Holdings resulted in separate tendering for Avon County Council contracts by the two subsidiaries. Nevertheless, such moves have not been blocked.[21]

Criticism has thus been raised concerning the controls to promote fair competition. More fundamentally, some have also questioned the very logic of applying such legislation to the bus industry. Alan Townsin[22] comments that agreements between operators have existed since the earliest days and that the effects were not necessarily harmful to the customer. Joint operation made sense, for example, where two operators had a garage at either end of a route. A bus started out from each base for the first morning journey and returned there with the last evening journey. Thus, they would 'simply continue all day running "opposite" each other, passing at the mid-point, giving passengers an even headway'. Townsin contrasts this approach with that which has often resulted from the 1985 Transport Act:

> If operators are expected to think of competition in terms of 'attacking' the opposition, then the obvious way to do it is to run just in front and hence one gets the ludicrous situation . . . where three buses an hour leave Sheffield for Leeds but all three depart within a ten-minute period. Which of the two principles is better tuned to the public interest?[23]

Alternative Policies for Transport

The opposition parties in the UK have rejected the Conservative government's *laissez-faire* approach to transport. **Labour**, the party which originally nationalized the railways and other key transport undertakings, has opposed the policies of 'rolling back the State' discussed above. Nevertheless, it accepts that competition for the supply of some transport would benefit consumers, if properly regulated and controlled – especially through State franchising authorities. The remaining State undertakings would also be freed from the restrictions which have denied them access to private capital, for example by allowing British Rail to lease rolling stock. The overall emphasis is on a comprehensive, planned approach. The Labour Party has outlined its alternative policies for transport:

> We will transform transport policy by ensuring, for the first time, that all road, railway, aviation, shipping and inland waterways projects are judged on the basis of their environmental, social and economic impact . . . . We will end the deregulation of buses, introduce bus priority measures integrated with new rapid transit systems within a 'green light' programme designed to encourage people to transfer to public transport.[24]

Labour's interventionist approach, tempered by the 'new realism' of the 1990s, is illustrated by the party's strategy for the railways, prepared in advance of the government's privatization White Paper. As part of wider proposals for regional government, Labour would establish Regional Transport Authorities with powers to franchise rail operations. This would reduce the role of central government to the setting of general objectives covering financial, commercial, quality, social, employment, environmental and safety aspects. The existing rail business such as InterCity would continue to own their own rolling stock, traction and some station facilities. They would be expected to collaborate closely with each other and with other public and private businesses.[25]

A State track authority would provide the infrastructure and control train movement, thereby promoting efficiency and a 'level playing field' for controlled access to the permanent way. This approach would also allow investment in road and rail to be assessed on the same basis, using criteria to evaluate environmental benefits, safety, community impact, and potential for economic regeneration. Unlike the Conservatives, Labour envisage a track authority that would receive public subsidy, because of the wider benefits of encouraging passengers and freight to use rail.

The **Liberal Democrats** embrace an interventionist approach, with an emphasis on making transport clean and efficient, on conserving energy and on tackling congestion. The 1992 Liberal Democrat Election Manifesto announced: 'By expanding the provision and quality of public transport and reducing dependence on the private car, we will improve travel efficiency and protect the environment.'[26] Their policies include investment in public transport, increasing its frequency of service, speed and safety, and reducing its cost to the individual, 'especially in isolated rural areas where need is greatest'. Light Rapid Transit and other schemes will be encouraged in urban areas. The party also promises immediate improvements to the rail network, including a commitment to construct a high-speed link from the Channel Tunnel to connect with the major rail routes to the North and West, as well as an extension of electrification. Like Labour, the Liberal Democrats oppose the privatization of British Rail, but support access for private operators to the network, while giving British Rail the freedom to raise investment capital on the open market.[27]

The **Scottish Nationalist Party** and **Plaid Cymru** also favour intervention in the wider context of self-government for Scotland and Wales within the European Community. As independent countries they would need to build and upgrade international links. These would include airports and air services, direct high-speed rail links to the Channel Tunnel, seaports and ferry services.[28] There would also be investment to bring about a reorientation of internal transport and communications to develop national unity.

It has been stressed that private capital has been mobilized for the development of projects which were formerly funded by the public sector. Thus new airports and even motorways and railways are being financed commercially. Nevertheless, the location of transport terminals and the routing of ways often raise a complex set of problems and issues which must be resolved by central government. The political leaders of the country must give due consideration to the advice of the various Civil Service departments and national agencies. The views of many different interest groups must be sought. In theory, the government should evaluate the alternatives and strike an appropriate balance, arriving at a rational decision based on an objective appraisal of the costs and benefits.

State Intervention and National Infrastructure

The opposition parties have offered alternative policies. Nevertheless, the general election of 1992 brought the Conservatives a fourth term of office, with a commitment to completing the transition to a market-led economy. As a result, central government has become less involved with the funding and co-ordination of transport operators. Carriers are given a loose rein to exercise their commercial judgement in providing transport services. The role of the State therefore focuses on quality licensing and other forms of **non-economic regulation**, discussed in part III. The State must also exercise controls to **safeguard the customer**, as outlined above. There is another important area where the influence of central government remains strong – decisions concerning the **provision of national infrastructure**.

The development of an international airport illustrates both the theory and the practice of decision-making. Firstly, the general policy framework for **major airports** in the UK has been fairly consistent in the postwar era, and there is still a considerable degree of political consensus. Nick Lewis[29] has summarized central government's principal planning-related objectives:

(a) To foster a strong and competitive British airline industry by providing enough airport capacity where it is needed.
(b) To minimize the impacts of airports on the environment generally, and to ensure that land-use planning and conservation policies take fully into account both the development needs arising from airports and environmental consequences.
(c) To ensure that all UK airports continue to maintain the highest standards of safety in accordance with internationally accepted rules and standards.

The question of where new or expanded airports should be located has, however, proved more difficult to resolve!

Some locational issues relate to airspace and aircraft movements:

(a) Account must be taken of the safety and efficiency of civil and military aircraft movements. Responsibility for air traffic planning and management rests with National Air Traffic Services – an organization which is jointly operated by the Civil Aviation Authority[30] and the Ministry of Defence.
(b) Defence considerations may also be significant. A large international airport may well affect military establishments which have special airspace requirements. Firing ranges may have danger areas reaching to a height of 15,000 feet or more.[31] This necessitates an input from the Ministry of Defence guided by the North Atlantic Treaty Organisation.
(c) Any proposal to build a new airport, or expand an existing one, will raise the issue of aircraft noise.[32] With regard to operational factors

including runway alignment, departure routes, and the forecast number/type of aircraft, an assessment must be made of the areas and communities which will be affected. Responsibility for issues relating to aircraft noise rests with the Department of Transport, in consultation with the Department of the Environment and local authorities.

Other locational issues relate to development on the ground:

(a) Airports cannot be too remote from the urban markets they serve. Surface access is therefore an important issue. Motorways and trunk roads are the responsibility of the Department of Transport, but local authorities are responsible for other roads which are likely to be affected by the increased traffic. As roads become more congested, attention focuses on rail access. British Rail and urban metro operators therefore become involved in the planning process.

(b) Airports generate employment, both inside and outside their boundaries. Account must be taken of the scale and type of labour required as airports develop. They can help revitalize regional economies where unemployment is high. The UK lacks a statutory framework for regional planning, but such issues are of considerable importance to local authorities, and their forums such as The London and South East Regional Planning Conference (SERPLAN) which advise the Department of the Environment.

(c) Account must also be taken of the actual physical development on the ground – how and where the airport can be built. Due regard must be given to policies of restraint such as Green Belts and National Parks. But airports inevitably change the character of an area. Local authorities make their views known, since they have powers and duties under planning legislation, and represent local communities. Nevertheless, 'national interest' may override local considerations. Planning Inquiries into proposals for major airports are chaired by an independent Inspector who reports back to the Department of the Environment and the Department of Transport. The final decision to permit or refuse rests, however, with the government of the day.

The history of the search for a suitable site for London's Third Airport suggests that the decision-making process is far from rational. Back in 1961 an Inter-Departmental Committee of the Civil Service was appointed to consider the requirements for a Third London Airport and, after evaluating 18 sites, recommended Stansted. Central government accepted this advice in 1964, but local objections led to a Public Inquiry, and the Inspector's report recommended against the proposal.[33] After a great deal of debate inside and outside Parliament, a Royal Commission (Roskill), several changes of government, the proposal and rejection of further sites, the wheel turned full circle. In 1980, on the invitation of central government, the British Airports Authority (now BAA plc) submitted an outline planning application to develop Stansted. After a record 258-day Public Inquiry in 1982–3, approval was given and work finally began in 1986. In his summary of overall conclusions, the Inquiry's Inspector Graham Eyre QC made the following comment: 'The history and development of airports policy on the part of administration after administration of whatever political colour has been characterised by ad hoc expediency, unacceptable and ill-judged procedures, ineptness, vacillation, uncertainty and ill-advised and precipitate judgements.'[34] The uncertainty over future provision of air infrastructure continues with the search for an additional runway in South-East England.

Conclusion

Central government policy for transport underwent a fundamental and comprehensive revision after 1979, when a pro-free market Conservative government abruptly ended a period of over 30 years during which the State had played a dominant role in transport and other sectors. Privatization, deregulation and a reduction in the public sector's share of national income have radically changed the environment in which transport operators conduct their business. The role of the State has shifted towards non-economic regulation, and controls to ensure 'fair play' between commercial operators, and thus to protect the interests of passengers and freight shippers. Some infrastructure projects of national significance are now being financed wholly or in part by the private sector. Nevertheless, central government will continue to exercise its judgement concerning the actual location or route of such schemes.

Notes

1   Smith, A. (1776) *The Wealth of Nations*, p. 158 (1986 edition): Penguin.
2   Ibid. p. 159.

3 See discussion of quantity licensing in road transport in chapter 9.
4 The Conservative Manifesto (1992) *The Best Future for Britain*, p. 9.
5 Adapted from Robertson, J. (1986) 'The Challenge of Change' in *Transport*, June, p. 115.
6 Ibid. p. 10.
7 Ibid. p. 6.
8 Ibid. p. 35.
9 Robinson, D. (1992) 'Major Opportunities for Private Finance' in *Transport*, January/February, p. 13.
10 Ibid. p. 13.
11 Ibid. p. 12.
12 The Conservative Manifesto, op. cit. p. 13.
13 See discussion of Transport Users' Consultative Committees in chapter 17.
14 British Rail Board (1992) *The British Rail Passenger's Charter*, p. 5.
15 The Post Office (1992) *Putting the Customer First*.
16 HMSO (1992) *New Opportunities for the Railways: The Privatisation of British Rail* Cmnd 2012.
17 HMSO (undated) *Office of Fair Trading: Working For You* pamphlet published by OFT.
18 Townsin, A. (1989) 'Is the Office of Fair Trading Unfair?' in *Coaching Journal*, February, p. 13.
19 Office of Fair Trading (1989) *Beeline*, November 89/3.
20 Robinson, D. (1989) 'Where will it all End?' in *Transport*, September, p. 198.
21 Yearsley, I. (1990) 'Much Change and Fixed Fortunes?' in *Transport*, July/August, p. 180.
22 Townsin, A. (1989) op. cit. p. 12.
23 Ibid.
24 Labour's Election Manifesto (1992) *It's Time to Get Britain Working Again*, p. 22.
25 Salveson, P. (1992) 'A Labour Rail Strategy' in *Modern Railways*, April, pp. 187–189, also in *Travel Sickness: The Need for a Sustainable British Transport Policy*: published April 1992 by Lawrence and Wishart.
26 The Liberal Democrat Manifesto (1992) *Changing Britain For Good*, p. 28.
27 Ibid.
28 Plaid Cymru (1992) *Tuag at 2000*, p. 19: Election Manifesto.
29 Lewis, N. (1990) 'Airport Planning – What is it?' in *The Planner*, 24 August, p. 13.
30 See explanation of the role of the Civil Aviation Authority in chapter 11.
31 Department of Trade (1979) *Report of the Study Group on South East Airports*, p. 18.

32   See discussion of the measurement of aircraft noise in chapter 19.
33   Department of Trade, op. cit. p. 2.
34   Department of the Environment and Department of Transport, *The Airport Inquiries 1981–3 – Extracts from the Report of the Inspector Graham Eyre QC*, p. 9.

14

Europe and the Single Market

The governments of the UK and the other 11 Member States of the European Community (EC), are co-operating to dismantle the internal barriers to trade. This will allow the free movement of people, goods, services and capital. Clearly, such aims have important implications for transport. This chapter reviews the progress which is being made towards a Common Transport Policy, focusing on the examples of road haulage and air passenger transport.

A Common Transport Policy?

When the Treaty of Rome was signed in 1957, the founders envisaged a truly united Europe. The Treaty attached considerable significance to transport and its role in promoting European integration, devoting a whole chapter to the subject. Yet, for nearly 30 years, the Member States were generally unwilling to co-operate in order to achieve a Common Transport Policy. In theory, the EC recognized that the 'Single European Market' (SEM) could never be achieved without a fair and workable system to facilitate the intended 'free movement'. In practice, however, transport within Europe was fragmented. Member States each shielded their national carriers from all 'foreign' competitors. Furthermore, there was a general lack of standardization of vehicle hardware, practices and procedures, particularly in road transport.

Indeed, progress had been so slow that in 1984 the European Parliament (the EC's directly elected assembly) started legal action against the Council of Ministers (the transport ministers of the 12 Member States), for failing to implement the transport objectives of the Treaty. The Court of European Justice (the EC's judiciary) upheld the case. From the mid-1980s there was, therefore, renewed pressure to work towards a Common Transport Policy.[1]

The **Single European Act** reaffirmed the objectives of the Treaty of Rome, and set out the reforms which would be necessary to make these concrete. It was signed by all Member States in 1986. The Act deals with many aspects of public policy, but contains three fundamental principles which have direct relevance to transport. These are: the removal of internal frontiers, liberalization and harmonization.

(a) Removal of internal frontiers
The aim is to create a trading area without internal frontiers, covering the whole of the EC. Until completion of the SEM, the customs authorities of each Member State carried out checks at their national frontiers, controlling movements from other EC States as well as non-EC States. Many of these checks could have been carried out elsewhere but the borders have been convenient control points. They include checks on:

(i)   compliance with national indirect taxation, e.g. duty on spirits and value added tax (VAT);
(ii)   plant and animal health and measures to combat drug smuggling, terrorism, the spread of dangerous diseases, illegal immigration etc.

Not all these frontier controls were abolished on the deadline of 31 December 1992, but the reforms bring far-reaching changes to lift the physical and fiscal barriers between EC states. As the Confederation of British Industry and TNT Express have commented: 'The objectives of the proposals will be to speed up the movement of goods across borders, allow carriers and transport users to schedule vehicles and predict transit times accordingly. The effect of this faster movement will be to create a more efficient transport industry.'[2]

(b) Liberalization
Liberalization aims to promote free competition between transport carriers of all Member States. In other words, this should eventually bring about deregulation on an international scale within the EC. Carriers will be allowed to transport people and goods:

(i)   from other Member States back to their own;
(ii) between other Member States;
(iii) within other Member States.

These rights have generally been denied to foreign operators through protectionist transport policies, such as permits and quotas. Each Member State has generally given preference, sometimes a monopoly, of trade to its own carriers.

The restrictions on free movement have created an inherent inefficiency in transport within the EC. For example, UK hauliers taking exports to Germany have been denied backloads on their return trips. At the same time, German hauliers taking exports to the UK have faced similar restrictions in taking goods in the opposite direction. It is anticipated that the elimination of such unprofitable empty running, together with the spur of open competition, should lower fares/tariffs and raise the quality of service to customers of passenger and freight transport.

(c) Harmonization

Harmonization aims to create a 'level playing field' within the EC. It is recognized that the benefits of (a) and (b) could be negated if 'invisible' barriers remained. Different rates of vehicle excise duty, for example, would give an unfair cost advantage to carriers from States with low duty. And different technical standards could be used by some states as a form of 'back door' protectionism to benefit their own carriers. It is also recognized that economies of scale could be gained if, for example, new buses and coaches were built to common specifications and railway operators were to use compatible traction equipment and signalling systems.

Common policy is therefore important to harmonize a number of critical aspects of transport operation:

(i)   fiscal policy, e.g. vehicle excise duty, fuel tax, motorway tolls;
(ii) subsidy, e.g. State support to seaports and airlines;
(iii) standards and regulations, e.g. vehicle weights and dimensions, drivers' hours and noise standards.

The following sections review progress towards these aims in two modes: road haulage and air passenger transport.

Example of Road Haulage

Road transport is the dominant mode for freight within and between EC countries. Furthermore, hire and reward (as opposed to own account) operators now carry over 80 per cent of goods moved by road between Member States. Liberalization and harmonization of EC haulage should therefore play an important role in improving the efficiency and quality of physical distribution for manufacturers and retailers. As Brian Colley of the Road Haulage Association has commented, international lorry movements have been 'controlled by a cumbersome and restrictive permit system'.[3]

This was based upon bilateral permits, which allowed operators to carry loads from one country to another. Thus, pairs of States exchanged an agreed number of permits each year. These were then distributed to hauliers undertaking international work in the country concerned. There were also a limited number of multilateral, Community-wide permits which authorized their holders to undertake unlimited international journeys within the EC.

The permit system was completely at odds with the Treaty of Rome. Inherently wasteful of resources, it undoubtedly added to the distribution costs of freight carried across national boundaries within the EC. Yet, for many years, proposals to dismantle it were strongly resisted by some Member States. After much negotiation, an agreement was eventually reached by the Council of Ministers. In 1988 it was resolved that the permit allocation would gradually be **liberalized**. This would lead to complete **abolition** of the permit system by 1993.

Thus, the liberalization of haulage between EC States has been carried through in accordance with the agreed timescale. In contrast, the extension of **cabotage** rights to hauliers of other EC countries has made only modest progress. In the context of haulage, cabotage means the right of a haulier registered in one country to carry domestic traffic in another. The UK government favours a fully liberalized regime for cabotage. Nevertheless, there is opposition to such proposals from some UK hauliers who consider such competition to be unfair. David Lowe and others have stressed the opposite point of view:

> These bodies in purveying such doom, fail to acknowledge the fact that while foreign hauliers will be able to come to Britain and steal

business from under the noses of local hauliers, our hauliers will just as easily be able to cross the Channel and appropriate domestic transport work in Europe, hitherto considered to be the exclusive domain of the local haulage fraternity.[4]

It is recognised that competition within a liberalized Single Market cannot be fair without **harmonization**. Standards for maximum vehicle weights and dimensions have shown considerable variation between Member States. Common standards for vehicles operating on international routes were agreed for implementation by 1993, with one exception. The governments of the UK and Ireland have been granted derogation (an extended period) to introduce the EC weight limit, having argued that time is needed to strengthen bridges to accommodate the heavier weights. At the end of 1998, however, we must increase the weight limit to 40 tonnes for five- and six-axle trucks, increased to 44 tonnes if working on Combined Mode operations. At present the UK limit for the largest articulated vehicles is 38 tonnes.

There are considerable differences in the level of taxation and duties. The French, for example 'operate low vehicle excise duty systems but impose road tolls, while UK operators pay 14 times more vehicle excise duty than the Italians'.[5] Harmonization of vehicle taxation will be phased in. The long-term proposals have not yet been agreed, but there is a general aim of pooling resources into a central EC road fund, which would be redistributed to Member States in proportion to the use of their roads by road freight operators. Duty on diesel fuel will also be harmonized. The European Commission has proposed a standard level of fuel oil tax, based on a weighted average.

Quality licensing will be based on a common EC standard. The basic requirements will be similar to the UK O Licensing system discussed in chapter 10: professional hauliers must be of good repute, of appropriate financial standing and professionally competent. Drivers' hours regulations have also been harmonized. Nevertheless, there are disparities in the action which is taken in different Member States where infringements occur. In the UK, the driver may face a heavy fine and suspension of his LGV Licence. Furthermore, the operator may also be fined and may even lose his O Licence. Elsewhere the penalties can be less severe. A uniform approach to all these aspects of road haulage is necessary to ensure fairness. The remaining anomalies must be eliminated to allow all EC hauliers to compete on the same footing, with similar cost structures and the same safety and other technical standards.

Example of Air Passenger Transport

The demand for passenger transport between European cities is expected to increase substantially as trading and cultural ties become closer. Fast rail links will provide an alternative mode on some routes, but it is anticipated that, in general, air traffic will continue to grow. During the 1980s some frequent fliers drew unfavourable comparisons between the highly regulated intra-European services and their counterparts in North America. As outlined in chapter 11, deregulation in the United States had brought benefits with regard to price and service quality on those routes where airlines were competing for market share.

Liberalization of scheduled air services within the EC was, however, disappointingly slow until the mid-1980s. Whereas air charters for Inclusive Tours (package holidays) had been allowed to develop under free market conditions, scheduled services were subject to restrictive quantity licensing. Bilateral Air Service Agreements generally eliminated price competition, ensured that capacity sharing was on a strictly 50:50 basis and limited market entry to State-owned flag carriers. Many of the latter received subsidy from their governments, yet there was little evidence that this benefited the average customer.

Some Member States were, however, prepared to encourage moves towards the creation of a more competitive commercial environment. By the late 1980s, liberal bilaterals had been agreed between the UK, Holland, Ireland and, to a lesser extent, Belgium. Furthermore, efforts are now being made towards the goal of 'freer skies' throughout the EC. Nevertheless, the European Commission and Council of Ministers is aware of the shortcomings, as well as the successes of full-scale deregulation. Experience in the United States helped to inform and guide policy in the EC. Furthermore, the financial difficulties of airlines throughout the world in the early 1990s created an unfavourable climate.

Two packages of economic liberalization in 1987 and 1990 brought only marginal benefits from the consumer's point of view. A third package agreed in 1992, however, is far-reaching in its scope. It has the potential to encourage much greater competition on intra-European routes, and thus to widen choice for air passengers. In essence, EC airlines will:

(a) have the freedom to set their own fares;
(b) be able to fly between any airports in the Community;
(c) be free to operate domestic services within another Member State.

The poor financial performance of many airlines, combined with the high operating costs in Europe mean, however, that dramatic price reductions are unlikely. As Betts and Gardner have commented 'the notion that deregulation will send fares crashing in Europe could not be more misleading'.[6] Furthermore, there are important safeguards. A proposed fare can be filed one day and applied the next. At any time, however, the regulatory authority from either end of the route may object that the fare is either **unreasonably high** with regard to the airline's costs, or else so **unreasonably low** as to be deemed predatory. Thus, 'much will depend on the speed of the EC arbitration process in the event that one country decides to veto an air fare'.[7]

Capacity sharing between airlines was relaxed from 1987 and finally abolished in 1993. With regard to **market entry**, the opportunities for Member States to designate more than one airline to fly a given route were progressively increased to allow multiple designation. Finally, uniform licensing criteria were adopted under the 1992 agreement. The way has therefore been paved for airlines to take up the 'Fifth Freedom' rights discussed in chapter 11 – that is the right to carry traffic between two other Member States. Cabotage, the right to carry traffic between points within another Member State, is being implemented more slowly. From 1993 to 1997 airlines will be allowed to fill up to 50 per cent of the seats on a given flight in this way – that is, to take on passengers on a foreign stopover. This will lead to full liberalization of cabotage in April 1997.

The process of creating freer skies within the SEM is well advanced. It is fully appreciated, however, that some controls are necessary to guard against the misuse of freedom, especially by large, well financed carriers. Since the early 1990s, amendments to EC legislation have allowed the European Commission to take swift action to prevent one airline using anti-competitive tactics against another. These controls are based on the principle of 'cease and desist'. Furthermore, the Commission has kept a watchful eye on proposed mergers, interlocking share arrangements and strategic alliances. It is still uncertain, however, if EC airlines will be allowed to join forces in some way to compete in global markets. Such a strategy would enable them to improve their effectiveness against the much larger American carriers. Nevertheless, it could reduce the amount of real competition within Europe, and thus undermine the essential principles of EC-wide liberalization.

With regard to the principle of harmonization, there is already a high level of conformity concerning equipment and practices on a worldwide basis, through the International Civil Aviation Organisation (ICAO).[8] With regard to Air Traffic Control, Member States are now co-operating to make more efficient use of airspace through a unified 'Eurocontrol' system. With regard to financial support to national airlines, there have been considerable anomalies. Whereas British Airways is now a privately-owned commercial airline, receiving no financial help from the UK government, other flag carriers such as Spain's Iberia have received substantial State assistance.[9] In principle, at least, State aid is prohibited under Article 92 of the Treaty of Rome, except in special circumstances. In order to ensure fair competition current subsidies to national airlines should therefore be ended. The following case study assesses the prospects for Greece's national airline in the freer skies of the European Community.

Case study: Olympic Airways

Olympic Airways now faces a difficult transition from State-owned, subsidized flag carrier in a highly regulated environment to self-sufficient airline in a competitive market. Until 1991, the airline was directly accountable to the Minister of Transport and was regarded primarily as a public utility. Since the early 1990s, however, Greece's pro-free market government has loosened these ties and has stated its intention to sell 49 per cent of the equity of Olympic Airways to the private sector.

By European standards, Olympic is a medium-sized airline. It has 34 aircraft for its international services:

- 4 × Boeing 747s
- 2 × Airbus A300–600s
- 8 × Airbus A300s

- 11 × Boeing 737s
- 3 × Boeing 727s
- 6 × Boeing 737–400s

There are plans to acquire a further ten aircraft during the mid-1990s. This fleet operates over an extensive network, including long-haul routes to America, Africa, Asia and Australia, and short-medium-haul routes to other European destinations and the Near/Middle East. The domestic operation of Olympic Airways provides scheduled services to and between the Greek Islands, with Athens as the hub.

The international services have been of benefit to Greek businesses, to public administration, and to foreign trade. Some routes, particularly those to Northern Europe, have assisted the development of tourism – a key sector of the national economy. It should be stressed, however, that scheduled services carry less than one-third of this holiday traffic – Greek government policy has allowed foreign charters to attain a dominant position. The domestic services provide a speedy alternative to transport by ferry for Greek nationals and for foreign tourists alike.

Hitherto, most of Olympic's routes have been tightly regulated. Liberalization within the EC has ended this protective regime, and other EC airlines will be free to compete on routes to and from Greece. By the same token, the Greek national airline will have the opportunity to operate new scheduled services, for example from regional airports in Northern Europe directly into Greek destinations. The domestic services, for the time being, enjoy protection, but these too may eventually face competition, when cabotage rights are offered to foreign carriers.

In 1992 Olympic Charters was set up as a wholly-owned affiliate of the parent airline. This should provide scope to expand into the holiday charter market. Nevertheless, inbound tourism to Greece is highly seasonal. This creates difficulty with the utilization of aircraft and other resources. Imaginative marketing initiatives, such as off-season short breaks in Athens, should offset this a little. In general, Olympic's scheduled services have carried a relatively small proportion of high-yield business traffic. Recent successes with the introduction of a premium Olympian Executive Class service suggest that there may be opportunities for growth on certain routes.

Although its fleet is relatively modern, there is a need to acquire the latest high-capacity, fuel-efficient aircraft in order to compete effectively. Olympic also needs to acquire information technology to develop Computerized Reservation Systems and other airline administration. There is an urgent need for infrastructure renewal to relieve capacity constraints and to upgrade facilities at Athens. The proposal to construct a new airport by 1997 is therefore welcome news to Olympic Airways. The airline's cost structure has suffered from relatively high staffing levels, though the establishment is now being reduced through a policy of non-replacement as employees leave or retire. It plans to reduce the workforce by 5 per cent per annum during the mid-1990s.

In summary, Olympic Airways is likely to experience some daunting challenges in its established markets. Competition may come from other European flag carriers, including British Airways, which is now in private ownership and has a fleet over seven times the size of Olympic. Challenges may also come from independent scheduled carriers and from charter airlines which may decide to diversify and operate scheduled services. Nevertheless, the relaxation of State control, the proposed injection of private capital, and the more liberalized environment, will present exciting opportunities for innovation and development.

Conclusion

The creation of a Single Market without internal frontiers represents a significant landmark in progress towards the unification of Europe for trading purposes. The fundamental aim of 'free movement' between Member States will be achieved through the principles of liberalization and harmonization of passenger and freight transport operation. It is anticipated that these measures will further stimulate traffic growth, creating new opportunities for transport operators and benefits for consumers. Nevertheless, the case of air passenger transport suggests that firm checks and controls are sometimes necessary to ensure that the new-found freedoms are not misused by large and well-financed operators.

Notes

1   Owen, R. and Dynes (1990) *The Times Guide to 1992: Britain in a Europe without Frontiers, a Comprehensive Handbook*, pp. 164–5: Times Books.

2   Confederation of British Industry and TNT Express (1990) *Transport and Distribution*, p. 7: CBI.
3   Colley, B. (1990) 'Looking for Acceptance by All' in *Transport*, May, pp. 117–121.
4   Lowe, D. (1989) *The Transport and Distribution Manager's Guide to 1992*, p. 58: Kogan Page.
5   Confederation of British Industry and TNT Express, op. cit. pp. 26–7.
6   Betts, P. and Gardner, D. (1992) 'Clouds over Open Skies' in *The Financial Times*, 24 June, p. 14.
7   Ibid.
8   See discussion on quality licensing and ICAO in chapter 11.
9   See Burns, T. (1992) 'Iberia Turns in Further Losses' in *The Financial Times*, 15 July, p. 30.

15

Local Government

This chapter explains the status and role of local government, and its relationship to central government. It assesses the influence of local authorities, and how this has changed in recent years. The discussion focuses upon the ways in which a local authority can shape the pattern of local transport provision and land use within its geographical area.

Status and Role of Local Government

In the earlier part of the nineteenth century, local government consisted of a patchy and disparate collection of ad hoc boards and agencies concerned with particular functions – public health, education, streets, sewers and so on. By the beginning of the twentieth century, however, this had evolved into multi-purpose local authorities, which provided comprehensive geographical coverage of the country. The elected councillors of cities such as Birmingham, Leeds and Liverpool often showed a great deal of reforming zeal in improving the conditions of life for their more disadvantaged citizens, and civic pride in the quality of the services provided.

The term local government has never implied, however, that such Authorities are free to decide what functions they carry out. They are subject to many constraints which determine what they can and cannot do. Local government is required to do as **directed**, or as **allowed** by central government. This is set out in detail, through national legislation, regulations and other statutory instruments. Local authorities have:

(a) Duties – to carry out certain prescribed functions;
(b) Powers – which enable them to carry out specific functions if they wish to do so.

For many years, a substantial proportion of the income of local authorities was derived from a form of local taxation known as the rates. This was based on a notional valuation of properties within each area. The local authority, in determining its annual budget, would then decide the level at which this would be set. In order to control public spending, however, local authorities which central government considered to be overspending were progressively penalized, and eventually 'capped', thus establishing an absolute upper limit. Then, the rate system was abolished altogether, and replaced by a Community Charge, or Poll Tax, to which all eligible residents were required to contribute at a flat rate, regardless of ability to pay. This proved so unpopular (and difficult to collect in some areas), that it was replaced by a Council Tax, based on banded property values. Local firms also contribute, although this is now centralized through the Uniform Business Rate.

Local government may also raise revenue by directly charging the users of the services they provide. Thus, in transport, off-street car parks and on-street meters provide a source of income. Nevertheless, a local authority's parking charges are generally set with a view to managing demand, as part of a wider transport strategy, rather than to maximize income. Thus, a Council wishing to attract shoppers to a particular retail centre may offer parking at a nominal charge or even free to short-stay users. Likewise, a Council may wish to encourage visitors to a congested historic town to use a park and ride scheme – transferring to public transport for access to the centre.[1]

Before the 1985 Transport Act, some local authorities and PTAs also used public transport fares as a means of managing demand. Before the Act, those with municipal bus fleets could decide how much revenue should be recovered from users, meeting any deficit by subsidy. Some encouraged the municipal operator to recover the full cost, whereas others had a policy of high subsidy and low fares.[2] The object was to encourage the use of buses as part of a strategy which emphasized public transport for its environmental, social and economic benefits. Today, however, the Authorities no longer have this discretion. Nor can they plan or co-ordinate the services, except the residual, non-commercial ones which they choose to subsidize.

As well as Council Tax and user charges, sources of income for local government include borrowing, sale of assets and the various grants administered through the Department of Environment and Department of Transport, discussed in the chapter 16. All of these are closely supervised and controlled by central government. Thus, the tight framework of legislation and financial constraints means that the discretion allowed to Authorities is restricted, in transport as in other functions. It would be wrong, however, to view them merely as passive agents of central government.

Elected councils decide policies according to the philosophy of the controlling political group and the particular problems and opportunities of the areas concerned. The latter include:

(a) Demographic and social aspects – for example, population size, structure and geographical distribution, social, racial and cultural mix.
(b) Local economy and employment pattern – for example, the type of industry and jobs available, the level of unemployment among the resident population, the level of commuting into and out of the area.
(c) Environment and amenity issues – for example, whether the Authority covers urban centres, inner urban, suburban, semi-rural or rural areas, whether townscape or landscape requires special protection and enhancement, the extent to which car traffic and other road vehicles can be accommodated.

Nevertheless, the role of local authorities has been changed substantially, and their influence reduced as a result of the Conservative Government's pro-free market policies since the early 1980s. Since their nineteenth-century origins, local authorities in the UK played a major role in transport provision. Under the 1870 Tramways Act, for example, they purchased and constructed their own tramway systems and later ran municipal bus undertakings in order to provide comprehensive service networks. Later, airports, seaports and other operations were added. As explained in chapter 2, however, these have become 'arm's length' companies. Some have been privatized already and the government intend that the remainder will also pass into private ownership.[3]

In essence, the role of local government with regard to public transport has been transformed from one of direct provision to one of securing services not provided commercially. Compared to other countries, including those in Continental Europe and in North America, this seems a somewhat marginal and residual role. Nevertheless, UK Authorities are responsible for important transport functions which are particularly vital to the well-being of less mobile sections of local communities.

The following case study illustrates the range of services carried out by a County Council, and how they are co-ordinated to ensure maximum efficiency and effectiveness of service delivery for the user.

Case study: Devon County Council Transport Co-ordination Centre

Devon, in the South-West of England, has several major urban areas, including Exeter and Plymouth, which are large commercial centres. Much of Devon is, however, rural and thinly populated with a pattern of small villages and market towns. Its coastal resorts such as Torbay and the Dartmoor and Exmoor National Parks are accessible via the M5 motorway and attract many car-borne tourists. The mild climate has also attracted a large number of retired people, and pensioners represent over a third of Devon's resident population.

The area therefore presents a range of issues which relate to transport. Good road access is important to the local economy but high traffic levels may adversely affect the environment. Public transport may help to relieve this stress. Many of the county's residents are wholly dependent on public transport. Some have special needs. Yet such services are unlikely to be provided commercially, especially in rural areas. The County Council intervenes to help satisfy these transport requirements, but must do so as efficiently as possible.

The Transport Co-ordination Centre (TCC) has been set up as a corporate unit to provide the planning and management of transport services for all the County Council's departments. The TCC is therefore the focal point for the Council's own requirements for the transport of passengers, meals, small goods, office removals, fleet management, vehicle hire and the provision of subsidized local bus services. Three key aspects of the TCC's work are illustrated as follows:

(a) Supported local bus services

The county has approximately 160 contracts for non-commercial bus services. These services are subject to competitive tenders, which are generally let on a net subsidy (minimum cost) basis, the operator making an estimate of revenue in his submission and keeping all money taken. Supported services are prioritized by a ranking system which takes into account the functions the service undertakes, numbers of passengers using the service, the cost per passenger and other features such as rural accessibility. These produce a points total for each service showing its relative value.

An annual survey is carried out on all services, usually in April, to update the ranking system and to plan 'good housekeeping' economies. Additionally surveys are carried out as required to consult passengers about proposed changes and during the summer on those routes subject to a seasonal increase in patronage. Recently acquired electronic ticket machines should also help to increase the amount and quality of information available. All supported services are monitored at least once every six months in order to ensure the contract is being operated to the county's specification. In addition to this programmed monitoring, services may be monitored in response to passenger complaints.

(b) Local bus and rail publicity

The 'DevonBus' logo was adopted to indicate county-supported bus services and public transport information. Timetable leaflets are produced for all supported services and where more than one operator runs between common points. During the summer, timetable booklets are produced for the North Devon, Sidmouth and Seaton and Dartmoor areas, aimed primarily at visitors. A comprehensive timetable book has not been produced since deregulation as the number and frequency of changes to services mean that any such publication becomes out of date extremely quickly. Research has also shown that the number of people seeking information for all of the county is extremely small. A comprehensive DevonBus map has, nevertheless, been produced, and is updated every year.

Roadside information is provided on all supported routes and at certain other interchange points, updated by county staff. Bus stops are also provided where necessary, all information and bus stop signs bearing the DevonBus logo. A bus help-line has also been established. This provides information for all local bus, rail and coach services within Devon. This is the only comprehensive source of information within Devon, as many operators will only answer enquiries about their own services. Some local rail services have also been promoted jointly with British Rail Regional Railways, and sometimes other agencies such as the Countryside Commission and the Rural Development Commission. This includes the themed 'Tarka Line' from Exeter to Barnstaple, which has been marked for walkers and cyclists as part of a 'green tourism' initiative.

(c) Public transport for the elderly and disabled
People who are disabled or have some difficulty using conventional public transport are not able to benefit from the Council's support of local bus services. The County Council seeks a partnership with locally-based groups in the provision of schemes for disabled and elderly people. Assistance may therefore be given to District Councils, Parish Councils and community/voluntary bodies. Initiation, promotion and development of such schemes is progressed by the TCC, and, in appropriate cases, the County Council will fund up to 50 per cent of the net cost. Over £100,000 per annum is now committed to transport provision for the frail elderly and disabled.

These include 'ring-and-ride' schemes, using tail-lift vehicles, which operate on specific days from specific areas. Passengers book in advance and are picked up at their door, journeys being routed according to demand. In many cases the vehicles have been integrated with social services and school transport, thereby maximizing the benefits of multiple use. For example, the vehicles are used to collect school children with significant handicaps on a daily basis before they are used for ring-and-ride. Voluntary car schemes have also been set up to complement ring-and-ride, catering for more individual journeys – irregular demands to destinations other than urban centres. In both types of scheme, co-ordination and booking systems are a key feature.

Planning and Highways

Local authorities also have important powers and duties for planning and highways. As locally-elected bodies, it is appropriate that they should be the prime agents for town and country planning – deciding whether a particular site should be developed for a particular land use. In order to ensure that such decisions are equitable, and to safeguard the wider national interest, however, there are various ways in which the Secretary of State for the Environment can intervene to override such local decisions. As highways authorities, they are also responsible for the network of local public roads, their construction and maintenance, as well as traffic management. Again, the national interest may prevail where necessary. In this case, the Secretary of State for Transport has certain powers, and is responsible for the national network of motorways and trunk roads.

Since 1947, permission has been required to carry out any activity defined in the town and country planning legislation as 'development and other use of land'. This refers not only to **new buildings and operations**, such as housing schemes, office developments, mining, quarrying and so on, but also to **change of use**, such as the conversion of a redundant unit on an industrial estate into a retail store or indoor sports centre. Both types of development may have implications for transport – generation of additional traffic, car parking, loading/unloading of goods vehicles, access by public transport and so on. Such issues may be assessed and taken into account, along with other matters, when a planning application is made. In most cases, this decision rests with the local authority for the area concerned. Thus, a local authority has the power to:

(a)   **grant** planning permission, subject to a set of conditions;
(b)   **refuse** planning permission, stating the reasons for doing so.

If dissatisfied with the Authority's decision – because the application has been turned down, or because the conditions are too onerous – the applicant has the right to appeal to the Secretary of State. The latter will appoint an Inspector from the Department of the Environment to assess the merits of the case and, if necessary, a Public Inquiry will be held.[4] Having considered the Inspector's report and recommendations, the Secretary of State then has the power to reverse or change the local authority's previous decision, or else to dismiss the appeal. Applications for major developments of wider national interest, such as large international airports, may be 'called in' by the Secretary of State, that is they will bypass the local authority.

Land use changes, then, may affect the transport system. New transport infrastructure may also affect the pattern of land use. A major highway constructed through open country may well create pressures to develop the 'green field' sites along its route, especially near the junctions. Such sites often present attractive locations for out-of-town shopping developments, for example. Thus, a superstore or hypermarket in a prime position may have a large catchment area – the potential to attract many thousands of car-borne shoppers within easy driving distance. Such a site will have plenty of space for convenient parking and good access for delivery vehicles. Nevertheless, the traffic so generated may overload the new highway, causing congestion. If the highway was built as a bypass or relief road, this would defeat its very purpose!

It is apparent, then, that land use planning and highway programmes are closely interrelated. There is a need for local authorities to take a longer-term and consistent approach to both. The policies and proposals should also be set out clearly and explained so that the public can know and understand the local authority's intentions for the area concerned. The statutory document which provides such information is known as the development plan. County Councils have a duty to prepare such documents, known as **Structure Plans**. These bring together the policies and broad proposals for land use and transport, looking forward 15 years or so into the future. They will indicate, for example, town centres in the county where a net increase in retailing, office development and so on would be acceptable, and those where it would not. They might also indicate the general areas of the county where additional housing of a particular type is needed – for example small, affordable units suitable for single people and couples.

County Structure Plans provide the basic framework for the more detailed **Local Plans**. The latter are mostly prepared by the second-tier District Councils. They set out the policies and proposals for land use change, referring to specific sites which are indicated on a large-scale Ordnance Survey-based map. These are related to any programmed improvements to highways and other transport infrastructure. For example, a Local Plan for a town centre may set out a programme to create a more attractive shopping environment by giving pedestrians priority on certain streets and providing rear servicing to shops and off-street car parks. It may establish which sites are suitable for redevelopment, and which features of the townscape should be protected and enhanced – historic buildings, open spaces, trees and so on.

In London and the major conurbations – Manchester, Merseyside, Tyne and Wear and so on, a curious situation has arisen regarding the preparation of development plans. In 1986 the government abolished the Greater London Council and the Metropolitan Counties, thus eliminating the first-tier County authorities altogether, leaving the Boroughs and Districts as the sole tier of local government. The former Structure Plans for the largest population centres of the country also disappeared. The Boroughs and Districts were required to prepare **Unitary Development Plans** (UDPs) for these areas, under the strategic guidance of the Secretary of State for the Environment. These UDPs, once adopted, will supersede all previous plans. Thus, in the case of London, 33 Boroughs are each formulating their separate UDPs. There is a London-wide planning forum, with representatives of all these authorities, known as the London Planning Advisory Committee (LPAC). But, as its name suggests, its purpose is to advise the Secretary of State and it has no executive power.

Conclusion

Local authorities have responsibilities for the well-being of the areas which they administer, and to which they are democratically accountable. Although many factors are beyond their control, they must take account of social, economic and environmental issues. Since transport has implications for all of these, local authorities often seek to influence the level and quality of transport for the benefit of their citizens. The scope for such intervention is, however, determined by the powers and duties conferred on them by central government. It is also strongly influenced by the financial resources available to them.

Notes

1 See discussion on park and ride schemes in the context of subsidies for conservation of the environment, in chapter 16.
2 See discussion of economic regulation and fares policy in chapter 9.
3 See also discussion of Conservative Party Manifesto commitments in chapter 13.
4 In most cases, however, this is not necessary, and the matter is dealt with by written representations.

16

Grants and Subsidies

Central and local government, as well as the EC, offer various forms of financial support to transport. These enable unprofitable services to survive. The State may also favour a particular mode or type of operation, making it cheaper than it would be in a pure free market economy. This chapter examines the reasons why such grants and subsidies are provided. It reviews the procedures and criteria used to guide resource allocation in particular examples. In a case study of Manchester Metrolink Light Rapid Transit, it shows how a large capital grant has been awarded for a private sector scheme.

Reasons for Grants and Subsidies

As emphasized in chapter 13, the UK has experienced a long period of restraint of public expenditure. In many cases, the government has looked to the private sector to operate transport on a commercial basis. Nevertheless, some grants and subsidies remain, as they do in the most pro-free market economies, such as the United States and Hong Kong. A variety of reasons has been used to justify the allocation of public funds to the transport sector, and to particular modes.

(a) Military/Defence
Efficient transport systems are essential for the movement of troops and equipment. The Roman roads were primarily built to establish and defend the empire. In the 1930s, the fascist dictatorships in Germany and Italy financed the construction of motorways with the same object in mind. Merchant shipping, seaports, civil

aviation and airports are also important for military logistics. Furthermore, they are vital in maintaining supplies to a civilian population isolated by an enemy power. Railways also have strategic importance. Countries with large territories and extensive borders, such as the People's Republic of China, recognize the importance of transport for national defence.

(b)   Economic development

Good transport systems are essential for trade and economic development. At international level, the EC allocates finance for infrastructure including road, rail and inland waterway projects, especially those which assist geographically peripheral and disadvantaged parts of Europe. At national level, governments may subsidize transport which may act as a catalyst for the generation of wealth and employment. This includes the support given to air transport by relatively poor, developing countries. Improvements to national transport infrastructure, including motorways and trunk roads, fast rail links, and domestic air services, may be subsidized in order to assist remote and disadvantaged regions. At local level, areas of industrial decline and high unemployment may be revitalized by investment in new transport facilities. Thus, urban metros and Light Rapid Transit systems may help regenerate inner city and former dockland areas by attracting new business and jobs.

(c)   Efficient use of resources

Assistance may be given to modes of transport which make good use of scarce resources. A commuter railway, for example, can move more people more quickly, more reliably and using less urban land than a road corridor. It may be difficult, perhaps impossible, for a large city to function efficiently without rail-based public transport. New or upgraded rail infrastructure may relieve heavily congested roads on parallel routes. In some countries, urban bus services are subsidized, since they make much better use of roadspace than private cars. State subsidy may also provide scope to plan and integrate public transport services, including those of different modes.[1] Again, this can allow better use of resources and make the whole system more attractive to passengers. Some forms of transport make efficient use of energy resources: the sharp increases in fuel prices in the 1970s encouraged State investment in public transport in North America, Japan and elsewhere.

(d) Conservation of the environment
In environmentally-sensitive areas such as historic centres, and National Parks, it may be desirable to encourage the use of public transport. Financial support may therefore be given for schemes such as park-and-ride facilities, which allow people to park their cars and then catch a bus or train into the area. The State may also offer incentives to divert some freight traffic from roads to railways and inland waterways. For example, under the 1974 Railways Act, Section 8, grants have been awarded towards the cost of private sidings, rolling stock and so on, where firms can demonstrate clear environmental benefits to the areas concerned. Subsidy can be used to encourage forms of transport which create less atmospheric pollution and do less harm to the global environment. It can also be used for the development of transport systems which reduce accidents and create safer, more pleasant surroundings for pedestrians and cyclists.

(e) Social equity
Public transport services which are unprofitable may justify financial support to provide a basic level of mobility for people who depend upon them. Thus, bus, rail, and even air services to remote rural communities may be subsidized. Since the money is allocated to the operator to provide the service, the transport will be available to all passengers at a subsidized fare. Alternatively, some forms of assistance go directly to the user. Certain groups within a community cannot pay the full market price for the transport they require. Thus, schoolchildren, students, senior citizens and others may receive the benefit of subsidized travel. Some groups may have special needs – notably those with disabilities. If public transport vehicles and the services they provide are accessible, such groups may also receive subsidized travel permits. If not, however, it may be more appropriate to support special forms of transport such as 'ring-and-ride' minibuses.

The remaining part of this chapter illustrates how central government finance is obtained for various types of local transport. It reviews the procedures for obtaining grants, and the methods for determining how they are spent. The first example is the annual review of policies and programmes for overall spending on transport by local authorities, which may be supported by a Transport Supplementary Grant. The second is a special one-off grant which may be made available for large-scale public transport infra-structure projects under Section 56 of the 1968 Transport Act.

Transport Supplementary Grant

Chapter 15 outlined the various functions performed by local government with regard to transport. In total, these may represent a significant amount of their total annual expenditure. As well as the income derived from local taxation (Council Tax), charges for services, sale of assets, and authorized borrowing, grants may be obtained from central government on an annual basis.

Firstly, local authorities receive a yearly contribution from central government towards current spending, known as the Block Grant. This is calculated by the Treasury with reference to each Authority's spending requirements, as measured by the Grant Related Expenditure assessment (GRE), as well as their potential to raise their own resources. As the title 'Block Grant' suggests, it is a general grant towards all local government services, and is therefore not specific to transport or any other function. Thus, it is up to the elected Council to decide how it should be divided up between the various spending departments.

In contrast to the Block Grant, the Transport Supplementary Grant (TSG) is specifically earmarked for certain types of transport expenditure. Thus it cannot be spent on any other local government service. TSG may be made available from central government if the projected expenditure of the local authority exceeds a specified level known as the 'threshold'. The grant was first introduced in 1975.

Before 1975, the procedures for obtaining central government finance for local transport had lacked co-ordination. Projects were assessed individually, on their own merits, with no requirement for local authorities to state their overall transport policies. The TSG system was originally based on the philosophy that local transport should be viewed comprehensively, in the wider context of land use planning. The objectives were to:

(a) promote the development and execution of comprehensive trans-port plans by the first-tier Authorities;
(b) eliminate bias towards capital or current expenditure or towards particular forms of expenditure;

(c) distribute central government grant in a way that reflected, as far as possible, the needs of individual areas;

(d) reduce the degree of detailed supervision by central government over individual schemes.

At first, the system allowed the first tier of local government – the County Councils – considerable discretion. Authorities could choose, for example, to enhance the role of local bus and rail services and spend less on highway construction, or vice versa, according to their policies. They could obtain TSG for a wide variety of purposes including public transport, highways, traffic regulation, parking provision and freight handling. In order to assist forward planning management of resources, counties were required to prepare an annual document known as the Transport Policies and Programme (TPP).

A TPP is, in effect, a local authority's formal 'bid' for its share of the nationally-allocated TSG. The TPP must include:

(a) estimates of expenditure for the following financial year;

(b) a statement of transport objectives and strategy covering 10–15 years;

(c) a medium-term five-year expenditure programme to implement the strategy, rolled forward annually;

(d) a statement of past expenditure and physical progress of implementation with a review of the extent to which the programme is meeting desired objectives.

In 1985, however, the criteria for allocated TSG were radically changed. Expenditure on public transport in England is no longer eligible for TSG,[2] and only certain types of capital expenditure on roads may receive grants. Current expenditure is now subsumed into Block Grants. In determining how much of an Authority's expenditure to accept for TSG, the Secretary of State will consider the extent to which the roads affected are of more than local importance, and the extent to which people living or working in the Authority's area would be relieved of the effects of heavy through traffic. Given the severe financial constraints, expenditure on local transport has been greatly reduced, not only for public transport, but also for road schemes.

Leicestershire, in the East Midlands, a County Council with a fairly typical pattern of expenditure, reviews the programme of highway construction in its TPP:

It is not an extravagant programme. Local highway planning in recent years has been a continuous process of paring down both the number and scale of previous proposals, to try to meet reduced financial horizons. The Structure Plan, for instance, was instrumental in deleting many previously hoped for proposals, the slim chance for construction of which could not be reconciled with the blight their retention was causing. The schemes that remain comprise mainly single carriageway ground level roads, which are long overdue and are urgently needed to cope with the traffic that is, or will be, generated by new development arising from increased population.[3]

'Section 56' Grants and Light Rapid Transit

Large scale public transport infrastructure schemes have been treated separately from the TSG/TPP system. Under the 1968 Transport Act, grants have been given by central government towards the cost of schemes such as the Tyne and Wear Metro in North-East England. Currently there is a great deal of interest in this source of finance to part-fund Light Rapid Transit (LRT) schemes which have now been proposed for over 40 cities in the UK.

As Professor Peter Hall and Carmen Hass-Klau have commented, 'despite what might appear to be the worst climate for new public transport investment in over 30 years – cuts in public spending, escalating financial tensions between central and local government, and deregulation of bus services – the last few years have been a flurry of planning for rapid transit schemes in cities and urban conurbations'.[4] Nevertheless, as Richard Tomkins' report for *The Financial Times* has emphasized, the Department of Transport's budget for road schemes is more than 100 times greater than its budget for light rail schemes. In other European countries, highway and public transport schemes are assessed on a more comparable basis. As a result, half the Western European cities with a population of more than 0.6 million have some form of rapid transit. In Britain, however 'only two schemes are in the pipeline – the Sheffield Supertram and the Midland Metro'.[5]

Rail-based LRT systems use tracked, light, electric vehicles. With a high power-to-weight ratio they can climb steep inclines. They can also negotiate sharp curves and therefore weave their way through city streets. They have fast acceleration and are capable of speeds of 80 kph. Running on reserved track or through underground tunnels, they can therefore offer speedy access to the heart of a city centre. They have a higher carrying capacity than a bus, typically accommodating about 200 people (sitting and standing) in an articulated unit, with scope for coupling two or more units together.

Where LRT systems are segregated from road traffic, on their own right of way, technology now enables the vehicles to be completely automated. LRT systems in Lille, Vancouver and London Docklands, for example, are operated with computer-controlled, driverless trains. This is a significant advantage in countries where labour represents a high proportion of operating costs and staff may be difficult to recruit, especially to work the unsociable hours required by public transport. Automated LRT can therefore operate at a high frequency throughout each working day, late into the evenings and at weekends, thereby generating considerable off-peak leisure traffic to and from city centres.

There are, however, certain disadvantages which should be borne in mind. Compared to buses, LRT systems' routing is inflexible. And, being unable to overtake, the breakdown of a vehicle may cause serious delays and disruption along the route. As the consultants Steer Davies Gleave have pointed out,[6] LRT is really only appropriate along traffic corridors with relatively high traffic flows – 10,000 or more passenger movements per hour at the peak, by all modes. At the other extreme, traffic flows in some large cities are too great for LRT, making conventional 'heavy' rail more appropriate. In general terms, LRT may be suitable for cities with a population size of between 0.5 million and 3.0 million.[7]

Nevertheless, LRT is pollution free and can therefore improve the quality of urban environments. It also consumes very little land for its ways and terminals, compared with urban roads and car parks. LRT schemes have attracted people to public transport along transport corridors where their journey times and reliability are better than private cars. Although lacking the privacy and door-to-door convenience of private cars, they can provide a stress-free journey without parking difficulties. Well designed LRT systems can offer a smooth, comfortable ride in heated/air conditioned vehicles. Some have low level floors, which can provide access for disabled people from street level. They have the potential to change the popular image of public transport to that of a clean and convenient means of conveyance for all social classes.

The following case study illustrates a successful application for finance under the 1968 Transport Act, Section 56, and explains how the original proposal for a public sector project changed, to become a unique partnership between government and private sector capital.

Case study: Manchester Metrolink Light Rapid Transit

Greater Manchester, in North-West England, with a population of just over 2.5 million, has proved a very suitable candidate for LRT. The government approved a Section 56 grant for Phase One of the 'Manchester Metrolink' project in October 1989. This was for 50 per cent of the eligible cost of the £112 million scheme. The Transport Minister welcomed this important and innovatory scheme. In April 1992, the first section of Metrolink opened for public service.

The Central Business District (CBD) of Manchester is a regional centre, and was designated as such in the Structure Plan. Nevertheless, its relative importance was weakened through strong competition from several sub-centres within the conurbation and beyond, where town centre developments had diverted office, retail and other activities. A major problem was that transport into and within central Manchester was poor. Motorists found roads congested and parking inadequate. Buses were also delayed by heavy traffic. Local rail services needed investment for modernization, and suffered from a long-standing problem – the networks to the North and South were not connected. Proposals to link the two rail terminals can be traced back over 150 years – they have included elevated and underground railways, and even a monorail, but none attracted sufficient finance.

The last attempt was in the early 1970s – a proposal for a full-sized railway tunnel linking Piccadilly station in the South with Victoria in the North, the 'Picc–Vic' scheme, but an application for Section 56 funding was deferred, and the tunnel concept was abandoned in 1977. The Metrolink alternative of converting existing British Rail heavy rail lines to Light Rapid Transit, and linking the two termini by street level running, arose from an evaluation of a number of lower cost options. The British Rail local services, subsidized by Greater Manchester PTA, had ageing rolling stock and other life-expired equipment. Comprehensive conversion to LRT would be more cost-effective than piecemeal replacement on a like-for-like basis.[8]

By the early 1980s, the severe economic recession brought unemployment in Manchester to a critical level. Not only had manufacturing and distribution industries declined in the inner areas, as in many other UK cities, but the service industries in Manchester's CBD were performing poorly compared with national trends. Overall, employment had declined from 160,000 full-time equivalent jobs in the mid-1960s to only 100,000 in the early 1980s.[9] Some commercial property proved hard to let and remained vacant It was feared that an upswing in the economy would not bring sufficient growth in new service sector jobs to compensate for those which were being lost in traditional industries.

It was recognized that improvements to transport access would improve the regional centre's competitiveness. LRT, combined with highway and traffic management schemes to reduce the number of road vehicles in the CBD, would create a more attractive environment for shopping, leisure and other city centre activities. A consultant's report in 1983 identified six corridors suitable for LRT, linked at the centre by tracks along streets, many of which would be wholly or partially pedestrianized. This would bring business to the city centre. It would also act as a catalyst for the regeneration of obsolete buildings and derelict land along the routes. As a prestige project it would raise the confidence of the business community in Manchester. The scheme was progressed. Phase One would convert the line to Bury, ten miles to the North, and link it to the line to Altrincham, seven miles to the South-West.

The benefits of the LRT scheme can be summarized as follows. Metrolink would:

(a) improve passengers' journeys to and across Manchester City Centre;
(b) link together the northern and southern rail systems;
(c) offer overall financial and economic benefits for the area;
(d) reduce the revenue support needed for local rail services;
(e) improve access to shops and businesses;
(f) encourage development of leisure, recreation and tourist facilities;
(g) provide better links with BR's local and InterCity networks;
(h) help create jobs in British industry.

The detailed proposals for Phase One of Metrolink were submitted to the government for authority to proceed, and for assistance with funding. The estimated costs were assessed against the wider community benefits including those outlined above. Using the criteria for cost-benefit appraisal, David Graham, Director

MANCHESTER CITY CENTRE

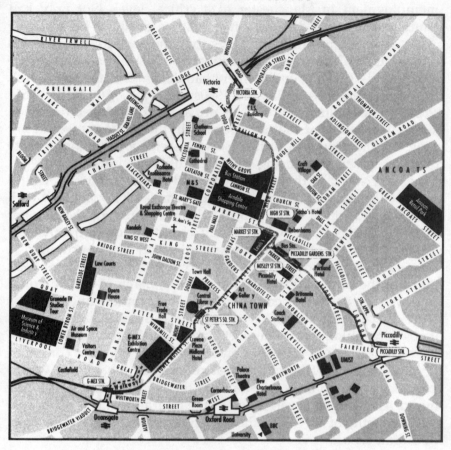

METROLINK

Greater Manchester Metro Limited

Metrolink House, Queens Road, Manchester M8 7RY. Enquiries Telephone: 061 205 2000

Plate 16.1   Metrolink: making tracks in central Manchester, courtesy of Greater Manchester Metro Limited

General of Greater Manchester PTE commented: 'Latest figures for Metrolink in Manchester show that the financial return on every pound invested will be in excess of £2.30.'[10] After the initial application had been made, however, implementation of the 1985 Transport Act brought far-reaching changes to the commercial environment for local transport, including deregulation and privatization.[11] The government therefore reviewed the whole basis upon which the Metrolink proposal would proceed.

As Ogden and Senior have commented, during the early years of the proposals the Passenger Transport Executive 'expected that it would be responsible for the creation and operation of any light rail scheme in Manchester'.[12] But, by the mid-1980s there was an overriding emphasis on private investment and commercial competition. Thus, the crucial change was that the government required the light rail proposal to be implemented by the private sector. The Section 56 grant was conditional on Metrolink being a private sector scheme, with one contractor being responsible for the entire project – design, build, operate and maintain (DBOM). Through a process of competitive tendering, the contract was eventually won by a consortium known as the GMA group. Thus, after receipt of the one-off capital grant, Metrolink is being run as a commercial enterprise.

Conclusion

Transport may be desirable or necessary in the public interest yet commercially unviable without financial support. Thus, grants and subsidies are required. The reasons for such assistance from the State are varied, and persist even in the most pro-free market economies. Nevertheless, the UK government's policy of 'rolling back the State' since 1979 has meant that the criteria for grants and subsidies have become more rigorous. In many cases, the level of support has been reduced. In recent years, new arrangements have been developed, with the aim of securing value for money, and much greater involvement by the private sector.

Notes

1 See discussion on the systems concept and integration of public transport in chapter 6.

2   In Wales since 1982 TSG became payable on capital expenditure only, and from 1985 has been confined to schemes costing over £5m.

3   Leicestershire, C.C. (1989) *Transport Policies and Programmes*, p. 11.

4   Hall, P. and Hass-Klau, C. (1987) 'Time for a fresh look', *Transport*, pp. 250–3 December.

5   Tomkins, R. (1992) 'Survey: Light Rail Schemes', *The Financial Times* 6 April, p. 23.

6   Steer Davies Gleave (1991) *Buses Mean Business*, p. 13. Bus and Coach Council.

7   Ibid.

8   Abbot, J. (1984) 'Manchester: Investment Needed Now' in *Modern Railways*, April, p. 215.

9   Arthur, J.M.H. (1985) *Public Transport and Employment Generation: The Light Rapid Transit Scheme in Central Manchester*: GMC information paper (unpublished).

10   Graham, D. (1991) in *Metrolink Official Handbook*, Introduction, p. 5: Transport Publishing Company.

11   See discussion of the 1985 Transport Act and its effects in chapter 9.

12   Ogden, E. and Senior, J. (1991) in *Metrolink Official Handbook* Concept to Tender, pp. 8–9: Transport Publishing Company.

Part V

Influence

17

User Bodies

This chapter examines the role of user bodies, – organizations which represent the customers of passenger and freight services. Some are statutory, having been established by Act of Parliament with specific duties to perform. Yet there are many others which have been set up on a voluntary basis, supported by public-spirited individuals and organizations who wish to see improvements in the services they use. Why then, has the transport industry attracted so much attention from the organized consumer?

Choice or Voice?

User bodies exist to provide a 'voice' for the customer, especially where their choice is limited or non-existent. The service may be poor or indifferent. Yet complaints may be ignored because the supplier knows that the customer has little or no alternative – a truly captive market. A 'watchdog' organization may therefore be required to ensure that the users' views are made known and taken into account.

A free marketeer might assume that user bodies have come into being simply to placate the customers of State monopolies, and in other situations where competition has been artificially blunted. The restoration of a contestable market would result in freedom of choice and consumer sovereignty, rendering user bodies redundant. It could be argued that 'voice' is no substitute for choice. Competition, or the threat of it, would provide a much better motivation for the supplier to focus attention on customer needs and wants.

There are, however, some important objections to this argument with regard to the transport industry. Firstly, the individual customer is often in a weak bargaining position, even in a free market. A passenger journey or freight shipment may be subject to unacceptable delay or otherwise fail to satisfy the user's expectation of reasonable service. The aggrieved customer may be able to take his/her business elsewhere, but the damage will already have been done. There may therefore be a need for an independent body to **investigate individual cases**. With or without competition between operators, a user body may serve as a channel for complaints, comments and suggestions.

There may also be a need for an independent body to **monitor the policies and performance** of transport operators. Whether or not competition exists, a user body may serve the useful function of reporting on service changes and assessing the likely implications for users. It may also carry out independent surveys to examine various aspects of service delivery such as the level of cancellations, early and late running, and the quality of customer information. Such analysis can be compared with the caseload of enquiries from dissatisfied customers.

A user body may also provide a **forum for discussion** and constructive criticism of the services provided by transport operators. Representatives of different customer groups, in both passenger and freight transport, may use this forum to explain their particular requirements. Consideration can be given to people whose needs cannot be met commercially, and services which require grants and subsidies as described in chapter 16. Statutory user bodies report their findings to the central or local government agencies who sponsor them. Voluntary user bodies lack these formal channels of communication, but are often skilled at public relations, and make their views known to those in public office through lobbying.

The consultation and dialogue between user body and supplier of transport can be productive, leading to benefits for both parties. User bodies often possess a wealth of knowledge and expertise. Their advice can lead to service improvements which provide a higher level of customer satisfaction. Although user bodies have little or no executive power, their influence can be considerable. The following examples from the various modes of transport suggest that voice and choice can be complementary.

Statutory User Bodies

Amongst the longest established, and best known of statutory user bodies are the **Transport Users' Consultative Committees** (TUCCs). They were originally set up in 1947, when large sections of the transport industry were nationalized. They were created as watchdog organizations to provide a voice for the customers of State-owned monopolies. Formerly multi-modal in their remit, their title is now somewhat misleading since they deal almost exclusively with rail passenger services.

The members of the TUCCs are appointed by, and report to, the President of the Board of Trade, who has overall responsibility for consumer affairs. They are funded by the same Ministry and have their own permanent staff. These arrangements give the TUCCs a fair degree of autonomy, and in particular, independence from a Secretary of State for Transport who has direct responsibility for the main operator – British Rail.

The eight TUCCs are regionally based, covering British Rail services and other networks such as the Tyne and Wear Metro and Manchester Metrolink. They cover England, Scotland and Wales, but there are separate arrangements for Northern Ireland.[1] The TUCCs handle a considerable case load of complaints, comments and suggestions from the travelling public. These individual cases are referred to them where the passenger is dissatisfied with the response that he/she has received from British Rail or another operator. Where the TUCC considers the passenger's case to be justified, the user body can make representations on their behalf. The operator may then be persuaded to offer an apology, and perhaps to provide some form of compensation, if appropriate. In some cases a full and clear explanation is sufficient.

TUCCs keep a watchful eye on the railway operators with regard to the quality of service they provide, and general policy matters. The latter include timetable changes, the passenger environment on trains and at stations, facilities for people with special needs, and so on. They also monitor various aspects of performance, including punctuality, level of cancellations, and overcrowding.[2] They are consulted on many issues as a matter of course. They also initiate their own surveys and commission studies and reports as they think fit and as their budgets permit. The TUCCs are, however, technically debarred from considering fares, under the Transport Act 1962. The important issue of value for money is, therefore, beyond their official remit.

The statutory user body for the capital is the **London Regional Passengers Committee** (LRPC). This organization was set up in 1984 to perform the same role as the TUCCs, but to cover a broader range of public transport services – not only British Rail, but also London Underground, Docklands Light Railway, Victoria Coach Station and all bus operators. With regard to the latter, however, the government's consultation paper *A Bus Strategy for London* (1991), suggests that if the proposed deregulation of services and privatization of London Buses is carried through, LRPC may lose this role.[3]

Members of LRPC include representatives of local passenger groups, industry and commerce, women's organizations, local tourist boards and organizations representing senior citizens and disabled people. Unlike the TUCCs, the LRPC holds its meetings in public, and its minutes and reports are widely distributed. Thus it has cultivated a high profile, and has lobbied operators and local authorities on a range of issues. It has played an active part in major accident inquiries, including those into the fire at King's Cross Underground station in 1987 and the commuter train collision at Clapham Junction in 1988.

As watchdog organizations, the TUCCs and LRPC may raise objections and criticize the operators' policies and performance. Thus, on some issues, their stance may be adversarial, sometimes confrontational. It should be emphasized, nevertheless, that this is not always the case. There are some important issues such as action to combat personal assaults on passengers and staff, or to curb vandalism and graffiti, where the operator and user body have a common cause. The latter have always been very supportive of cases for greater public investment and subsidy, and have shown their appreciation of operators' initiatives such as station refurbishment and customer care training for staff.[4]

There is one specific issue, however, where the TUCCs and LRPC must distance themselves from the railway operator in order to adopt a quasi-judicial role. If British Rail, London Underground or the Docklands Light Railway wish to close a passenger station or line in their region the Committee is required by law to consider any objections which are raised and report to the government on the hardship that would be caused if the proposals were put into effect. The proposed closure cannot be implemented unless the government has given consent, having considered the Committee's report and any recommendations it may contain.

The work of the TUCCs and LRPC is, by its nature, area-specific. The broader picture for the national network of mainland Britain is reviewed by the **Central Transport Consultative Committee** (CTCC). The members of the latter include the Chairmen of the TUCCs and LRPC. It has permanent staff who collate area information, so as to monitor British Rail services as a whole and to identify key issues and problems. Thus in the words of the CTCC's own annual report, the organization 'monitors the national performance and policies of British Rail as these affect the paying customer. It has the legal right to make representations to the British Rail Board or to the government, and will press for improvements where necessary'.[5]

The Passenger Transport Authorities (PTAs) may, if they wish to, establish their own **Local Transport Advisory Committees** (TACs), under the Transport Act 1968. Some PTAs such as Merseyside have done so, primarily to provide a forum for discussion. Members of TACs may include local councillors and representatives of organizations such as pensioners' groups and chambers of commerce from the locality. They review a wide range of consumer matters relating to public transport, but, as their title suggests, their function is purely advisory and they do not normally deal with individual complaints. Their role as watchdog organizations is therefore somewhat limited, but their views and opinions are valued, both by the operators and by the local authorities who sponsor them.

Airport Consultative Committees (ACCs) were set up under the Civil Aviation Act 1968 to encourage discussion of all matters affecting the development or operation of airports and aerodromes. ACCs have been established for each of the seven airports owned by BAA plc and for nearly 40 others. They represent the interests, not only of airport users, but also of the people living or working in the surrounding areas.[6] Thus, their membership may include airlines, freight forwarders, regional tourist boards, local authorities, amenity groups, trade unions and so on.

There is also a national user body which represents the interests of all customers of air transport (as opposed to airports and aerodromes). Its role and functions are discussed in the following section.

Case study: Air Transport Users Committee (AUC)

Originally set up in 1973, the Air Transport Users Committee (AUC) assumed its current name and terms of reference in 1978: 'to make reports and recommendations to the Civil Aviation Authority for furthering the interests of air transport users including the investigation of complaints against the suppliers of air transport services; to co-operate with any airport consultative committees which are charged by airport proprietors with furthering the interests of air transport users inside their airports'.[7] Members of the AUC are appointed by the Civil Aviation Authority, who provide the funding. Its staff consists of the Director General, his personal secretary and three other executives.

The AUC's Annual Report for 1990–1 reviewed a very difficult year indeed for the air transport industry, adversely affected by the Gulf War and its aftermath and a worldwide downturn in economic activity. During that year, the Committee responded to some dramatic changes in the commercial environment for airlines and in the regulatory environment for Europe. In particular, there were the proposals for the third stage of liberalization in the EC, described in chapter 14.

On this issue, the AUC stated its unequivocal support for competition as: 'the best possible guarantee that users have choice – a choice between airlines, a choice of service, and a choice of fares. The authorities should thus interfere as little as possible with the workings of the marketplace and regulation should be confined to the lightest of touches.' They went on to argue, however, that there are important provisos: 'there must be effective competition policy for the Community to ensure that airlines do not misuse new found freedoms to the disadvantage of consumers or to eliminate competition unfairly; and above all, governments must be made to stand back from the industry and state subsidies should be stopped'.[8]

AUC also offered their enthusiastic support for the Secretary of State for Transport's removal of the Traffic Distribution Rules for Heathrow in March 1991 – an important step allowing the entry of American, United and Virgin Atlantic to London's premier airport.[9] The consequent stepping up of competition on transatlantic services would be to the benefit of consumers. The AUC has, however, advised that measures should be taken to ensure that vital domestic and short-haul services are not squeezed out of Heathrow.[10]

The AUC emphasized that lack of infrastructure remained a

Table 17.1 Air Transport Users Committee: analysis of complaints received in the year ended 30 September 1991 Figures for 1989/90 in brackets

	Airlines	Travel Trade	Airports	Total
Tickets	156 (147)	148 (169)		304 (316)
Flight Cancellations and Delays	175 (220)	20 (24)		195 (244)
Baggage	134 (170)	6 (4)	1 (1)	141 (175)
Reservations	50 (51)	76 (86)		126 (137)
In-Flight Service	105 (99)	5 (1)		110 (100)
Overbooking	79 (62)	9 (9)		88 (71)
Airports/Air Terminals	55 (40)	5 (7)	11 (14)	71 (61)
Tariffs	42 (43)	27 (35)		69 (78)
Schedules	43 (35)	20 (18)		63 (53)
Safety	40 (46)	– (–)	1 (–)	41 (46)
Security	12 (10)	1 (–)	1 (1)	14 (11)
Cargo	5 (6)	2 (1)		7 (7)
Other	2	2	1	5
Total	898 (929)	321 (354)	15 (16)	1234 (1299)

Source: Air Transport Users Committee, 1991a[14]

significant barrier to greater competition between airlines. With regard to capacity in the air, they recognized and appreciated the Civil Aviation Authority's determination to progress its own long-term investment programme which 'by the mid-90s will produce greatly improved capacity for flights to and from the South East as well as for aircraft overflying the British Isles'.[11]

With regard to capacity on the ground, the AUC has pressed for an early decision to build a new runway in the London area. It represents consumer interests on the Secretary of State's Working Group on Runway Capacity to Service the South-East (RUCATSE), and has expressed its disappointment with the lack of progress: 'That the Government continues to evade making decisions on this vital matter by a variety of devices is little short of scandal. Continuing delay risks surrendering the UK's position of strength in civil aviation to our continental competitors, who feel no such inhibitions.'[12]

Air safety is also an important matter of concern for the AUC. In April 1991 the Committee expressed its disappointment at the Civil Aviation Authority's decision not to require the provision of passenger smokehoods on UK-registered aircraft, and its policy of discouraging airlines from providing them: 'Moreover, development is in such an early stage that it cannot yet place much faith in what appears to be the Authority's preferred solution to the problem of cabin safety – the provision of on-board water spray systems.' Thus AUC have registered their disagreement with the CAA's policy on these issues and have conveyed their views to the Authority's Chairman.[13]

As stated above, AUC's terms of reference include the investigation of complaints. An analysis of the Committee's caseload for the year ending 30 September 1991 is shown in table 17.1. The total of complaints was less than 1,300, a relatively low number when compared to the annual passenger throughput of UK airports, which has approached 100 million in recent years. As emphasized in the AUC's Annual Report, the user body: 'does not set out to be a complaints bureau, since this would be quite beyond its present resources'.[14] The Committee has therefore adopted a rather low profile, especially when compared to the TUCCs and LRPC described above. Nevertheless, it responds sympathetically to the many requests it receives from air transport customers. AUC acts as an 'honest broker', and has secured an acceptable outcome for aggrieved passengers in a high proportion of cases.

Voluntary User Bodies

In addition to the statutory user bodies discussed above, there are many others which have been set up voluntarily. Some are concerned with transport for people with special needs such as the elderly or those whose mobility is impaired by a disadvantage such as blindness, deafness or arthritis. For example, the London Dial-a-Ride Users' Association publicize the problems experienced by people dependent on a specialized form of transport for which demand greatly exceeds supply. Their surveys have shown that even the initial telephone call to book a journey requires persistence and patience. In general, the user then faces a long wait before a driver and vehicle becomes available.

Rail passengers have also formed voluntary user groups in order to protest against closure proposals or to campaign for better service. Supporters of the Settle and Carlisle Line, for example, have successfully defended their railway for nearly 30 years. In Essex, a user group drawn from six town and parish councils has sought improvements on the eastern end of London Underground's Central Line. The group has articulated dissatisfaction with ageing rolling stock and frequent service failures on a line which urgently requires modernization. In practice, many such groups work with national organizations such as Transport 2000 and the Railway Development Society.

As John Cartledge has commented, outside London and the PTA areas 'formal provision for bus user representation is patchy in the extreme'. A few counties such as Lancashire, and some districts such as Hertsmere in Hertfordshire, have experimented with area consultative committees similar to the TACs described above. Some bus operators, such as Go-Ahead Northern, have established user panels.[15] In some cases groups of passengers have formed their own local organizations. The National Federation of Bus Users provides guidelines for people wishing to set up such a group. As with the voluntary user bodies for rail, however, their existence often depends upon the enthusiasm and sustained commitment of a few individuals who are prepared to give up their spare time.

With regard to freight, a number of voluntary user bodies have been set up to represent firms who are customers of transport operators. For example, at the Port of Felixstowe described in chapter 6 'a Port Users' Association provides a voice for the various sectoral interests. The user body has some 200 members who are divided into categories, each of which has its own elected representative on the council of the Association. The categories include shipowners and liner agents, forwarding agents, domestic and international hauliers, and other port-related companies such as chandlers, ship repairers, accountants, solicitors and so on. The Association negotiates directly with the Port of Felixstowe, HM Customs and Excise and other official bodies. Its role is to secure the best possible conditions for the port and its users. In doing so the Association has contributed to the success of Felixstowe, for example in the development of the Port's world-renowned computer system – FCP80.[16]

Freight transport in the UK is a highly competitive industry. In general, the customers have a choice between various operators and sometimes between different modes. Nevertheless, the freight shippers have recognized the advantage of forming organizations in order to represent common interests. In particular, 'shippers' councils' provide a countervailing force to the shipping conferences described in chapter 12. Nationally the shippers' councils are represented through the Freight Transport Association – a trade association-cum-user body[17] which represents the interest of own account transport operators such as manufacturers and retail firms and the users of third party freight transport of all modes.

Conclusions

User bodies perform important functions as guardians of customer interest, especially where one supplier has a monopoly or near-monopoly of a public utility such as transport. Their role is no less important where markets have been opened up to competition. To be effective 'watchdogs', user bodies must thoroughly scrutinize the operator's business strategy and criticize shortcomings in service delivery. Yet this need not lead to hostile confrontation. There may well be issues where open discussion and co-operation will bring tangible benefits to both operator and user.

Notes

1   A statutory Transport User body for Northern Ireland was created in 1967. It covered all surface transport services within the province, as well as sea and air links to Northern Ireland. In 1984, however,

its responsibilities were transferred to the General Consumer Council for Northern Ireland.

2   Since formal quality of service targets were set for British Rail in 1989, the TUCCs have played an even greater role in this respect.

3   Department of Transport (1991) *A Bus Strategy for London*: Consultation Paper, HMSO.

4   A good example of co-operation between rail operator and TUCC is described in Stewart, V. and Chadwick, V. (1987) *Messages for Management from the Scotrail Challenge – Changing Trains*, pp. 114–16: David and Charles.

5   Central Transport Consultative Committee (1990) *Annual Report*.

6   Department of Trade (1981) *Guidelines for Airport Consultative Committees*.

7   Air Transport Users Committee (1991a) *Annual Report 1990/1*: AUC.

8   Air Transport Users Committee (1991b) *Annual Report 1990/1*, Press Notice, p. 2: AUC.

9   See discussion of the removal of the Traffic Distribution Rules from Virgin Atlantic's point of view in chapter 5.

10   Air Transport Users Committee (1991a) op. cit. p. 9.

11   Air Transport Users Committee (1991b) op. cit. p. 3.

12   Ibid. pp. 3–4.

13   Ibid. p. 4.

14   Air Transport Users Committee (1991a) op. cit. p. 25.

15   Cartledge, J. (1991) 'Consumer Representation in Public Transport', unpublished working paper for the Independent Transport Advisory Group.

16   Port of Felixstowe (1992) *Port Journal*, p. 83.

17   See general discussion of trade associations in chapter 18.

18

Trade Associations

Just as the customers have user bodies to represent them, so the employers and owners of transport undertakings have trade associations. This chapter examines the functions performed by trade associations in the transport industry, and assesses their influence. Such organizations clearly exist to further the interests of their members. Do they also benefit the customer and society in general?

The Role of Trade Associations

As explained in parts III and IV, competition between transport operators has been stimulated through the outright abolition, or relaxation, of economic regulation. In the UK, deregulation has been extended from road haulage to express coaches and buses. Domestic air services have been liberalized, and new franchising arrangements will introduce competition for the supply of passenger services by rail. Some international services have also been opened up to greater competition, notably within the European Community. The commercial environment encourages rivalry between transport operators. Yet, there are also sound reasons why those same carriers should co-operate on certain issues. As Edmund Gubbins comments: 'as transport becomes fragmented by deregulation, very competitive and attacked by environmental pressure groups, collective action will be needed in many policy areas if the voice of that industry is to be heard'.[1]

Internal functions of trade associations include the negotiation of special rates with suppliers – services such as vehicle recovery and insurance. They help their members to keep themselves informed and up to date with issues such as developments in technology and changes in the law and regulations. They may also offer advice to individual members on a wide range of matters, including human resource management, business expansion and marketing – some assistance may be free to members, or else available at a lower rate than outside consultants would charge. Trade associations may provide training and other personnel-related services. Some have a special function as negotiators in relations with the trade unions. In the case of the International Air Transport Association, the organization has played a particular role in economic regulation through its 'Traffic Conferences' of air carriers.[2]

External functions include the creation of a platform for discussion and debate. Thus, operators who might be active rivals in particular transport markets come together through the association. They may formulate a common view on a specific issue such as the need for improvements in vehicle design or the infrastructure they use, or to face a common threat such as the imposition of onerous or ill-conceived regulations, increases in tax or duty and so on. Where there is a general consensus of opinion among the membership, a trade association may instigate a campaign to further their collective interest. Thus, the association may lobby government, the civil service, international organizations such as the European Commission and agencies of the United Nations. They may also seek to influence public opinion, directly through promotion such as advertising, and indirectly through the news media and other channels of communication. Thus, public relations is a vital function.[3] Table 18.1 lists some important trade associations of transport operators in the UK and at international level. The rest of this chapter provides three examples – explaining their role and the range of activities they perform. It also examines a number of campaigning issues in which they are currently involved.

The Chamber of Shipping

Previously known as the General Council of British Shipping, the organization reverted to its original name, 'The Chamber of Shipping', in 1991. As the trade association of British shipowners

Table 18.1   Trade associations of transport carriers

UK organizations	Mode(s)
Bus and Coach Council (BCC)	Road passenger transport
Chamber of Shipping (formerly General Council of British Shipping)	Sea transport
Freight Transport Association (FTA)	All modes of freight transport, mainly own account
Road Haulage Association (RHA)	Hire-and-reward road freight transport

International organizations	Mode(s)
International Air Transport Association (IATA)	Air transport
International Chamber of Shipping (ICS)	Sea transport
International Road Transport Union (IRU)	Road passenger and road freight transport
International Union of Railways (ICS)	Rail transport
International Union of Public Transport (UITP)	All modes of local public transport

and shipmanagers, the Chamber 'promotes and protects the interests of its members, both nationally and internationally'.[4] Its membership comprises 140 companies, managing nearly 800 ships.[5] As Alan Branch comments: 'Because of its comprehensive membership it is able to speak for the whole industry. It is not directly involved in commercial affairs of individual companies but tries to set the climate in which shipping can best trade and operate as a free enterprise competitive industry.'[6]

The organization's governing body is the Council of the Chamber of Shipping – a committee of 40 people representing the wide range of members' interests. This is supported and advised by the President's Committee. Five Section Committees represent the diverse commercial sectors of British shipping:

(a) Deep Sea Bulk;
(b) Deep Sea Liner;
(c) Ferry and Cruise;
(d) Offshore Support Vessel;
(e) Short Sea Bulk.

Various Policy Committees represent the different functions of the organization. These include:

(a) Defence;
(b) Employment Affairs;
(c) Foreign Shipping;
(d) Maritime Law.

The Director General of the Chamber heads the trade association's staff establishment. As the Chamber is keen to point out, the Merchant Navy is important for national defence. It is also important for the balance of payments, representing an important 'invisible export'. It is a source of employment, with some 18,000 officers and ratings on Chamber member vessels. During the 1980s, however, the British fleet experienced difficult trading conditions and underwent fundamental rationalization.[7] In 1980, 30 per cent of the UK's imports by sea were carried on UK flag vessels, but by 1990 this had declined to 17 per cent.[8] There has been a strong trend towards 'flagging out' British owned vessels: 'In 1985, 75 per cent of the British owned tonnage was on the UK register. By June 1991, this figure had fallen to only 25 per cent. The main beneficiaries of this shift in the last two years have not been the Crown dependencies or the British Dependent Territories but ship registries in the rest of the world.'[9] The Chamber comment that under the circumstances, British shipping has shown remarkable resilience, despite the favourable fiscal regimes enjoyed by many of its competitors.[10]

It was emphasized in chapter 12 that shipping has largely developed under free market conditions, with far less State intervention than other modes such as air transport. Nevertheless, the Chamber is closely involved in discussions over any new legislation affecting the owners of British ships. It has maintained political neutrality, advising and negotiating with the government of the day.[11] It also supports the UK government in action against countries which discriminate against British shipping. Today, as progress is made towards a Single Market, European Community policy has significant influence. Thus, the Chamber and its colleagues in the European Community Shipowners' Associations (ECSA) argue the case for their members' interests. The Chamber supports the aim of increasing the number of ships under EC flags and the number of EC seafarers, but is doubtful that in its present form the proposed EC common flag 'EUROS' will have this effect. More positively, the Chamber welcomes the progress towards liberalization of cabotage for mainland and offshore operations, and later for trades with islands. Together with ECSA, it has worked for block exemption for liner consortia from EC competition rules, which would otherwise prohibit such commercial agreements.[12] The Chamber has successfully argued that ferry operators should continue to sell duty-free products for a substantial period beyond 1992.

Safety and environmental issues are also important aspects of Chamber policy. Liaison with the International Maritime Organisation[13] is therefore important. Directly or indirectly through the Department of Transport, the Chamber offers advice on the formulation and development of conventions such as Safety of Life at Sea (SOLAS). Yet the Chamber is also involved in initiatives which go beyond the requirements of these international standards. For example, it produces a quarterly newsletter *Health and Safety Aboard Ship* and safety posters for shipboard distribution. Together with the seafarer unions, it organises an annual safety competition. Ideas taken from the best entries are often used in the production of health and safety literature. In 1990, the Chamber published its 'Environmental Code', thus acknowledging the role of responsible self-regulation.[14] The Code emphasizes the stringency of existing safety and environmental controls, 'which in many cases are well ahead of those applying to land-based operations'.[15] Amongst other requirements, each member company should formulate a policy on the environment and audit it on a regular basis. This should include the prevention of pollution from oil, noxious liquids, dangerous goods, sewage and so on.

Until recently, the Chamber was directly involved in industrial relations as the employers' representative on the National Maritime Board. In 1990, however, shipping became one of the first industries in the UK to break away from national negotiations for pay and conditions of employment. The Chamber also administered the Merchant Navy Establishment (MNE). It was responsible for selecting, reuniting, and shore training most ratings employed by the Merchant Navy, and also played an important part in reuniting deck and engineer cadets and policy for officer training.[16] In 1990, however, the six offices of the MNE closed, marking the end of an organization set up in 1947 to end casual employment in the industry.[17] At its peak in 1949 the MNE had 50 offices and supplied 300,000 officers and ratings. Since 1990 the Chamber's 'Sealife Ltd' has operated as an employment agency for the supply of seafarers. The Chamber is also represented on the Merchant Navy Training Board which oversees policy on entry standards and training.

The public relations function of the Chamber includes promotional activities to raise the profile of the industry, and to increase awareness of its importance to the nation. In 1990 the Chamber was represented on a Government/Industry Joint Working Party on British Shipping, which was chaired by the Secretary of State for Transport. The report concluded that the industry is 'a vital national asset. After years of contraction, it is lean and fit . . . . The Gulf Crisis has brought back into sharp focus our strategic defence needs for British ships and British seafarers.'[18] Taking its cue from the positive tones of this official study, the Chamber stepped up its campaign for measures to facilitate the necessary investment in modern vessels and for training youngsters for service at sea. A new logo was adopted, and a campaign slogan 'The Seaway to Success'. A video and book were produced to show the diversity and professional skills which contribute to the industry in the 1990s. A series of events was organized in ports all over the country. Local schoolchildren and adults were invited to attend exhibitions and presentations and to go on board a range of ships.

The Bus and Coach Council

The Bus and Coach Council (BCC) is the trade association of road passenger transport (with the exception of taxis and hire cars). Corporate membership is open to bus and coach operators. This includes local bus, express coach, private hire, tour and charter firms. Some of these are operators with very large fleets, including the London Bus, Metropolitan, and ex-National Bus companies. Nevertheless, some are very small firms, especially those in coach-hire operations. Associate membership is open to vehicle manufacturers and other associated suppliers. The overall aim of BCC is 'to watch over, promote and encourage the interests of members and to promote the consideration and discussion of all questions affecting directly or indirectly the road passenger transport industry'.[19] BCC's governing body is the Council. Prior to deregulation and privatization of the bus industry, BCC members were grouped into four – the nationalized sector, the transport executive sector, the local authority sector and the coach and independent bus sector.[20] Since these categories became irrelevant, a new structure was devised to provide a balanced representation of operators in the conduct of the Council's affairs. BCC opted for a new structure based on fleet size:

(a)   Section A, up to 50 vehicles.
(b)   Section B, up to 750 vehicles.
(c)   Section C, over 750 vehicles.

Each section has its own National Committee, with other relevant committees reporting in. Like the Chamber of Shipping, the BCC's Council is supported by a Policy Committee and specialist functional committees, which include:

(a)   Traffic;
(b)   Technical and Engineering.

The day-to-day operation of BCC is handled by the secretariat headed by the Director General.[21]

As explained in chapter 9, a period of rapid change and instability, with a series of take-overs and mergers, followed implementation of the 1985 Transport Act. By the early 1990s the structure of ownership was becoming more stable, but the Gulf War and deepening economic recession brought many difficulties, especially for international coach operators[22] and others in the leisure markets. Although both express coach and local bus services (outside London) have been freed from economic regulation, the industry is governed by stringent and complex quality licensing covering safety, competence and environmental aspects of operation, as discussed in chapter 10. BCC makes sure that its members' views are made known to central and local government, as well as the European Commission. In recent times BCC's representations resulted in the requirement that local authorities should consult operators before installing speed humps or width restrictions on bus routes within the new 20 mph zones. The BCC sought assurances from the Department of Transport that coaches would not be confined to the inner two lanes of the widened M25 motorway. Implementation of the European Community Directive on harmonized driver licences followed a long process of consultation to ensure the best arrangements for bus and coach operators.[23]

As the BCC's Annual Review stresses, 'because British bus and coach operators take safety very seriously, they have one of the most enviable records in the world'.[24] The trade association has made its own contribution – for example since European Road Safety Year in 1986, many of members have pledged support for the BCC Code of Conduct for Drivers, relaunched in 1991 to encourage safe and professional standards. BCC's safety programme for children – Buscode – introduced 1990–1, includes printed materials, stickers and badges which urge children to take care on and around buses. This campaign has reached a quarter of a million children.

BCC continues to emphasize the environmental advantages of using buses and coaches. Yet it also recognizes that irresponsible operators can damage the industry's reputation. Co-operation between the BCC and Westminster City Council resulted in a scheme to report coach firms who park illegally, leave their engines running or block up streets. BCC's journal *Platform* reported that where the local authority considered residents' complaints justified, the matter would be taken up with the trade association: 'BCC has agreed that it will ask members to explain themselves and if necessary apologise if they have broken BCC's Code of Practice on coach parking in London'.[25]

In the summer of 1992 Westminster City Council agreed to lift the evening ban on coach parking along Victoria Embankment and Park Lane for an experimental six-month period. The effects would be closely monitored by an independent survey team jointly funded by the local authority, BCC and the Department of Transport. The Council made it clear that further relaxation beyond this period would depend upon improved coach parking and driving practices and increase in the income from coach parking meters. BCC commented that their members should lead by example and uphold the trade association's Code of Practice for the Operating and Parking of Tourist Coaches.[26]

BCC provide a variety of services for members. These are

especially useful for smaller operators since the trade association effectively provides economies of scale, either by offering services itself, or by negotiating some discounts and special arrangements with suppliers. BCC's 'Bus and Coach Services' range from insurance and pensions to bulk fuel purchasing and antifreeze. BCC provides training services and advice. It also offers briefings on diverse subjects which have covered, for example, a national anti-congestion campaign, seatbelts and the new system of driver licensing. It provides reference materials such as a popular coach parking map of London. It offers a comprehensive operational advice service. BCC have no direct involvement in negotiations with the industry's trade unions, though they may provide advice to operators on various aspects of human resource management.

Through a 'Mutual Aid' scheme, members can call for each other's help when they get into difficulties on the road, and membership provides access to commercial recovery services. Its Bonded Coach Holiday Scheme offers a comprehensive bonding package protecting holidaymakers of operators who join. These various facilities for members may also be said to benefit the customers, since they undoubtedly serve to raise efficiency and professional standards in the industry. The trade association also addresses the needs of customers more directly – BCC have worked with the Department of Transport on a Code of Practice for handling customers' complaints. For some years, it has published the booklet *Getting Around By Bus and Coach – a guide for people with disabilities*, now in its third edition.

In 1990 BCC launched a major initiative to promote buses as a cost-effective, and sometimes overlooked means of tackling urban congestion. An action plan of 18 demonstration projects, costed out at £17.5m, was formulated. BCC members were actively involved in presentations to Ministers, Members of Parliament, local authorities and other policy-makers. Using the campaign slogan 'Buses Mean Business', BCC stressed the advantages of buses over cars and, in some cases, over rail-based systems.[27] By February 1991, the campaign had received the formal support of the Transport Minister Roger Freeman, under whose chairmanship a working group was established to identify towns where the demonstration projects could be run. The proposals have been supported by politicians of all parties, and have also been commended by organizations such as the National Federation of Bus Users.[28]

Road Haulage Association

The Rcad Haulage Association (RHA) is 'an independent non-political organisation to promote and protect the interests of the hire and reward sector of the haulage industry'.[29] It represents those professional hauliers who carry other people's goods to and from factories, shops, warehouses and so on. It has a membership of over 11,000 hauliers, many of which are sole traders with less than four vehicles. Many of its members are small operators who need a great deal of advice and help.[30]

The RHA is governed by a National Council – a committee of 50, elected to reflect the diversity of the industry. The Council elects from its members an Executive Board which directs policy and activities. There are 13 National Groups, which represent the various sectors of road haulage. Thus members may join a group appropriate to their particular business. These include:

(a) Car transporters;
(b) Express parcels, warehousing and distribution;
(c) General haulage;
(d) International.

The National Council and Board are supported by four Standing Committees:

(a) Careers and Training;
(b) Infrastructure;
(c) Security;
(d) Vehicle Standards and Engineering.

The RHA has a Head Office, with its Director General, and seven District Offices, each administered by a District Manager and his/her staff.

As emphasized in chapter 9, haulage in the UK is highly competitive, with over two decades' experience of the rigours of a deregulated market. The deepening economic recession further intensified competition in the early 1990s. The pressure on haulage rates was exacerbated by high interest charges, increased and fluctuating fuel prices and late payment by customers. The RHA's Annual Report 1991 commented that the road haulage sector, 'the barometer of the economy, has suffered more than its fair share of pain. The sadness is that we have seen many, long established, family firms fail under the pressure of the recession.' It points to the particular difficulties created where large companies, as customers of the haulage industry, have taken advantage of the situation and used their buying power to reduce rates. The RHA comment: 'Sadly there are hauliers who are prepared to . . . "buy work" and until they can be convinced of the futility of this practice, it will be difficult to improve rates.'[31]

The RHA has pressed for legislation to require payment of interest on unpaid bills after a specified time. It has continued to express its concern about 'phoenix' companies in the haulage industry. A firm ceases to trade by calling in the receivers, but subsequently starts trading again under a new name, but with the same people, vehicles and premises, thus escaping its debts and leaving its creditors without hope of payment. The RHA has objected to the O licence applications from such firms and would like the regulations to be tougher. The RHA acknowledges the increasing influence of the European Commission on the haulage industry and continues to maintain links in Brussels through its participation in the International Road Transport Union (IRU). It has argued strongly, for example, for harmonization of fuel tax and vehicle excise duty within the European Community.[32] At local level it maintains a dialogue with local authorities, especially over highways and planning matters, and participates in consultations over traffic management proposals which affect haulage operations.

As with the Chamber of Shipping and the Bus and Coach Council, the RHA gives safety and environmental issues a high priority. Recent initiatives have included, for example, an Environmental Code of Conduct emphasizing responsible behaviour by road hauliers. It has stressed that 'diesel is a cleaner fuel than petrol', and welcomed the 1992 Budget 'with its more conciliatory attitude to taxing the fuel'. It is, however, concerned that prejudiced opinion can do much harm to its members' interests: 'The uninformed constant attack on the haulage industry must be countered.'[33] The RHA has, for example, expressed dissatisfaction with procedures by which Licensing Authorities deal with environmental objections to Operators' Licences.[34] In the trade association's opinion, there have been cases where their members have been required to accept restrictive conditions as a result of unsubstantiated and misleading evidence from local residents and pressure groups.

The benefits of joining the RHA include professional advice on vehicles and other equipment and a wide range of members' services. RHA members can take advantage of loan schemes, including short-term borrowing to spread the payment of Vehicle Excise Duty over the year. There is also a breakdown and recovery scheme, with a nationwide network of over 1,500 contractors which are inspected and approved by the RHA.

The RHA also assists its members in industrial relations and other human resource management matters. It facilitates the employers' side of negotiations under the Joint Industrial Councils.[35] Thus, although it does not actually negotiate on their behalf, it conducts the arrangements which allow meetings to take place. The District Managers also provide support and advice to members. Without this service small haulage firms, in particular, would find it difficult to keep abreast of employment law and all its complexities. Thus, 'many members have saved themselves a great deal of trouble, and a lot of money, by using the RHA industrial relations service, before taking action'.[36] Potential legal minefields for the haulier include sickness pay, equal pay, health and safety, redundancy and short-time working.

Conclusions

The evidence suggests that trade associations in transport have done much to raise professional standards. In modes such as coaching and road haulage which have many small firms, operators are able to obtain supplies and support services at favourable rates. Improvements in efficiency and service quality should therefore be passed on to the customer. Professional codes of conduct cover safety, environmental and other matters. These encourage members of a trade association to set a good example. Such self-regulation does, however, rely on voluntary co-operation, and those firms who chose not to join the association cannot be expected to participate. Trade associations in the transport industry have developed considerable skills in promoting the views of their members. Some have the resources and access to government which allow them to lobby persuasively and effectively. They have every right to further the interests of their members in this way, but since some trade associations have a more powerful voice than others, it can be argued that successful lobbying by one mode or sector of the industry might well be at the expense of another.

Notes

1   Gubbins, E. (1988) *Managing Transport Operations*, p. 264: Kogan Page.
2   See discussion on economic regulation in air transport in chapter 11.
3   See discussion on public relations in transport in chapter 5.
4   The Chamber of Shipping (1991) Annual Report, p. 2.
5   Ibid.
6   Branch, A. (1981) *Elements of Shipping*, fifth Edition, p. 104: Chapman and Hall.
7   The Chamber of Shipping op. cit. p. 35.
8   Ibid. from table, p. 36.
9   Ibid. pp. 35–6.
10 Ibid. p. 36.
11 Branch, A. op. cit. p. 104.
12 See discussion of shipping conferences and liner consortia in chapter 12.
13 See discussion of the work of the International Maritime Organization in chapter 12.
14 See discussion on self-regulation in the transport industry in chapter 10.
15 General Council of British Shipping (1990) *Environmental Code*: GCBS.
16 Branch, A. op. cit. pp. 104–5.
17 The origins of this labour supply function actually date back to 1891.
18 Government/Industry Joint Working Party on British Shipping (1990) *Challenges and Opportunities*: GCBS.
19 From the Memorandum and Articles of the Bus and Coach Council.
20 Bell, G., Bowen, P. and Fawcett, P. (1984) *The Business of Transport*, p. 291: Macdonald and Evans.
21 Bus and Coach Council (1988) Annual Review 1987/8, pp. 6–7: BCC.
22 Bus and Coach Council (1991) Annual Review 1990/1, pp. 2–4: BCC.
23 Ibid. p. 11.
24 Ibid. p. 9.
25 Bus and Coach Council (1990) *Platform*, Volume 13, no. 9, p. 9.
26 Parkes, J. (1992) 'Coach Operators on Trial in London as Evening Parking Ban is Relaxed' in *Platform*, June, p. 3.
27 Steer Davis Gleave (1990) *Buses Mean Business – the Solution to Urban Congestion*: BCC.
28 Bus and Coach Council (1991) op. cit. p. 10.
29 Road Haulage Association (1992) 'What is the Road Haulage Association?', press release.
30 Bell, G., Bowen, P. and Fawcett, P. op. cit. p. 290.
31 Road Haulage Association (1992) Annual Report and Accounts 1991.
32 See discussion on harmonization in chapter 14.
33 Road Haulage Association (1987) Annual Report and Accounts 1986.

34 See discussion on environmental objections to O Licences in chapter 10.
35 The Joint Industrial Councils have a much reduced role in wage bargaining nowadays. While they are still strong in Scotland and parts of the South, the total number of Councils has reduced considerably. The trend in wage bargaining is away from national or regional agreements towards bargaining at plant level.
36 Road Haulage Association (1987) op. cit.

Part VI

Futures

19

Environmental Issues

The development of transport is closely associated with economic growth and rising affluence. Nevertheless, all modes of transport have adverse effects on the physical environment. This chapter examines a wide range of environmental problems associated with the transport sector. It considers how they affect the quality of life, and the implications for the health and well-being of people, plants and animals. It examines the issue of how such problems can be evaluated, and what action, if any, can be taken.

Adverse Effects

Developments in transport bring greater personal mobility and allow a better range of commodities to be distributed to consumers. Some, such as private jet aircraft, are enjoyed by a privileged minority. Others, such as Light Rapid Transit systems, benefit a larger section of society. Transport is an important sector of the economy. In the more affluent, industrialized countries, it typically represents between 4 and 8 per cent of Gross Domestic Product, and accounts for between 2 and 4 per cent of jobs.[1] In less wealthy countries transport is generally seen as a catalyst for economic growth.

Over the past few decades, however, there has been increasing public concern over the detrimental effects of transport which can do serious harm to the environment. There are some who even question whether the material benefits justify the sacrifices, especially where these sacrifices are distributed unevenly within society and between geographical areas. Those who suffer the problems may not experience the benefits. Furthermore, it is argued, consideration should be given to conservation of the physical environment upon which future generations will depend. Such concern was expressed, for example, in the elections to the European Parliament in 1989 when Green Party candidates received significant numbers of votes in most EC countries. There has therefore been pressure to translate such beliefs into action through political programmes at local, national and international levels.

With regard to the transport sector, a number of serious environmental problems can be highlighted:

(a) **Noise/vibration** – This may adversely affect the quality of life, disturb sleep patterns and add to mental stress. Buildings and other structures may be damaged over a period of time by some types of vibration, such as that caused by commercial vehicles and railways.

(b) **Atmospheric pollution** – Harmful gases and particulates (small particles) may cause respiratory diseases and other serious health problems. They may even alter the climate and hence the ecology of regions. The damage which may be occurring to the earth's ozone layer is partly attributed to increasing road traffic and aircraft movements.

(c) **Water pollution** – Harmful substances may poison water-courses, lakes and seas, causing damage to marine life and to the health of human beings. In recent years, a number of large-scale pollution incidents have been caused by shipping accidents.

(d) **Visual intrusion/danger** – The intrusion of transport operations (including road traffic), may have an adverse impact on residential neighbourhoods, historic towns, attractive countryside and other sensitive areas. Not only might the visual qualities and character of such places be diminished, but the danger to pedestrians and cyclists might be considerable.

(e) **Severence of land and communities** – The construction of new ways and terminals, e.g. major roads and railway depots, may divide up land holdings such as farms, sometimes making them unviable. They may also sever communities by creating a physical barrier which is dangerous, or impossible to cross.

A fundamental point is that in a pure free market system, the various costs imposed on the environment are not borne by the transport undertaking itself. Economists sometimes describe these disadvantages as 'negative externalities'. Since the costs are not internalized by the polluter one might argue that the transport service is offered at too cheap a price. In other words the passenger fare or freight tariff takes no account of the economic costs which have been imposed.

To take a very simple example, steam locomotives deposited large quantities of soot on people's clothes, buildings and so on along the route, yet the cleaning bills were seldom paid by the railway operator. Pollution of the sea by oil tankers, or by the flushing out of ships' fuel tanks, may adversely affect fishing industries and tourism at beach resorts. Residential property values might fall as the result of increased noise levels near an expanding haulage depot or other vehicle base.

Conflicts and Decision-Making

A solution advocated by some economists would be to 'make the polluter pay'. In other words, the extent of the damage should be assessed by an impartial third party and an agreed formula used to calculate the amount of money needed by way of compensation. Better still, the polluter would be required to eliminate/ mitigate the problem, doing so at his own expense. This principle may hold good in certain circumstances. There are however a number of drawbacks which limit its more general application:

(a) **Clear identification of cause and effect** – Firstly, it may be difficult or impossible to isolate the source of the environmental problem and to prove cause and effect. Atmospheric pollution, for example, is often the result of emissions from many separate sources. In a city these might include many thousands of private cars and commercial vehicle operators, as well as other modes of transport and industries such as factories and coal-fired power stations.

(b) **Distance factors** – This is further complicated where the source is geographically distant from the effects. Pollution of the atmosphere, and of the sea, may drift for hundreds or even thousands of miles. International action would therefore be necessary to administer a scheme of compensation.

(c) **Time factors** – A further difficulty is that the effects may take years to build up to a point where they can no longer be tolerated, for example disturbance from traffic noise experienced by residents on a busy road. The effects may also be cumulative, as in damage to historic buildings from vibration and atmospheric pollution.

(d) **Measurement and conversion to a monetary value** – Some adverse effects are difficult or impossible to measure in any objective fashion. Although there may be some common agreement concerning the evaluation of traffic noise and so on, there is no agreed scale for measuring the effects of visual intrusion, such as the impact of a motorway in an attractive landscape or a seaport on a scenic coastline. Many features of the physical and natural environment are effectively 'zero priced' since they have no immediate economic value to mankind. Their loss would therefore go 'undetected'. As Harry Conway concluded,[2] this problem has arisen with many natural resources: 'The difficulty comes from the fact that the natural environment has long been regarded as "free". It has a zero-priced supply because no market place for what it provides really exists . . . . Since it has no market price, there are no limitations on its consumption.'

In practice then, the State and its agencies may have to act as arbiter to establish and enforce environmental standards. In other words, quality regulation may be necessary. This approach may be appropriate where the nuisance can be readily quantified and action taken. For example, where the noise standards for motor vehicles are exceeded, a fine may be imposed. In applying such environmental standards the State may allow certain exceptions to the general rule. For example, the Anglo-French supersonic aircraft Concorde was excluded from UK noise regulations, presumably because of its significance to the aerospace and civil aviation industry. Other countries took a different view! The Greater London lorry ban was introduced to give some relief to residents on certain routes in the evenings and at weekends. Operators of road freight vehicles could, however, apply for exemption plates which would provide immunity from the ban. In theory, these were to be granted where the operators had little alternative, such as those delivering fresh produce to wholesale markets. In reality, such exemption plates were granted very liberally.

Where the effects on the environment cannot readily be quantified, a different form of arbitration is required. As outlined in chapter 15, land use changes defined as 'development' are regulated under town and country planning legislation. Thus, the State identifies and evaluates the environmental implications of a proposal – such as an aerodrome for general aviation. These are balanced against other factors, including the economic benefits. If the proposal is considered wholly unsuitable, planning permission may be refused. Alternatively, conditions may be imposed to ensure that the hangars, terminals, control towers etc. are as sympathetic and unobtrusive as possible, within the constraints of safe operation.

Limitations might also be placed on the type of aircraft allowed and on the hours of operation, so as to minimize disturbance to people living in the surrounding area.

With regard to motorway and trunk road proposals, a different procedure is followed. Firstly the programme for additions to the national highway network is announced by central government, usually in the form of a White Paper. Alternative routes are then compared using the Department of Transport's modelling technique known as 'COBA'. This provides a method of evaluating the costs and benefits of each alternative using a common benchmark. As Stuart Cole has explained, the costs which COBA takes into account are:

(a) capital costs, including land purchase, construction and temporary facilities such as diversions;
(b) maintenance cost savings on existing roads and future costs incurred on maintaining the new road.

The only benefits which COBA takes into account are:

(a) journey time savings;
(b) savings in vehicle operating costs;
(c) accident cost savings.[3]

These alternative proposals, and the preferred route, are then presented to affected parties and the general public, section by section. A Public Inquiry is conducted by the Department of Transport and objectors have the right to make their views known. They may even suggest further alternative routes, but they cannot question the underlying principle that a road should be built, since this decision has already been made by central government. Such inquiries do, however, provide some opportunity to identify and discuss qualitative aspects, for example the effects on:

(a) landscape beauty;
(b) species of flora and fauna;
(c) ancient monuments and historic buildings;
(d) the viability of farmland;
(e) the character of small settlements.

Many environmentalists would argue, however, that the whole procedure is unsatisfactory. COBA takes into account only a very

limited set of benefits and focuses on those which accrue to the
road user. The environmental factors are not given due consideration until the Public Inquiry stage, by which time a considerable
amount of work has been put into the planning and design of the
road proposals. Furthermore, the modelling technique does not
allow investigation of the scope for diverting traffic to another
mode of transport, such as investment in an under-used railway
along a particular corridor.[4]

So far, the discussion has emphasized the range of environmental problems associated with transport, the possibility of measuring
these adverse effects and the process of regulation and decision-
making whereby conflicts are resolved. The following section
provides a more detailed discussion of one environmental issue
which has attracted considerable attention over the past 30 years
– the disturbance caused by aircraft noise around major airports.
It examines the various ways in which the problem is being
tackled.

Example of Aircraft Noise

The nuisance of aircraft noise has often brought a hostile reaction
from people living close to major airports. Pressure groups have
publicized the issue and lobbied government at local and national
level. In a few cases protest movements have staged violent demonstrations, as at Narita Airport, Tokyo. Politicians, especially those
with constituencies near major airports, have, in turn, demanded
action against aircraft noise by governments and international
agencies. In one sense, noise disturbance is subjective: some individuals may be mildly irritated, whereas others experience acute
distress. Nevertheless, social surveys of reaction to aircraft noise,
notably sleep disturbance, show spatial patterns which correspond
with the alignment of flight paths, aircraft movements and the
type of aircraft overflying residential areas. Efforts have been made
to develop a scientific method of measuring aircraft noise which
broadly correlates with the results of social surveys.

The noise impact of a particular type of aircraft, following a
given take-off procedure on a given departure route, can be plot-
ted as a 'noise footprint'. This is based on the empirical evidence
of recordings made using noise meters with microphones mounted
in strategic positions on the ground. The scale of measurement

generally used is the 'perceived noise decibel' (PNdB). Yet actual noise disturbance is taken to be the product of the noise of individual aircraft movements and the number of these movements over a period of time. For this reason, a composite measure is used. Since 1961 the two factors have been combined as the Noise and Number Index (NNI). The resulting NNI contours give an indication of the areas worst affected.

The UK government, like many others, recognizes that aircraft noise is a serious environmental problem which requires action by the State, by aircraft manufacturers, by airlines and by airport authorities. Nevertheless, it does not wish to impede the expansion of civil aviation:

> There are, of course, conflicting interests and the aim is to achieve a workable compromise. It is clearly not possible to shut down all airports and stop civil flying completely. Apart from the fact that a great many people wish to fly on business or pleasure, civil aviation makes a vital contribution to our national economy. Some 18 per cent by value of our exports are sent by air. The task is to maintain a fair balance between the interests of the people who live near airports and the benefits of air transport to the nation as a whole.[5]

By far the most satisfactory way of tackling aircraft noise is by **reducing it at source**. Considerable progress has been made since the earlier generation of jet airliners, built in the 1960s and early 1970s. They can now be made quieter by fitting them with 'hush kits'. More significantly, quieter engines such as the Rolls Royce RB 211 are used to power modern aircraft such as the Lockheed Tristar and some versions of the Boeing 747 and 757. In spite of an increase in seating capacity of the order of 300 per cent, noise levels experienced on the ground can be as little as 50 per cent of earlier jet aircraft. In order to reap the benefits of such technological developments, noise regulations have been agreed through the International Civil Aviation Organisation (ICAO), with common standards for member countries.[6]

Another approach to the reduction of aircraft noise is through **operational measures**. This includes departure procedures. Pilots are required to take off and climb at the steepest angle compatible with safety, at or near maximum power. On landing, it is desirable to adopt a 'continuous descent approach' in order to avoid flying low and level over residential areas. Bearing in mind the problem of sleep disturbance, the hours of flying may also be regulated. Quotas or complete bans on night flying may be introduced. Another operational method is to route aircraft so as to avoid overflying the most densely populated areas wherever possible, especially in the earlier part of the climb. 'Noise Preferential Routes' may therefore be established through Air Traffic Control. It should be stressed, however, that these form a centre-line, rather than a precise track. Aircraft will tend to wander slightly either side of this line within the tolerances of navigational aids, wind and flying technique.

Finally, the problem can be alleviated on the ground through **noise insulation**. Grants towards the cost of insulating residential property in the worst affected areas have been made available, using double glazing to deaden the noise. Such grants have been recovered from airport authorities who will, in turn, pass the cost on to airlines and thus to their customers. Such financial compensation provides an example of the principle of making the polluter pay discussed above. It should be pointed out, nevertheless, that noise insulation is not a wholly satisfactory solution – residents may wish to open their windows and their enjoyment of gardens and open spaces such as public parks may also be impaired by the intrusion of aircraft noise.

In general terms, however, the example of aircraft noise provides some cause for optimism. The NNI contours around major airports such as London Heathrow and London Gatwick are now shrinking despite a substantial increase in the volume of airline traffic carried. This can be attributed mainly to the increasing proportion of quieter modern aircraft, which carry considerably more passengers per aircraft movement. Nevertheless, some other environmental problems present a more disturbing prospect. Their effects are much more widespread and long-lasting than aircraft noise.

Atmospheric Pollution and World Issues

The transport sector is not the only cause of air pollution. Nevertheless, it is a major contributor. A study for the European Conference of Ministers of Transport and Organisation for Economic Co-operation and Development (OCMT/OECD) concluded that in industrialized countries, particularly in urban and densely populated areas, human activities are responsible for almost all air pollution, of which transport sources make up about 50 per cent. Thus 'a major proportion of overall health effects resulting from air pollution can therefore be attributed to the transport sector, and mainly the road transport sector'.[7] Toxic emissions with serious consequences for human health include:

(a) **Carbon monoxide (CO)** – Ninety per cent of all CO emissions originate from transport, mainly private cars. In higher concentrations, which may occur in urban areas under particular climatic conditions, it causes loss of productivity at work and general discomfort. It restricts the supply of oxygen to the bloodstream, and hence to body tissue. It can affect the central nervous system, impairing co-ordination, vision and judgement. It can worsen conditions associated with diseases of the heart, lung and circulatory system.

(b) **Lead (Pb)** – Added to high octane fuels, it can affect the kidney, liver and reproductive system, as well as blood formation. At higher concentrations it can impair the brain – children being particularly at risk. It is also suspected of having other consequences, especially as a carcinogen. Fiscal incentives for non-leaded petrol in the UK and other countries should help, but it is highly poisonous and can damage human health at very low levels of concentration.

(c) **Hydrocarbons (HC) and Organic Compounds** – Some have serious adverse effects – symptoms include eye irritation, coughing and drowsiness. Some appear to be carcinogenic, and are particularly associated with leukaemia.

(d) **Nitrogen Oxides (NOX)** – Damage to health includes blood and respiratory disorders. They can also damage plant life, including forests and farm crops.

These and other poisonous gases and substances in the atmosphere have been the subject of considerable public concern. In some badly-polluted cities such as Los Angeles and Tokyo, action and controls have measurably reduced the local levels of some toxic emissions and air quality has improved. In the United States, for example, unleaded petrol contributed to a fall in lead emissions from transport sources of 68 per cent between 1975 and 1983.[8] Yet overall, there is little cause to rejoice. Processes are more complex than was once thought to be the case. Some emissions undergo chemical change in the atmosphere, and may be carried long distances. One particular concern is the deposition from 'acid rain', which affects plant life, and hence the natural ecosystems.

There is also a great deal of concern over the destabilization of the earth's climate. The increased concentration of carbon dioxide (CO_2) is particularly associated with the burning of fossil fuels for transport and other activities. Carbon dioxide is not a pollutant since it is a natural component of the atmosphere, but its build-up may be causing a global increase in temperature (the greenhouse effect) with consequent rise in sea levels and implications for natural ecosystems. The build-up of chlorofluorocarbons (CFCs) is associated with chemical processes which seem to be thinning the ozone layer in the stratosphere. Unfortunately, CFCs can persist for 100 years or more.[9]

In some countries, environmental issues have gained a particularly high profile. In Holland, for example, concern over amenity and the quality of life, as well as issues such as global warming, are reflected in the National Environment Plan, published in 1990. This has established targets for reductions in emissions, including those for which transport is a major source.[10] Adopted in the same year, the Second National Transport Plan (SVV2+) was revised to take wider account of environmental issues. The Dutch government have accepted that the adverse environmental consequences would militate against any further substantial expansion of the roads programme. Thus, the planned investment is allocated with 38 per cent for railways, 14 per cent for other public transport, and 7 per cent for inland waterways. Elsewhere, particularly in the less developed non-OECD countries, environmental policy has less priority and greater weight is given to the goal of economic growth. Nevertheless, the concept of **sustainable development** has been widely publicized. Adopted by the World Commission on Environment and Development, it holds that 'the use of resources and the environment should not reduce the potential of these resources for future generations'.[11]

Transport and Energy Consumption

The sustainability of energy resources is a cause for particular concern. Research by the Organisation for Economic Co-operation and Development (OECD) suggests that transport activities account for about 30 per cent of total energy consumption in industrialized countries, and that they are almost wholly dependent upon oil. Road vehicles account for 82 per cent of total consumption by the transport sector, air 13 per cent, rail 3 per cent and inland waterways 2 per cent.[12] The two unprecedented increases in oil prices in the 1970s prompted many governments to focus on the need for energy conservation, and some introduced fuel efficiency measures. Nevertheless, from 1970 to 1987 average oil consumption by motor vehicles in industrialized countries rose by over 50 per cent. Furthermore, road transport's share of total final oil consumption increased from 34 to 47 per cent. The main reasons were the growth in traffic and vehicle numbers as well as the relatively low cost of motoring.[13]

The essential problem is that the oil basins are finite, and non-renewable. The length of time that they will last depends on the interplay of demand and supply. As Professor I.C. Cheeseman has commented, the salient factors are:

(a) the price that is paid for oil;
(b) the rate at which oil is used;
(c) the policy of the oil producers;
(d) the availability of alternative energy supplies.

He concludes that it seems 'reasonable from the evidence available that crude oil supplies will continue to be available in quantities that will not cause a catastrophic increase in price for the rest of this century and will be available at an inflated price for the first twenty years of the next century.'[14] The economic problems which resulted from the dramatic price increases instigated by the oil-producing countries in the early to mid-1970s provided a salutory lesson of the seriousness of the general supply problems which will occur in the twenty-first century.

How then, has this dependence on fossil fuels come about? It is closely linked with the process of industrialization and economic development. Manpower, horsepower, and windpower gave way to steam technology in the nineteenth century. Coal provided a high-density fuel which was convenient to distribute, store and handle for rail and sea transport. Then, in the twentieth century, development of the oil-fired internal combustion engine opened up new possibilities for road transport. Railway locomotives and ships could also be run on oil, and the second half of the twentieth century saw a huge expansion of air transport, which is wholly dependent on oil as a source of energy. Compared to coal, oil is even more convenient – as a liquid it can be distributed by sea/

rail/road tanker or by pipeline, and can be stored and handled using tanks and mechanical pumps. As a means of transmitting power, electricity has relevance for some modes. A particular advantage is that a variety of energy sources can be used to generate the power. In rail transport, the capital investment is economic for some trunk passenger and freight operations. Electric traction is also appropriate for urban metros and Light Rapid Transit. In road transport, however, it is limited (so far) to trolley-buses and certain battery-driven vehicles of limited range such as milk floats.

All this has had important implications for the process of urbanization. In pre-industrial society most of the population lived in rural areas and communities were largely self-sufficient. Most food and other necessities were grown and processed locally. The majority of people travelled only short distances for work and recreation, and did so on foot or horseback. Industrialization meant mass production and specialization of economic activities. Raw materials were transported by sea and land from all over the world to factories and plant where they were processed, and transported back to distant foreign, as well as home markets. There was a large-scale net migration of the population from countryside to the growing urban areas. Yet the industrial cities of the nineteenth century were still relatively compact, and the majority of their population still walked to work, public transport generally being too expensive for everyday use by working people. Nevertheless, the railways brought new opportunities for personal mobility where cheap fares were available for longer distance leisure and social journeys.

The twentieth century brought the widespread development of lower density suburbs as towns and cities encroached further into the countryside. At first, these followed the corridors of public transport routes, but later the freedom offered by the private car allowed a more dispersed pattern of residential development, especially in North America.[15] In the UK after the Second World War, planning policies designated 'green belts' to contain the growth of major urban areas, beyond which free-standing 'new towns' were built. In theory, the latter were supposed to be self-contained, with sufficient employment for the local population. Commuting distances would therefore be reduced. In practice, however, commuting patterns simply leap-frogged the green belts. Meanwhile the decline of traditional manufacturing industries led to an out-migration from inner urban areas, especially in the 1970s and early 1980s.

In the UK and other developed countries the more affluent commuters and their families have moved out, not to large settlements, but to small towns and villages in attractive countryside. Second and retirement homes are also located in the country, National Parks and coastal areas. The new 'sunrise' industries involved in new technology and information-processing are locationally mobile, and have also chosen, in many cases, to move out to a rural environment. Leisure and retailing centres have sought greenfield sites near trunk roads out of town. Thus, for the first time since the industrial revolution, the countryside is being recolonized. Professor Peter Hall has emphasized the importance of this dispersed decentralization for land use planning in a post-industrial age.[16] The demands placed on transport and energy resources are also of great significance for planning. Journeys are longer and follow more complex patterns. Passenger movement is made possible by private cars, and in general it is difficult or impossible to serve by public transport. Similarly, freight distribution is made possible by road vehicles, and transfer to rail is generally uneconomic and often impractical.

The search for cost savings has already encouraged greater fuel efficiency. This will become even more critical as scarcity of supply causes oil prices to increase. Immediate savings can be made by **vehicle operators** through more fuel efficient driving techniques. More car-sharing may also be practical and, in North America in particular, encouragement has been given to High Occupancy Vehicles (HOVs). In road freight, better routeing and scheduling through information technology can bring significant improvements in vehicle utilization. **Manufacturers** of private cars and commercial vehicles have responded by developing more fuel-efficient engines and aerodynamic bodies. Similarly, modern aircraft make more efficient use of aviation fuel. In the longer term, however, it is hard to escape the conclusion that action by **government** will be necessary. As a last resort fuel rationing may be necessary. A more strategic approach would, however, include positive encouragement for greater use of public transport, passenger movement and greater use of rail and water for freight where it is appropriate to do so. Governments may also assist research into alternative energy sources for motive power in transport as well as for other sectors. As yet, however, there are few signs of a technological breakthrough which could greatly reduce our dependence on fossil fuels.

Thus, unless alternative sources of energy can be developed in the near future and made economically viable, industrialized countries will face the daunting prospect of having to rely on fossil fuels which will become increasingly scarce and therefore expensive. It will be difficult to provide the transport to support current lifestyles with a decentralized and scattered population, and a dispersed pattern of economic activities.

In recent years, there has been greater recognition of the link between energy efficiency and **land use planning**. A study by Susan Owens of the University of Cambridge for the Council for the Protection of Rural England[17] concluded that planning policies must encourage 'the evolution of energy-efficient development patterns and transport systems'. Nevertheless, for several decades the opposite has been happening. 'Social and economic trends have interacted to make land use and travel patterns increasingly energy intensive and less sustainable.'[18]

Conclusion

The environmental problems arising from transport are truly diverse. Some have localized effects, whereas others have regional and even global implications. Some are brief intrusions, whereas others do lasting damage. The intensity of some adverse effects can be quantified and measured using fairly straightforward methods. Others are qualitative and involve subjective assessment. The example of aircraft noise suggests that concerted action by governments, manufacturers of equipment and transport operators may bring relief to those who suffer the environmental disadvantages. Nevertheless, it would be wrong to assume that technology-led solutions can be found in other cases. Air pollution is responsible for many serious hazards to human health and appears to be changing the world's climate and ecosystems. Yet it is only partially understood and more complex than was once thought. The concept of sustainable development seems to offer greater promise than short-term remedial action. Nevertheless, important issues, including our dependence on oil for most of the transport industry's energy requirements, raises serious doubts as to how the principle could be put into practice.

Notes

1   European Conference of Ministers of Transport and Organization for Economic Co-operation and Development (ECMT/OECD), (1990) *Transport Policy and the Environment*, p. 11: ECMT/OECD.
2   Conway, H. (1990) 'Environmental Compromise' in *Transport*, October, p. 243.
3   See Cole, S. (1987) *Applied Transport Economics*, p. 181: Kogan Page.
4   Rogers, K. (1991) 'More Roads? The Government's Roads Programme Reconsidered' in *The Planner*, 8 March, pp. 7–9.
5   Department of Trade (1983) *Action Against Aircraft Noise*.
6   See discussion of the role of ICAO in chapter 11, the standards are referred to as chapter 2 and chapter 3, these being relevant sections of Annex 16 to the Chicago Convention.
7   ECMT and OECD (1990), op. cit. p. 30, and subsequent discussion, pp. 30–45.
8   Ibid. pp. 33–4.
9   Ibid. p. 33.
10 Sturt, A. (1991) 'Taking the Integrated Route' in *Transport*, May/June, p. 74.
11 World Commission on Environment and Development (1987) *The Bruntland Report*, Green Paper.
12 European Conference of Ministers of Transport/OECD (1990), op. cit. p. 20.
13 Ibid.
14 Cheeseman, I.C. (1982) 'The Implications of Energy, Futures for Public Transport', *The Urban Transport Future*, p. 29, (ed. Young A.P. and Cresswell R.W.): Construction Press.
15 See discussion of congestion and urban development in chapter 20.
16 Hall, P. (1988) 'The Industrial Revolution in Reverse?' in *The Planner*, January, pp. 15–19.
17 Owens, S. (1991) *Energy-Conscious Planning*, p. 48, commissioned by the Council for the Protection of Rural England: CPRE.
18 Ibid.

20

Responses to Congestion

In the UK and many other countries, congestion impairs the performance of the transport sector. It can therefore retard the economy, disrupt social life, and harm the physical environment. The various modes of transport are affected in different ways, but the problems are almost universal and seem to be getting worse. This final chapter examines the underlying reasons for congestion, and explains why it is so hard to overcome. Focusing on the issue of urban traffic congestion, it explores a range of solutions which are now being implemented in various parts of the world.

Supply and Demand

Congestion occurs where the capacity of a transport system is overburdened by the level of traffic. As Mandy Bridge has commented, it 'seems simplistic to state that the existing infrastructure and system cannot cope with the increased demand being placed upon them. Yet, that basically is the problem.'[1] The nature of congestion varies from mode to mode. Nevertheless, there are some common principles which apply to the transport sector as a whole.

It was noted in chapter 3 that the output of transport cannot be stored, but must be provided as and when the customers require it. In other words, the product is highly perishable. Unfortunately, the level of demand is seldom uniform over time. Rather, it tends to fluctuate, with regular peaks occurring in a few hours of the day, a few days of the week, or a few weeks of the year. The capacity of the transport system must therefore be capable of carrying the traffic during those periods when demand is at its highest level.

Examples occur in both passenger and freight transport, and in every mode:

(a) Commuter railways must accommodate the high traffic flow which generally occurs for just two or three hours in the morning and evening peaks, Mondays to Fridays only. Furthermore, the flow is in one direction only – inwards or outwards.

(b) Deliveries to retail stores must anticipate the pattern of purchasing behaviour of the shoppers. Furthermore, as stressed in chapter 8, many products have a limited shelf-life, and the retailers will want to minimize the amount of stock they hold to reduce carrying costs.

(c) Vacational traffic, carried by scheduled and charter airlines from Northern Europe to the Mediterranean resorts, peaks at weekends during July and August. Air carriers transporting exotic fruit, vegetables and flowers must respond to a very short growing season.

In some cases, it may be possible to flatten out these demand fluctuations through marketing off-peak services and offering price discounts. For example, the cross-channel ferry services described in chapter 4 promote bargain breaks and day-trips during the winter season. In some cases, premium fares or tariffs can be used to discourage some people from travelling or sending their freight at peak times. Thus, InterCity railways may charge a higher fare on Friday evenings, or other busy times on certain routes. Nevertheless, there are limits on the extent to which passengers and freight shippers can reschedule their activities. Thus, the fundamental problem of having to respond to periods of peak demand cannot be eliminated. In almost all transport operations there will be times when the system is overloaded and put under stress.

Chapter 6 outlined the systems approach which emphasizes the interdependent elements of the whole. In transport systems these comprise the ways, vehicles and terminals which are necessary to provide a service. Change in one element will have implications for all others. Thus, a capacity constraint – a bottleneck – in one element will affect the system as a whole. In other words, the system's capacity is limited by the element which has the least ability to handle the throughput of traffic.

In air transport, for example, the system comprises the aircraft (vehicles), the runways, controlled airspace and air corridors (ways) and the terminals for passengers and freight at airports. Developments in aerospace technology and innovative marketing have enabled attractively low fares and freight tariffs to be offered on high-capacity jet aircraft. This has successfully tapped a latent demand for air transport, and over the past two decades traffic has increased dramatically on many routes. Unfortunately, however, the air transport system has been put under considerable stress in many countries, since the capacity has not been able to keep pace with demand.

Significant bottlenecks occur. Firstly, there is a limited amount of runway capacity. As noted in chapter 13, governments have been reluctant to permit new runways and other airport development, fearing unpopularity from local residents and other well-organized pressure groups. Efficiency in the use of available runways, and of controlled airspace, is achieved through Air Traffic Control. Some believe that technology will allow further progress to be achieved, but operations are governed by the accepted safety standards and rules for aircraft separation. At some airports, further constraints are imposed through the quotas or outright bans on night operation discussed in chapter 19.

On the ground, the throughput of passengers and freight is limited by the design capacity of terminal facilities. In international passenger terminals, the 'Busy Hour Rates' of the check-in, security search, passport control, and departure lounges must be taken into account. Despite computerization, the limiting factor is usually the check-in, since this generally has the lowest capacity.[2] Finally, consideration must be given to surface transport. Near many major airports the road, and in some cases the rail systems, are severely overloaded. Airport traffic mixes with other traffic, exacerbating congestion, especially on the main corridors from the airport to and from the city centre. Thus, airports with good surface access, such as London Stansted described in chapter 6, have a significant advantage.

The Supply of Transport and Private Enterprise

Chapter 13 emphasized the significance of the price mechanism in a free market economy. If effective demand for a commodity increases, and supplies run short, the 'natural price' will rise – in the short term, at least. This will then act as a signal to entrepreneurs to supply more of that commodity. Thus, equilibrium will eventually be restored, and the natural price will come down again, provided there is healthy competition between suppliers at the market-place. Thus, supporters of free market principles argue that private investment and commercial competition should prevail in transport, as in other sectors of the economy.

With regard to the vehicles of a transport system, there are some circumstances in which private ownership and deregulation can increase the supply and thus provide some relief to congestion. In Hong Kong, for example, privately-owned Public Light Vehicles (minibuses) gained market entry during a public transport strike in 1969, and continued to operate on free market principles. Some, identified by their livery, provide non-scheduled services. Neither their fares nor their routes are regulated. Thus, they respond flexibly to the interplay of demand and supply. A report by the Organization for Economic Co-operation and Development (OECD) concluded that these 14-seat vehicles 'have helped to deal with the travel demands which the more traditional forms of public transport could not cope with in the short term or at the heights of the peak period'.[3] Since minibuses share a common way, however, they are subject to traffic congestion along with other vehicles.

In the UK, deregulation of express coaches in 1980 allowed market entry to commuter coach operators into London. These can provide their customers with an acceptable alternative to overcrowded commuter trains, at a lower fare.[4] They also provide an alternative to the private car, making better use of roadspace per passenger carried. Nevertheless, coaches carry only a very small proportion of people who commute into the capital. And, as with the minibuses described above, a major drawback is that they share a common way. They have proved successful only on certain corridors, using radial motorways and trunk roads where traffic congestion is not too severe.

There may also be circumstances in which the increased supply of vehicles actually worsens congestion. Deregulation of domestic air services in the United States in 1978 brought increased flight delays at major hub airports, as described in chapter 11.[5] In the UK, bus deregulation in 1986 brought congestion to certain city centres such as Glasgow, where bus operators competed to pick up customers on busy streets. Some bus and coach stations, like airports, suffer from excess peak demand, while some bus and coach operators add to congestion on narrow streets by waiting and loading outside. Critics of the free market might argue that such developments in air and road passenger transport illustrate the problem of wasteful competition. Rival operators, often with low load factors on their vehicles, make inefficient use of ways and terminals. But to what extent can commercial enterprise help increase the supply of infrastructure?

With regard to ways and terminals, projects once thought possible only through public sector funding are now being built with private finance. As shown in chapter 13, these include very large-scale schemes including the Channel Tunnel, Light Rapid Transit, international airports, river crossings, motorways and relief roads. Even a trunk railway, the proposed Heathrow-Paddington Link, will be part funded by the private sector. All these infrastructure projects make (or will make) a significant contribution to the relief of congestion on heavily-used routes. Indeed, the roles of public and private sector have undergone such a reversal that it could now be questioned whether the State could allocate the scale of funding required. Not only is the public sector's share of national income being reduced as a principle of government policy in the UK, but the demand for infrastructure is rising at a very rapid pace, outstripping supply in many cases.

Closer examination suggests, however, that such schemes can seldom be free from State intervention. In particular, there are controls over competition, which are not usually applied to other industries. Firstly, there may be too little competition. In some transport, there is a danger that the owners of the infrastructure might abuse a position of actual or near-monopoly. In the case of BAA plc for example, strict rules apply to the prices that may be charged to the airlines and other users of their London airports. On the other hand, too much competition may create a climate of such uncertainty that nobody would be willing to risk their capital. Thus, in some cases, potential investors may require assurance that they will be granted exclusive rights to operate a tunnel, a river crossing, or a Rapid Transit System for a period, perhaps of several decades, to provide a more certain market base and an adequate payback period.

Other European countries have favoured a more balanced approach where the public and private sectors play a complementary role in the provision of transport infrastructure. As outlined in chapter 19, the Dutch government has adopted an ambitious National Transport Plan (SVV2+) which takes account of the need to protect and enhance the physical environment. Thus, the allocation of public finance is strongly slanted towards the railways, other public transport and inland waterways. Yet the private sector is also being encouraged to invest in national transport infrastructure, including the Port of Rotterdam and a new freight railway line. A partnership between the Dutch government and commercial enterprise is favoured in order to promote sustainable economic growth in a competitive Single European Market.

The European Commission itself has set up 'the Group 2000 Plus' with the task of examining the problems facing European Community transport, and making recommendations regarding future policy. The Group concluded that the increased movement of people and goods associated with completion of the Single Market will 'cause added stress to the already strained transport infrastructure'. It regretted that transport policy as foreseen by the Treaty of Rome had not been implemented, and that 'investment in transport as part of Gross National Product is at a record low'. European transport axes or major corridors should be identified by the EC in order to set standards on levels of speed, noise, safety and environmental pollution. As explained in chapter 14, subsidy to suppliers is not generally favoured by the EC because it distorts competition. Nevertheless, 'the exceptions are where long-term transport infrastructure is needed. Here, a mixture of public and private investment is necessary.'[6]

Demand Management: Electronic Road Pricing

The previous section has focused on the supply of transport and the question of whether free market principles can be applied to bring relief to congestion in various modes. To what extent can the demand side of the market be managed? With regard to road transport, an important difficulty is that the pricing system for use of roadspace is extremely crude, particularly compared to other modes. In many countries, such as the UK, payment of road tax for a vehicle (every 6 months/12 months) provides access to the entire road network, except for certain toll bridges and tunnels for which additional payment is required. Fuel tax may be more equitable, in that its payment bears some relationship to distance/engine capacity. These various methods cannot, however, use the price mechanism to manage the demand for roadspace at a particular place, at a particular time.

The case for 'road pricing' can be traced back to the nineteenth century. In 1964 a Ministry of Transport study chaired by Professor R.J. Smeed concluded that road pricing offered the most promising solution to traffic restraint.[7] At that time the technology was undeveloped, but today Electronic Road Pricing (ERP) has been tried and found to be effective. Furthermore, the case for it has never been stronger – traffic congestion is steadily growing. It is now generally accepted that road building and public transport improvements will not on their own solve the congestion problem; the general movement towards a market-oriented transport sector makes road pricing more appropriate.

The case for road pricing recognizes that the individual motorist takes account only of the marginal cost to himself. Quite commonly this is perceived as the fuel cost. As the Chartered Institute of Transport's study *Paying for Progress* has commented, the theory is quite simple: 'The more vehicles use roads the busier they get; after a while congestion sets in and a few extra vehicles lead to disproportionate delays for all – both the new traffic and that which was already there. This happens because the additional traffic takes no account of the delay it imposes on the relatively large number of existing road users.'[8] Selective charging would therefore price up the use of roadspace where and when congestion occurs.

Simple area licensing systems can require motorists to prepurchase a permit before entering a congested zone. This method has been used in Singapore since 1975. It has had the desired effect of reducing the number of private cars entering the central zone at the morning peak, initially by 75 per cent.[9] A similar method, known as 'cordon pricing', requires toll gates to be set up at entry points – a system introduced in Norway for the centre of Bergen in 1986, and Oslo in 1990.[10] Yet, manual systems involve physical checks and administration. Electronic Road Pricing has enabled permit cards and toll booths to be replaced by electronic monitoring and charging. This facilitates a much more flexible arrangement, allowing charges to be put up or down in order to target congestion at a particular place at a particular time.[11]

There are two main types of ERP. The first, known as Automatic Vehicle Identification (AVI) involves the fitting of an electronic number plate, allowing the movement of each vehicle to be traced. Data is captured using an electronic loop under the road surface. This enables a vehicle crossing into the zone to be identified.

Through roadside equipment, the code for the vehicle and details of locations and times visited enter a computer known as a communications controller.[12] The vehicle's keeper is then billed periodically – an arrangement similar to that used for household electricity and gas charges. This method was pioneered in a 12-month experiment in Hong Kong. The AVI system correctly identified 97.7 per cent of the tagged vehicles, and security features including closed-circuit television proved effective in detecting fraud.[13] Nevertheless, AVI proved unpopular from a civil liberties point of view, since there were fears over the misuse of electronic surveillance by the authorities.

The second type of ERP does not identify individual vehicles. Instead, an on-board meter makes a charge by deducting units from a stored value or 'smart' card. Signals from a beacon at the roadside can be used to register when the vehicle crosses into the cordon area. One device, linked to the vehicle's odometer, commences charging only when a combination of speed and distance travelled indicates that the vehicle is in a congested street. Proposals for implementing such a scheme are now well advanced for the city of Cambridge in the UK. This is part of a wider package including public transport and road improvements as well as more traditional traffic management. Such a strategy is considered necessary to maintain the economic prosperity and amenity of a historic city with narrow streets, where congestion is a serious problem, forecast to get worse unless appropriate action is taken.[14]

Congestion and Urban Development

Traffic congestion should be understood, not only in terms of the transport system and the use of its various modes, but also in relation to the pattern of land use and development. In North America between the two World Wars, mass-produced motor cars became affordable for a large section of the population, and motoring costs were low. The gridiron pattern of wide streets in urban areas facilitated motor traffic. Furthermore land was readily available, and there were few planning controls to restrict the growth of car-oriented low-density suburbs. In the postwar period the number of cars continued to increase, and a programme of highway construction accommodated the growth in demand on a 'predict and provide' basis. Nevertheless, in the 1990s congestion in many

North American cities has reached crisis proportions. Sometimes, a situation known as 'gridlock' occurs, and traffic ceases to flow at all.

Many European cities have inherited land use patterns from previous eras, and street patterns unsuited to motorized traffic. Typically, they spread out along radial public transport routes into the countryside, absorbing small towns and villages. In the UK, leafy suburbs developed around London and other major cities as mortgages became available for middle-class commuters and their families. These were built at a relatively low density on 'green field' land which was cheap, especially during the severe downturn in farming of the interwar period. It was not until after the Second World War, however, that car ownership began to rise to a significant level, and by this time a comprehensive system of town and country planning had been established. Land use policies, including the green belts described in chapter 19, were used to prevent reoccurrence of the disorderly sprawl of pre-war days.

The growth in road traffic did, however, create difficult problems for urban planning. An influential government study – *Traffic in Towns* (1963) – otherwise known as the 'Buchanan Report', examined the environmental problems of traffic congestion. By projecting the anticipated growth of traffic, and calculating the required capacity, the report illustrated the scale of road construction which would be required. This served to demonstrate that many large urban centres could not be adapted to accommodate all the demand for roadspace, even with very large-scale demolition and reconstruction. Nevertheless, during the 1960s and early 1970s urban motorways were built in cities such as London and Leeds, causing the dislocation of communities and a great deal of distress to the residents and businesses who remained. Unfortunately, they brought only short-term relief to congestion, as traffic filled the available roadspace.

As Carmen Hass-Klau has commented: 'Modern traffic congestion is clearly related to the desire to decentralise cities, to unrestricted promotion of motor vehicle use and to the incapability of adapting existing cities to the demands of car use.'[15] In London there was a fall of 2 mph in road speeds during the decade of the 1980s, reducing traffic flows to only 3 mph faster than they were in 1912.[16] As in many other major cities, congestion now extends over 7 hours of every working day over much of the metropolis, and over 12 hours in the central area.[17] Congestion is spreading out geographically into the suburbs and along the radial routes. Traffic on the M25 orbital motorway, built as a bypass around London, is often slow-moving, and sometimes stationary.

The economic waste associated with congestion has been highlighted in a report by the Confederation of British Industry (CBI), which also stressed the personal frustration and disruption of family life it can cause.[18] An increasing number of private cars in the capital continues to exacerbate the problem. A report by the Department of Transport in 1989 estimated a rise of between 22 and 34 per cent in car ownership in the capital by the year 2001.[19] As the Chartered Institute of Transport have commented, the car-owning resident population faces a major conflict of interest. 'The greatest flexibility to respond to the wide array of journey types is provided by the car, but this creates considerable stress and environmental problems. Journey times are uncertain; parking is difficult; pollution caused by noise and fumes is increasingly intolerable. These same problems create difficulties for the cyclist and pedestrian.'[20]

The London Planning Advisory Committee – the Forum of the 33 London Planning Authorities – commissioned Coopers & Lybrand Deloitte to investigate the capital's future competitiveness as a world city and how this could be sustained and enhanced. The study recognized that a world city must not only serve as a centre where international business can be conducted efficiently, but must also offer desirable residential areas and diverse and cosmopolitan cultural activity.[21] Transport is recognized as an essential part of the 'enabling infrastructure' of such a city. Reviewing the successes and failures of several world cities such as New York, Paris, Tokyo and Frankfurt, the study identifies five critical attributes for a world-class urban transport system:

(a) **Government** policy which allows strategic transport planning and effective implementation, especially through consistent funding.
(b) An efficient, high quality, safe and **integrated mass transit system**.
(c) A **fares system** which actively encourages people to use public transport.
(d) Efficient **highway networks** meeting demand, especially for freight, essential services and public transport, without becoming congested by car-borne trips which could be better made by public transport.
(e) Affirmative action to protect and improve the quality of life, particularly in respect of the adverse **environmental** impacts of traffic.[22]

Plate 20.1 Making Toronto a liveable metropolis, S.J. Shaw

The following case study examines the strategy of a North American metropolitan authority, and how it intends to tackle congestion and wider urban planning issues over the next 20 years.

Case study: Toronto – the liveable metropolis

Metropolitan Toronto is the centre of a region with a wide range of employment opportunities, the focus of Canada's financial sector and the seat of Provincial government. The city's strengths lie in its strategic location for international trade, the diversity of its economic activities and the skills of its workforce. Until the 1970s, Toronto's employment base was oriented towards freight handling and distribution around the harbour front and railhead, as well as the manufacturing industry and warehousing along the shores of Lake Ontario. But, as in other countries, these sectors have declined. In the future, a greater proportion of the city's economic growth will depend on the generation, handling and management of information. The emphasis, in planning for the year 2000 and beyond, will be on public intervention to create the conditions for a 'liveable metropolis' based on the three interacting components of:

(a) a healthy environment;
(b) economic vitality;
(c) social well-being.

Metropolitan Toronto's planning strategy emphasizes the significance of an integrated transport system in establishing an urban form to achieve these important goals.

Metropolitan Toronto's current population of approximately 2.3 million is expected to rise to between 2.5 million and 2.8 million over the next 20 years. The larger region of the Greater Toronto Area (GTA) has a population of 4 million, which is anticipated to rise to about 6 million. Hitherto, the rapid growth in areas of the GTA outside Metropolitan Toronto has created heavy traffic congestion and placed considerable development pressure on agricultural land and open space. This has been exacerbated by the low density of much of the residential development which is insufficient to support public transport. During the 1960s and 1970s there was an ambitious programme of highway construction, including elevated urban motorways. Capacity was increased to meet the growth in demand for use of private cars. Today, however, such large-scale road schemes have few supporters. Not only is the financial cost prohibitive, but the environmental cost is unacceptable. Furthermore, increasing the supply of roadspace while permitting the outward expansion of car-oriented suburbs only provided a short-term solution to the problem of congestion.

Metropolitan Toronto has therefore adopted a strategy of re-urbanization – reinvestment and redevelopment of the existing urban area making more efficient use of the available land and other resources. Rather than continuing to expand further outwards onto greenfield sites, the emphasis is now on urban planning to reduce sprawl; to reduce reliance on the private cars; to reduce loss of natural resources; and to reduce the infrastructure servicing costs. Re-urbanization will focus on three structural elements:

(a) A hierarchy of centres will be strategically located across Metropolitan Toronto, with high-density development in compact areas, and served by rail-based transport including rapid transit and subways (underground).
(b) Linear development as corridors along major streets, which can be served by high frequency public transport, including streetcar (tram) and bus.

(c)   An extensive system of green spaces to balance the re-urbaniza-
      tion of existing built-up areas, thereby conserving the natural envi-
      ronment and providing compatible opportunities for leisure and
      recreation.

The transport system is therefore a key element of the planning
framework for re-urbanization. Improvements are necessary to
accommodate population and employment expansion, to meet
changing travel needs and to support the aim of economic vitality.
Co-ordination and control is necessary to ensure that the transport
system is developed in a balanced way. A fundamental change of
emphasis 'from moving vehicles, to moving people is both desirable
and necessary. Expansion of the rapid transit system and increasing
its attractiveness as an alternative to the automobile for a wider
range of trip origins, destinations, and purposes, is a high priority.'[23] The concept of centres and corridors should improve the
balance between housing and employment on a local area basis,
and new employment should be encouraged to locate within 300
metres of rapid transit facilities.[24]

These principles are translated into policies and proposals in the
Metropolitan Toronto Official Plan, which is the legal framework
for managing and directing physical development. The 1980
Official Plan has recently been reviewed in the light of social and
economic change, as well as increasing awareness of environmental
issues. Changes in the political and administrative structure have
established a directly-elected body, with a broader mandate and a
greater emphasis on the 'regional interest'. With regard to public
transport, Metropolitan Toronto recognize the desirability of co-
operating with the other municipalities within the GTA and with
the Government of Ontario with regard to their 'Go Transit' rail
services. The feasibility of creating a regional and inter-regional
transit network with integrated scheduling, fares, and other
'systems' features, is being explored.[25]

Metropolitan Toronto has direct responsibility for the transport
system within the geographical area of its jurisdiction. This includes
the rail- and road-based public transport, metropolitan express-
ways (motorways) and arterial streets. It is also responsible for
licensing taxis, and shares responsibility for parking, pedestrian
and parking facilities with the second-tier local authorities. Thus,
integration of these components of the transportation system
with each other, and with transportation systems under other

jurisdictions, enables the mobility needs associated with people, goods and services to be met within Metropolitan Toronto and across the Greater Toronto Area.[26] The framework for urban transport in Canada is therefore very different to that in the UK conurbations discussed in chapter 15, where first-tier Metropolitan Counties have been abolished and public transport provision has been subjected to free market conditions through deregulation and privatization.

The policies and proposals of the Official Plan for Metropolitan Toronto include measures to ensure that transport capacity will meet forecast demand for the movement of people and goods. In the past, the main emphasis was on increasing the supply to meet observed and projected travel demand, including that for private cars. Today, however, it is becoming 'increasingly desirable and necessary to pursue the management of travel demand, while avoiding undesirable constraints on mobility'.[27] Thus, to meet the healthy environment objectives of reducing energy consumption and the emission of pollutants associated with car use, a reduction of vehicle-kilometres of travel per person-trip will be pursued by promoting and facilitating public transport, walking and cycling, increased occupancy of cars and shorter trips. The Draft Plan includes targets for the year 2011. These include an average reduction from 5.6 (1986) to 4.4 peak-period vehicle-kilometres of travel per person-trip within Metropolitan Toronto and the average increase in non-automobile modal share from 40 per cent (1986) to 50 per cent for peak period trips, from and within Metropolitan Toronto.

Although the current package of initiatives represents a fresh approach, notable for its comprehensiveness, the city's support for high-quality public transport is long-established. Following a 'boom-and-bust' period of private enterprise, municipal control began in 1921.[28] Under the Toronto Transit Commission (TTC) nine separate streetcar networks were unified with a single fare and free transfers, and the 1920s saw a $30 million programme of improvements and line extensions.[29] Bus and coach services were added, and after the Second World War TTC started constructing a subway system. The first section of its North-South line opened in 1954, and during the subsequent decade the subway acted as a catalyst for commercial development along its route, bringing new employment and tax revenue to the city. The first section of an East-West line opened in 1966, and also stimulated economic growth within walking distance of the subway stations. Some of the streetcar routes were abandoned, but in 1972 a decision was taken to retain the seven surviving routes, and during 1978–82 nearly 200 new streetcars were delivered, followed by over 50 articulated units 1988–90.[30]

The 1980s and 1990s have seen further expansion and upgrading of the multi-modal network in accordance with land use policy. When a Major Centre was proposed at Scarborough to the North-East of the Downtown area the developers favoured a rail-based link. Thus, a new line was built to connect with the Eastern terminus of the subway at Kennedy. Scarborough Rapid Transit is something of a showcase for new rail technology, with automated cars powered by linear induction motors using elevated guideways for 1½ miles of its 5-mile length. The line, which opened in 1985, now carries about 40,000 passengers per day, but this will increase substantially as Scarborough City Centre's employment level and residential population expands from 13,000 to about 60,000 in 2011, in accordance with the proposals in the Official Plan. Public transport is also playing its part in the regeneration of the old harbourfront area. The Harbourfront Light Rail opened in 1990, uniting the Downtown area with the redeveloped waterfront, with its mixture of apartments, offices, shopping, leisure and cultural facilities. Also in 1990, Metropolitan Toronto resolved to proceed with a new rapid transit route to link the Western end of the Harbourfront Light Rail with Bloor Street subway station to the North. Using a central reservation along a wide street, and following stringent environmental guidelines, the new Spadina Line is scheduled to open in 1996.[31]

Metropolitan Toronto has little or no control over global economics. Nevertheless, through its various functions as an urban authority it can influence a number of the factors which contribute to the quality of life enjoyed by residents and visitors. It competes with other cities in North America for a share of the growth associated with the 'idea-driven' industries and services. It needs the well-educated and well-trained people who drive these new economic activities. A liveable metropolis can do much to attract the economic growth and the people. The planning strategy of Metropolitan Toronto is to facilitate a civilized urban form with an integrated network of high-quality public transport to provide accessibility, and reduce the need for inefficient movement, especially unnecessary journeys by private car.

Conclusion

The rising affluence of consumers in developed countries is generating a huge increase in demand for transport. As a result, all modes show signs of strain at bottlenecks where demand exceeds supply. Worsening congestion causes much public concern, but no simple solutions can be offered. Throughout the world, there is a desire for personal mobility, especially that provided by the private car. Yet, neither town nor country can be physically adapted to accommodate the projected demand. Road space is in short supply. The use of cars must therefore be restrained and managed, perhaps through road pricing. Rising affluence has also brought an increased awareness of the need to protect and enhance the environment. The case of Toronto suggests that any serious attempt to combat congestion requires a comprehensive approach to transport of all modes, together with the planning of land use and amenity. This is both desirable and necessary to sustain the economic growth and quality of civilized living which consumers value as much as personal mobility.

Notes

1   Bridge, M. (1989) 'Which Way Congestion?' in *Transport*, September, p. 187.
2   Lewis, N. (1990) 'Airport Planning – What is it?' in *The Planner*, 24 August, pp. 13–14.
3   Organization for Economic Co-operation and Development (1988) *Cities and Transport*, Ch. 3, p. 48: OECD.
4   See discussion of express coach deregulation in chapter 9.
5   Stephenson, F.J. (1987) *Transportation USA*, p. 376: Addison Wesley.
6   Commission of the European Communities (1991) *Transport in a Fast Changing Europe*, ISEC/B10/91, pp. 1–4.
7   Ministry of Transport (1964) *Road Pricing – the Economic and Technical Possibilities*: HMSO.
8   Chartered Institute of Transport (1990) *Paying for Progress: A Report on Congestion and Road Use Charges* (executive summary): CIT.
9   Tan Swan Beng (1991) 'Singapore: Road Pricing Pioneer Prepares to go Electronic', in *Urban Transport International*, May/June pp. 24–27.
10 Chartered Institute of Transport, op. cit. pp. 10–11.
11 Hughes, G. (1992) 'The Cambridge Congestion Metering Scheme' in *Transport*, May/June p. 8.

12   Organization for Economic Co-operation and Development, op. cit. p. 53.
13   Chartered Institute of Transport, op. cit. pp. 12–13.
14   Hughes, G. op. cit. pp. 7–9.
15   Hass-Klau, C. (1990) 'Public Transport and Integrated Transport Policies in Large Metropolitan Areas of Europe' in *The Planner*, 25 May, p. 15.
16   Department of Transport (1989) *Traffic in London*: HMSO.
17   Hass-Klau (1990), op. cit. p. 15.
18   Confederation of British Industry (1989) *Transport in London: the Capital at Risk*: CBI.
19   Department of Transport (1989), op. cit.
20   Chartered Institute of Transport (1991) *London's Transport – The Way Ahead*, p. 7: CIT.
21   London Planning Advisory Committee (1991) *London: World City*, pp. 7–8: HMSO.
22   Ibid. pp. 128–9, my summary but authors' emphasis.
23   Metropolitan Toronto Planning Department (1992) 'The Liveable Metropolis – Metropolitan Toronto Official Plan, Internal Review Draft', p. 11: Metropolitan Toronto.
24   Ibid. p. 87.
25   Ibid. p. 16.
26   Ibid. p. 109.
27   Ibid. pp. 111–2.
28   Toronto Transit Commission (1989) *Transit in Toronto*, p. 11: TTC.
29   Ibid. p. 12.
30   Wickson, E.A. (1991) 'Toronto's New Light Rail Line' in *Light Rail Review* 2, pp. 63–65.
31   Ibid.

Questions

The following questions are reproduced by courtesy of the Chartered Institute of Transport. They are selected from the Qualifying Examination Paper 'Corporate Strategy and Policy in Transport'.

Self-assessment questions for part I

1.1 'An entrepreneur seeks out commercial opportunities which he exploits through innovation, energy and personal commitment. A manager ensures that the business delivers its output every day consistently, efficiently and reliably. In transport entrepreneurs have contributed to growth and development – managers have made the trains run on time.'
Discuss.

1.2 In what ways does the management of a transport company or undertaking differ from the management of other enterprises?
What would you, therefore, expect to be the most appropriate management organisation for a transport enterprise?
(Give examples when answering *both* parts of the question.)

1.3 The railways were the first large-scale industrial organisations. They adopted management structures based on those used in the armies of Western Europe and America. Such 'military' principles of management served the railways well for over a century, but now they may no longer be appropriate.
What do we mean by a 'military' organisation structure and what are its characteristics?
Why is it likely to be particularly suited to a railway company?
Is such an organisational principle relevant today? If so, say why, and if not, what would you recommend in its place?

1.4   In some forms of transport (especially air transport), the vehicles used and cost to the customer are virtually the same for all operators on a route. If you were one of several operators in this situation operating on a particular route, explain how you would go about obtaining more customers than your rival operators. Use *two* different modes of transport as examples, *one* freight and *one* passenger.

Self-assessment questions for part II

2.1   Explain the 'systems concept' as applied to transport. For your own country, discuss *two* examples, *one* for passengers and one for freight, where the 'systems concept' is already working or where it could be utilised effectively.

2.2   What is the function of a transport terminal? Use *three* different examples of passenger terminals and discuss their mutually common requirements, and the special requirements needed for each.

2.3   Describe the main features of a 'hub-and-spoke' transport operation, commenting on the role of the vehicles, ways and terminals. What do you consider to be the advantages and disadvantages of hub-and-spoke compared with other systems?

2.4   In former times the goods we purchased in the shops were generally presented just as they were produced. While there was some specialised distribution of perishable goods, most food, clothing and durables passed through a similar system of warehousing and wholesalers. The past two decades have seen a dramatic change in the nature of the goods to be distributed. Analyse these changes and the distribution technologies which have been developed to cope with them.
What are the demands now placed on the management of physical distribution by the market, and how have they been dealt with?

Self-assessment questions for part III

3.1   Twenty years ago virtually all public passenger transport, and a great deal of freight transport, was entirely regulated by governments. Why was this? How was such regulatory control exercised? In recent years there have been considerable moves towards deregulation. What are the arguments for this and to which modes of transport do they tend to apply?

3.2 How far is public passenger transport a suitable case for competition? Select two of the following – air transport, sea ferries, long distance coaches, local bus services, mini-buses – and describe what form competition between operators might take and what benefits and dis-benefits there might be for the consumer in both the short and long term.

In your two cases, do you foresee any requirement for the competition to be regulated?

If so what form would it take?

3.3 Air transport is worldwide and consequently requires international bodies to control it. State which two bodies do this and explain their nature and composition, how they function, and whether they liaise with each other.

3.4 Describe the structure and objectives of the International Maritime Organisation (IMO).

How far is it now meeting these objectives?

What are Liner Conferences and how do they work? Do they benefit the operator or the user, and why?

Given the rapidly-changing pattern of world trade and the substantial technological and marketing developments of the last two decades, how do you think international shipping will be organised in the future?

Self-assessment questions for part IV

4.1 (a) Why are some transport services subsidised?
(b) Describe the different ways in which subsidies can be provided.
(c) Explain why subsidised services can lead to inefficient operation and discuss how this can be overcome.

4.2 'Europe will never be a single market until there is a single transport system with a single set of regulations.'
Discuss.

4.3 Explain the reasons why a local authority might subsidise passenger transport in a rural area.
What do you consider the best arrangement to ensure value for money where such subsidy is provided?
Justify your answer by providing examples where appropriate.

4.4 There has recently been worldwide renewal of interest in Light Rail Rapid Transit Systems. What are the advantages of such systems and why are they particularly appropriate today?

Light rail also has certain disadvantages when it comes to dealing with, for example, competition or traffic peaks; how would you expect the management of such systems to achieve financial viability? (Please answer this question with reference to actual systems with which you are familiar.)

Self-assessment questions for part V

5.1   'User bodies are only required where there is a regulated market structure; where competition exists, user rights are naturally protected as the user has freedom of choice.' Discuss critically.

5.2   In transport, as in other industries, governments have established user bodies to help safeguard the interests of consumers.
Taking *one* such user body as an example, explain the organisation's role and its reporting structure.
On what issues has the user body criticised the transport operator's performance in recent times?
How can the operator and the user body work together for mutual benefit?

5.3   (a)   What is a Trade Association? Include in your answer a discussion of its organisation, aims/objectives, financing and role in the transport industry.
(b)   Illustrate your answer to part (a) by giving *three* examples of trade associations, commenting on the points raised in part (a).
(c)   Using your three examples, discuss whether Trade Associations are beneficial or detrimental to the customer.

5.4   How does membership of a Trade Association help the management to run a successful transport undertaking? Describe any possible disadvantages.
How can the management of such an undertaking mobilise consumer opinion through a Transport User Body or other channels of communication with its customers, in order to improve the quality of service and efficiency?
(Please give examples when answering both parts of this question.)

Self-assessment questions for part VI

6.1   The cost of a road system is probably many times the apparent expenditure by government and users. Typically governments have sought to recoup their expenditure through permits, licences and general taxation – crude methods which do little to regulate supply and demand.

What alternative methods of charging for the road system are available to governments, and how might they be administered? What are the main advantages and disadvantages of direct road pricing?

6.2 Discuss any *three* environmental problems associated with transport and explain how these may be tackled through government action. What methods are available to measure such environmental conflicts, and how may these be used to mitigate them?

6.3 For your own country, what form of 'energy shortage' is most likely to occur? Explain what problems this will create for the transport industry and discuss ways of overcoming these.

6.4 Through the world, major cities are suffering road congestion. This is not just inconvenient; it imposes real costs through delays, pollution and inefficiency. What do you consider to be the causes of this congestion, and how would you evaluate its consequences?

How might a transport authority, either national or local, act to alleviate congestion while at the same time improving mobility for people and goods?

Glossary

ASA Air Service Agreement. A reciprocal agreement between two countries governing various aspects of traffic rights for air services between them. In general, they cover the designation of airlines and gateway airports, as well as the frequency and capacity of services. In many cases they require the airlines concerned to agree fares and tariffs, which must be approved by both governments. ASAs are also known simply as 'bilaterals'.

Bill of Lading A multi-purpose document used in sending freight by sea. It serves as a contract of carriage, receipt, and evidence of ownership. A 'through' bill of lading is used for through transits by more than one carrier, including onward movement by another mode, e.g. for containerized cargo.

Breakbulk Ship A vessel built to carry non-containerized cargo such as loose pallet-loads, crates etc.

Cartel An association of businesses, formed in order to fix prices and otherwise restrict competition between them.

Capital Finance invested in a business, e.g. in its plant, vehicles, other equipment, inventory etc.

Carrier A transport operator, i.e. carrying passengers and/or freight by any mode of transport.

Cellular Ship A vessel built to carry ISO containers, having vertical cells with special guides for loading.

Charter A non-scheduled service where the whole vehicle with driver/ pilot etc. is hired by an individual or group.

Chartered Institute of Transport The premier professional body for transport managers in the UK, Commonwealth and other countries. Its members work in road, rail, sea, and air transport, as well as related fields of professional practice.

Classification Society An independent organization such as Lloyd's

Register of Shipping which surveys and inspects vessels to ensure sea-worthiness, as a service to owners, insurers etc.

Cold Chain Temperature-controlled distribution of food and other stock from production through the supply chain to the retail outlets where the items are sold to the final customers.

Combined Mode Inter-modal freight transport, especially road-rail, where each mode is used to its best advantage with regard to the overall effectiveness and efficiency of the through transit.

Conference, Liner A cartel agreement between shipping lines, specific to scheduled services on a particular route or 'trade'.

Consolidation The grouping together of freight consignments into larger units for onward movement. The term is sometimes used in the context of passenger transport, especially combining groups of airline passengers to make up a full-load charter flight.

Container A form of unit load consisting of a metal box for carrying freight on vehicles. Those built to the specifications of the International Standards Office (ISO containers) are designed for inter-modal transport by road, rail and sea.

CRS Computer Reservation System. A computerized airline booking system which provides real time information on flight times, seat availability, fares etc. Access can be gained by travel agents and other retailers using computer terminals on their own premises.

Diversify To spread or branch out one's business into non-core activities, e.g. a bus operator may also trade as a supplier of contract engineering services, offer driver instruction, vehicle recovery, van hire, consultancy etc.

Dwell Time The period of time while a vehicle is at rest at a terminal.

EC European Community. The association of European countries formed under the 1957 Treaty of Rome to foster economic co-operation and to liberalize trade between the Member States. The founder members were Belgium, France, Holland, Italy, Luxemburg and West Germany. Denmark, Ireland and the UK joined in 1973, Greece in 1981, Spain and Portugal in 1986.

EDI Electronic Data Interchange. A system of computerized order processing, where trading partners (e.g. supplier/retailer) can exchange information electronically, dispensing with the need for paperwork.

Entrepreneur An individual who initiates and carries out a business venture, bearing the risk of commercial success or failure.

Equity The shares issued by a limited company.

ESOP Employee Share Ownership Plan. An arrangement by which the employees jointly own equity in a company, and may benefit from profit-sharing.

Feeder A route or service which has a relatively low level of traffic flow, but 'feeds in' to a trunk operation, e.g. branch line railway.

FMCGs   Fast Moving Consumer Goods. Items of stock for personal and household use, where suppliers can achieve a high volume of throughput. These include breakfast cereals, detergents, toilet rolls etc.

Freight Forwarder   Agents who organize through transits of their customers' consignments. Their services are usually comprehensive, including arrangement of inter-modal transport, customs documentation, insurance etc. They act as intermediaries between shippers and transport principals (operators) and negotiate volume discount rates for freight transport.

Gateway Airport   An airport designated for international airline services.

Hub-and-Spoke System   A system of transporting either passengers or freight. Traffic is collected and carried by vehicles which are routed along radial routes (spokes) inwards to a central terminal (hub). The hub facilitates interchange (passengers) or transhipment (freight) before onward movement outwards along the spokes to the appropriate destination terminals.

ICAO   International Civil Aviation Organisation. The worldwide intergovernmental agency which promotes and co-ordinates the safe and orderly growth of air transport. It has special status as an agency of the United Nations.

IMO   International Maritime Organisation. The worldwide intergovernmental agency which promotes and co-ordinates safety at sea and other maritime matters including action to prevent pollution. It has special status as an agency of the United Nations.

Inclusive Tour   A leisure travel package supplied by a tour operator which generally includes flights, coach transfer and accommodation, with the benefit of a company representative to assist the customer when travelling and at the destination.

Integrated Carrier   A freight transport operator which has a dedicated fleet of vehicles of more than one mode, e.g. aircraft and road vehicles for express deliveries. Thus, the customers' consignments are carried exclusively within the operator's own transport system.

Interchange Facility   Terminal facility which allows passengers to transfer from one vehicle to another. In some cases this involves transfer between different modes, e.g. bus, taxi or car to trains at a railway station.

InterCity Railway   A main line passenger railway providing services between major urban centres.

Interline   An arrangement whereby passengers or freight can be transferred from one airline to another for onward movement.

Inventory Management   Management of a firm's stock of materials, parts, and finished products and their value, i.e. the total amount of capital tied up in stock.

JIT   Just-In-Time. A system of inventory management which minimizes inventory holding. The emphasis is upon reducing lead times, smoothing the flow of stock, and improving product quality and customer service.

LA Licensing Authority. The regulatory body for the road freight industry in the UK which issues Operator's Licences etc. Each LA is responsible for a Traffic Area and reports to the Secretary of State for Transport.

Laissez-Faire Government policy based on a free market philosophy, i.e. with a reluctance to intervene in the market-place.

Land Bridge An overland route for freight movements, as an alternative to a sea route, i.e. using rail and/or road transport, e.g. Trans-Siberian Land Bridge.

LGV Large Goods Vehicle. In conformity with EC unified driving licences, the term has replaced 'HGV' in the road freight industry.

Limited Company A form of ownership in which shareholders' liability is limited only to the extent of their equity holding. In a public company, shares can be bought by the general public, whereas in a private company they cannot.

Liner Freight or passenger ship which sails to a fixed route and schedule.

Local Plan A statutory land use plan, generally prepared by a District Council, which sets out policies and detailed, site-specific proposals for land use and transport, in accordance with the general context of the County Structure Plan.

LRT Light Rapid Transit. A light tracked urban public transport system using tramcar-type vehicles. These may use track on an exclusive right of way such as a central reservation or subway and/or mix with other road vehicles and pedestrians in urban streets.

Market Share The proportion of the total market in some commodity which is supplied by a particular firm, type of supplier etc. It is usually expressed as a percentage.

Marketing Mix The marketing ingredients which a firm blends together in order to influence customer demand in a particular target market. These ingredients are usually analysed under the headings: Product, Price, Place, Promotion.

Mode of Transport The method of moving passengers or freight, i.e. by road, rail, sea, air, or pipeline.

Monopoly A market structure where one supplier has exclusive possession of the trade in some commodity.

Multiple Retailer A retailing firm with many outlets, e.g. a chain of supermarkets.

Municipal A transport or other operation owned by a local authority, usually accountable to a committee of councillors.

Oligopoly A market structure dominated by a few large suppliers of some commodity.

Order Processing   The activities carried out by a supplier in response to a customer's request for stock.

Own Account   Operator who only carries goods in connection with his or her own business, as opposed to carrying goods for hire and reward.

Park-and-Ride   A facility which enables people to park their cars and interchange with public transport – either rail or bus. For example, commuters may be encouraged to use a car park at an outlying station and continue their journey into a city centre by train.

Partnership   A firm which is jointly owned by two or more people who take responsibility for its liabilities, according to a legal agreement.

PCV   Passenger Carrying Vehicle. In conformity with EC unified driving licences, the term has replaced 'PSV' in the bus and coach industry, with regard to drivers' regulations.

Piggyback   A form of bi-modal freight transport, where road trailers are carried on rail flatwagons.

Policy   Commitment to a particular approach on a specific issue, e.g. policy on customer service, safety at work, recruitment and training, noise reduction etc. The term is used both in politics and in business.

Positioning   Development of the Product and other elements of the Marketing Mix, in order to appeal psychologically to particular target markets.

PTAs   Passenger Transport Authorities. Policy-making bodies of local government for the metropolitan areas (major conurbations, e.g. Greater Manchester). Originally set up under the 1968 Transport Act and 1972 Local Government Act to plan and co-ordinate public transport within their respective areas. The 1985 Transport Act has reduced and restricted their influence with regard to local bus operations.

PTCs   Public Transport Companies. Companies which operate municipal public transport undertakings at arm's length from the local authorities who own their equity. An arrangement set up under the 1985 Transport Act.

PTEs   Passenger Transport Executives. The body of professional officers employed by PTAs to implement their policies.

Public Corporation   A transport or other operation owned by central government, where there is some separation of ownership from day-to-day management. Unlike a State department the staff are not civil servants.

Ring-and-Ride   A term used in community transport for a service which enables the user to telephone and arrange for door-to-door transport by minibus, taxi, car etc.

Ro/Ro   Roll-on/Roll-off. A ferry or deep-sea vessel which carries cars, coaches and/or 'wheeled' cargo, i.e. commercial vehicles.

RTW   Round-The-World. Independent shipping lines which provide express container services on routes which circumnavigate the world, with a limited number of ports of call.

Segmentation The process of identifying different groups of customers. Within each segment there will be common characteristics which distinguish the group from other types of customer.

Shipper A customer of a freight carrier, i.e. the person or agent sending a cargo consignment.

Shippers' Council An organization formed to represent the users of freight shipping services and to enhance their negotiating strength.

Sole Trader A firm which is owned and run by one person who takes full responsibility for its liabilities.

Sortation Process of sorting individual parcels for their correct destinations in an express delivery system.

State Department A transport or other operation owned by central government and directly accountable to a government minister, its staff being civil servants.

Strategy Plan of action. Originally a military term, in business or government it refers to the medium- or long-term planning framework, as opposed to short-term tactics.

Structure Plan A statutory development plan prepared by a County Council which sets out the policies and broad proposals for land use and transport, looking forward 15 years or so into the future.

Sustainable Development Prudent use of resources and the environment, so as not to reduce their availability and quality for future generations.

System An interdependent set of elements which work together to perform a common function.

Targeting, Market The process of assessing the potential of the various market segments, and selecting one or more which the firm is well placed to serve.

Terminal, Computer The equipment for transmitting electronic messages to/from a computer.

Terminal, Transport The access/exits points along the ways of a transport system, e.g. bus stops/stations, loading areas/bays for vans and trucks, railway stations and goods sidings, seaports/riverports/wharves and airfields/airports.

TEU Twenty-foot Equivalent Unit. A measurement equivalent to an ISO container which is twenty feet long, e.g. to express capacity of vessel, throughput of terminal etc.

TPP Transport Policies and Programme. A planning document prepared each year by County Councils where these exist, and by Borough/District Councils where they do not, i.e. in London and Metropolitan areas. They set out the context of transport policy and the programme of expenditure, as well as a statement of progress.

Trade Association An organization which represents the interest of a particular group of employers and owners in an industry. In transport these are mostly mode-specific, an exception being the Freight Transport Association which is multi-modal in its scope.

Traffic The passengers or freight carried by a transport operator.

Traffic Commissioner The regulatory body for the bus and coach industry in the UK which issues the Operator's Licences etc. Each Traffic Commissioner is responsible for a Traffic Area and reports to the Secretary of State for Transport.

Tramp Freight ship which sails neither to a fixed route or schedule, but may be hired or chartered at a negotiable rate.

Transhipment Facility Terminal facility which allows freight to be transferred from one vehicle to another. In some cases this involves transfer between different modes, e.g. lorry/train/barge to ships at a seaport.

Trunk A route or service which has a relatively high level of traffic flow, and forms the main artery of the network, e.g. main line railway.

TSG Transport Supplementary Grant. An annual grant from central government to local authorities for specified types of transport expenditure. Originally introduced in the mid-1970s to allow considerable local discretion, the type of scheme eligible for TSG has been narrowed down considerably since the mid-1980s.

UDP Unitary Development Plan. Following the abolition of the Greater London Council and Metropolitan Counties in 1986, the Borough and District Councils have been required to prepare UDPs as statutory development plans for their areas. These are prepared in accordance with strategic guidance from the Secretary of State for the Environment. Once adopted, UDPs supersede all previous plans.

Unit Load A collection of items which can be moved as one unit suitable for mechanized handling, e.g. a container. The term is used in contrast to loose cargo which is handled manually.

User Body An organization which represents the interest of a particular group of customers who use transport services. Some are statutory, having been set up through legislation, while others are voluntary.

Vehicle The means by which the traffic is carried. The term is used in a general sense to include road vehicles, railway rolling stock, vessels and aircraft.

Way The track or media on or through which the vehicles travel. They include roadways, railways, seas/rivers/canals, and airspace/airways.

Select Bibliography

Abbot, J. 1990: 'Management Set New Priorities after City Bus Firm Buy-Out'. *Urban Transport International*, May/June.

Barker, T. 1990: *Moving Millions*: London Transport Museum.

Bell, G., Bowen, P. and Fawcett, P. 1984: *The Business of Transport*: Macdonald and Evans.

Benson, D. and Whitehead, G. 1985: *Transport and Distribution*: Longman.

Betts, P. and Gardner, D. 1992: 'Clouds over Open Skies'. *Financial Times*, 24 June.

Blackstock, D. 1985: 'The Conference System v Independent Lines – A Freight Forwarder's View'. *Freight Forwarding*, November.

Branch, A. 1981: *Elements of Shipping*, Fifth Edition: Chapman and Hall.

Cheeseman, I.C. 1982: 'The Implications of Energy, Futures for Public Transport'. *The Urban Transport Future*, (ed. Young, A.P. and Cresswell, R.W.): Construction Press.

Chrzanowski, I. 1985: *An Introduction to Shipping Economics*: Fairplay.

Colley, B. 1990: 'Looking for Acceptance by all'. *Transport*, May.

Cole, S. 1987: *Applied Transport Economics*: Kogan Page.

Cooper, J., Browne, M. and Peters, M. 1991: *European Logistics – Markets, Management and Strategy*: Blackwell.

Cottham, G.W. 1987: 'Identifying the Market – The Yorkshire Rider Approach'. Chartered Institute of Transport Conference, 12 September.

Crandall, R. 1991: 'Crandall: Industry Outlook Gloomy'. Interview by Kimberley Smeathers in *IATA Review*, No. 3.

Fawcett, P. McLeish, R. and Ogden, I. 1992: *Logistics Management*: Pitman.

Faulks, R. 1987: *Bus and Coach Operation*: Butterworths.

Gialloreto, L. 1988: *Strategic Airline Management: The Global War Begins*: Pitman.

Gloag, A. 1989: 'Stagecoach: Exploiting Opportunities'. *Bus and Coach Management*, November.

Gubbins, E. 1988: *Managing Transport Operations*: Kogan Page.

Gutman, G. 1987: 'Slicing up the Far East Cake'. *Freight Forwarding*, May.

Hass-Klau, C. 1990: 'Public Transport and Integrated Transport Policies in Large Metropolitan Areas of Europe'. *The Planner*, 25 May.

Hayward, R. 1990: *All About Public Relations*: McGraw-Hill.

Hibbs, J. 1987: *The Bus and Coach Operator's Handbook*: Kogan Page.

Hibbs, J. 1989: *Marketing Management in the Bus and Coach Industry*: Croner.

Hind, D. 1986: 'Working on the Buses'. *Marketing*, 9 October.

Holloway, J.C. 1989: *The Business of Tourism*: Pitman.

Hopson, B. and Scally, M. 1989: *12 Steps to Success through Service*: Lifeskills Publishing Group.

Kelsey, A. 1986: 'Transport Finance and Investment'. Chartered Institute of Transport Occasional Paper.

King, Lord John 1987: 'The World's Favourite Take-Off'. *The Observer*, 25 October.

Lancaster, F. and Massingham, L. 1988: *Essentials of Marketing*: McGraw-Hill.

Lowe, D. 1989: *The Transport and Distribution Manager's Guide to 1992*: Kogan Page.

Middleton, V.T.C. 1988: *Marketing in Travel and Tourism*: Heinemann.

Owen, R. and Dynes, M. 1990: *The Times Guide to 1992: Britain in a Europe without Frontiers, a Comprehensive Handbook*: Times Books.

Owens, S. 1991: *Energy-Conscious Planning*: Commissioned by the Council for the Protection of Rural England.

Peters, T. 1988: 'Thriving on Chaos'. *Handbook for a Management Revolution*: MacMillan.

Peisley, A. 1990: 'The UK – Europe Ferry Industry and Strategies for the 1990s'. *Travel and Tourism Analyst*, No. 2: Economist Intelligence Unit.

Quarmby, D. 1987: 'Road Improvements – Identifying the Wider Benefits of Freight Distribution'. *Transport Economist*, summer.

Rushton, A. and Oxley, J. 1989: *Handbook of Logistics and Distribution Management*: Kogan Page.

Salveson, P. 1992: *Travel Sickness: The Need for a Sustainable British Transport Policy*: Lawrence and Wishart.

Shaw, S. 1990: *Airline Marketing and Management*: Pitman.

Shaw, S.J. 1991: 'Seeking Equality'. *Transport*, March/April.

Smith, A. 1776: *The Wealth of Nations*, (1986 edition): Penguin.

Steer Davies Gleave 1991: *Buses Mean Business – The Solution to Urban Congestion*: Bus and Coach Council.

Stephenson, F.J. 1987: *Transportation USA*: Addison Wesley.

Stewart, V. and Chadwick, V. 1987: *Messages for Management from the Scotrail challenge – Changing Trains*: David and Charles.

Index